WAR MOTHER

FRED VAN LENTE | STEPHEN SEGOVIA | TOMÁS GIORELLO | ANDREW DALHOUSE

CONTENTS

Collection Cover Art: David Mack

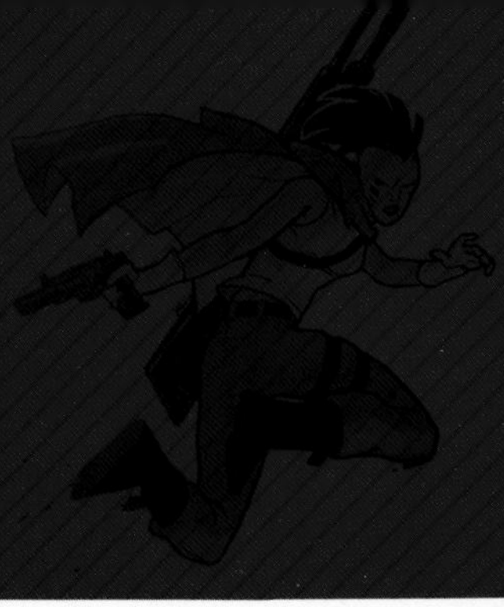

Assistant Editors: Lauren Hitzhusen (4001 A.D.: WAR MOTHER) and Ben Peterson (WAR MOTHER #1-4)
Editor: Danny Khazem (WAR MOTHER #1-4)
Editor-in-Chief: Warren Simons

VALIANT.

Peter Cuneo
Chairman

Dinesh Shamdasani
CEO & Chief Creative Officer

Gavin Cuneo
Chief Operating Officer & CFO

Fred Pierce
Publisher

Warren Simons
Editor-in-Chief

Walter Black
VP Operations

Hunter Gorinson
VP Marketing & Communications

Atom! Freeman
Director of Sales

Annie Rosa
Sales Operations Manager

Julia Walchuk
Sales Manager

Travis Escarfullery
Director of Design & Production

Jeff Walker
Production & Design Manager

Robert Meyers
Managing Editor

Peter Stern
Publishing & Operations Manager

Victoria McNally
Marketing & Communications Managerr

Charlotte Greenbaum
Editor

Benjamin Peterson
David Menchel
Editorial Assistants

Shanyce Lora
Senior Marketing & Digital Media Manager

Ryan Stayton
Director of Special Projects

Ivan Cohen
Collection Editor

Steve Blackwell
Collection Designer

Rian Hughes
Trade Dress & Book Design

Russell Brown
President, Consumer Products,
Promotions and Ad Sales

Caritza Berlioz
Licensing Coodinator

ALIANT

4001 A.D. #1

WAR MOTHER

FRED
AN LENTE

TOMÁS
GIORELLO

BRIAN
REBER

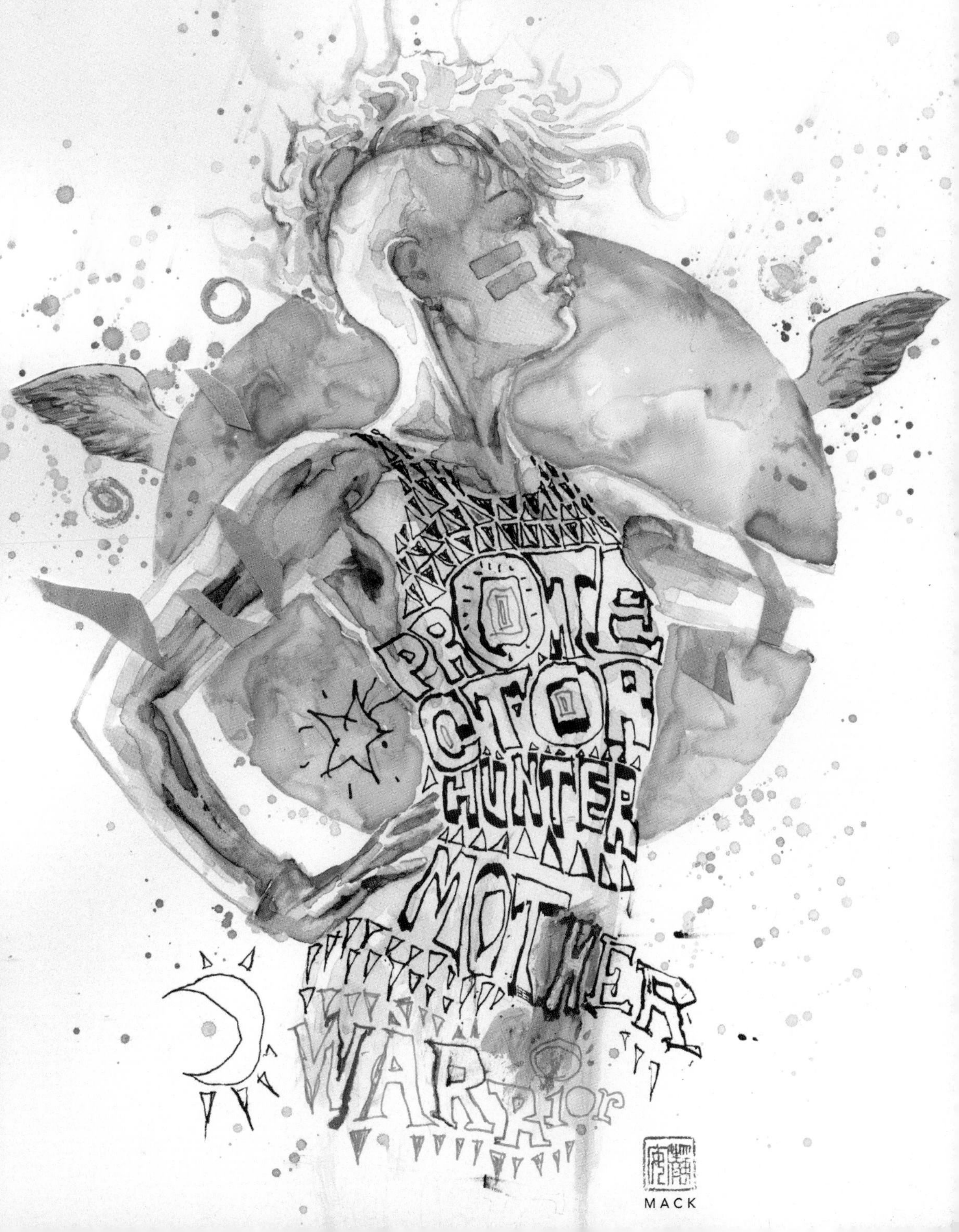
PROTECTOR
HUNTER
MOTHER
WARRIOr
MACK

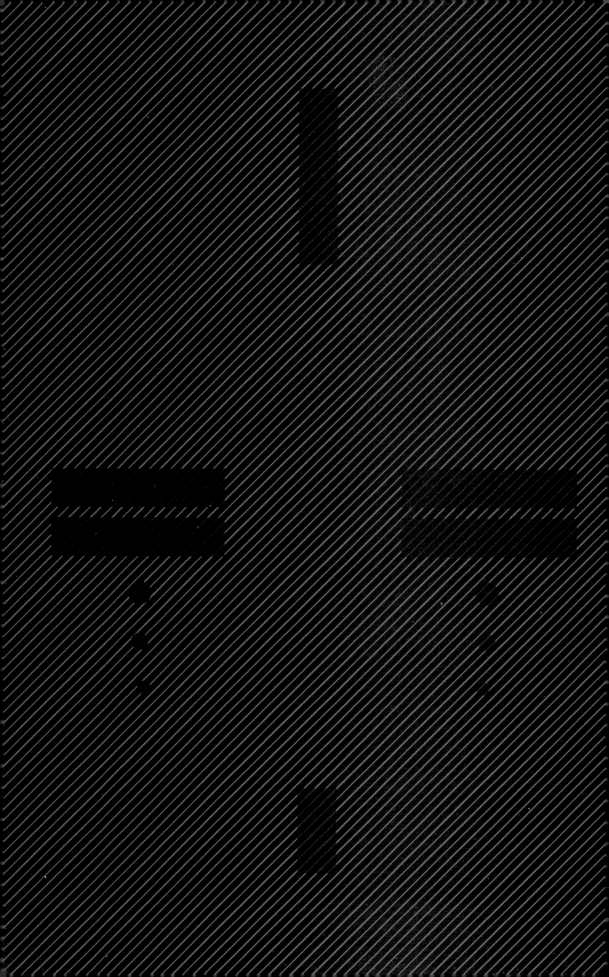

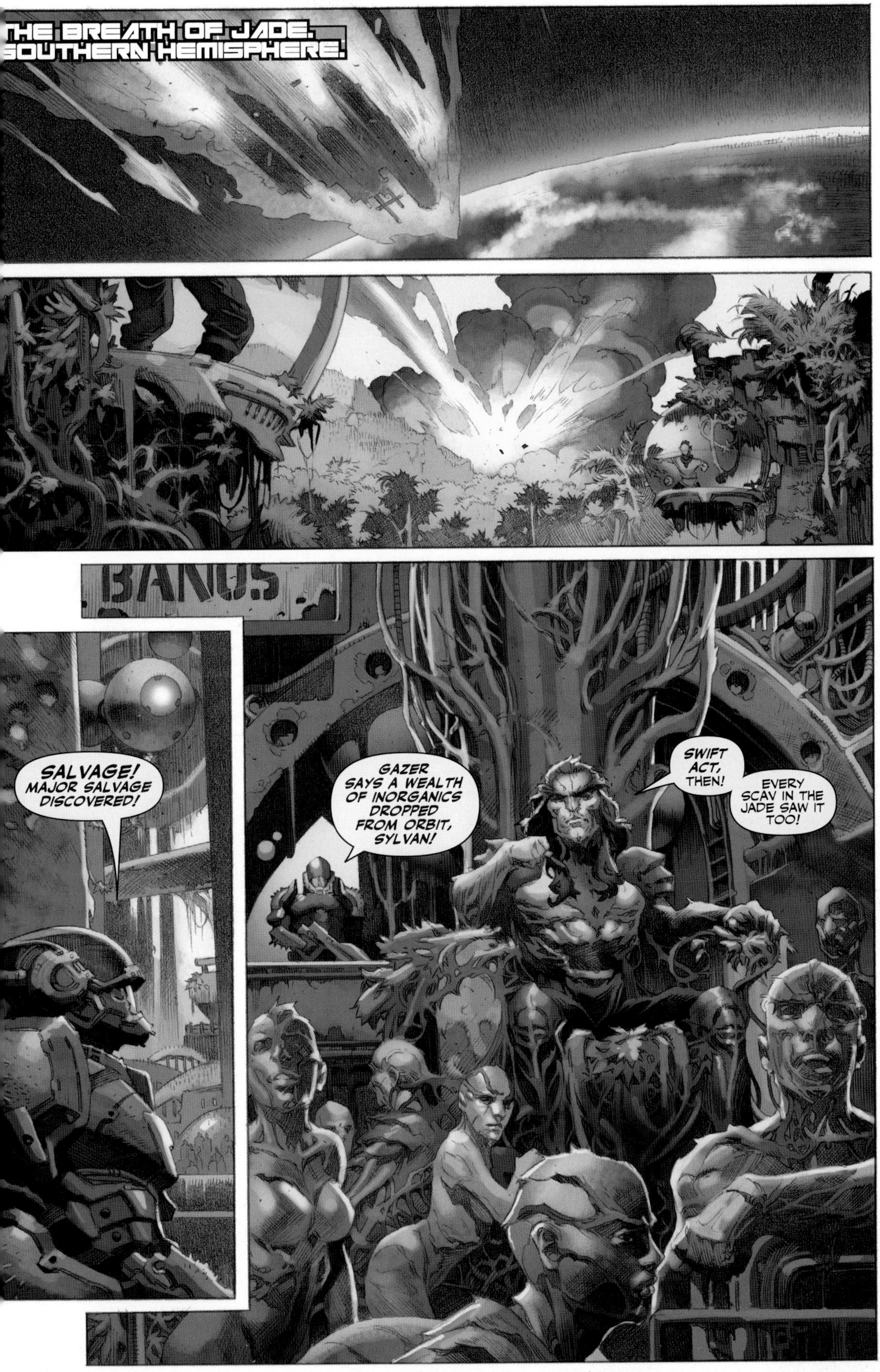
THE BREATH OF JADE. SOUTHERN HEMISPHERE.
BANOS
SALVAGE! MAJOR SALVAGE DISCOVERED!
GAZER SAYS A WEALTH OF INORGANICS DROPPED FROM ORBIT, SYLVAN!
SWIFT ACT, THEN!
EVERY SCAV IN THE JADE SAW IT TOO!

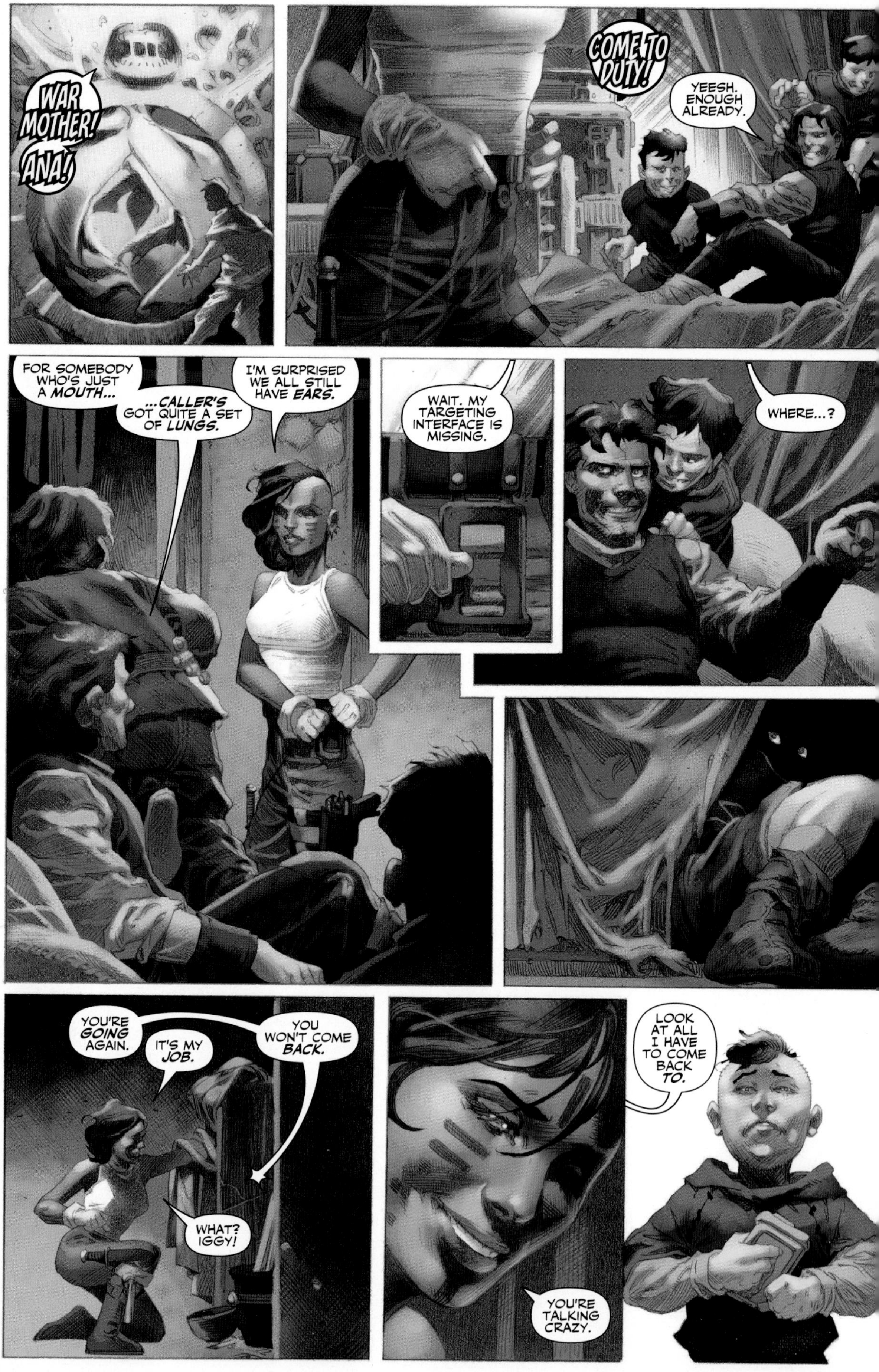
WAR MOTHER!
ANA!
COME TO DUTY!
YEESH. ENOUGH ALREADY.
FOR SOMEBODY WHO'S JUST A MOUTH...
...CALLER'S GOT QUITE A SET OF LUNGS.
I'M SURPRISED WE ALL STILL HAVE EARS.
WAIT. MY TARGETING INTERFACE IS MISSING.
WHERE...?
YOU'RE GOING AGAIN.
IT'S MY JOB.
YOU WON'T COME BACK.
WHAT? IGGY!
YOU'RE TALKING CRAZY.
LOOK AT ALL I HAVE TO COME BACK TO.

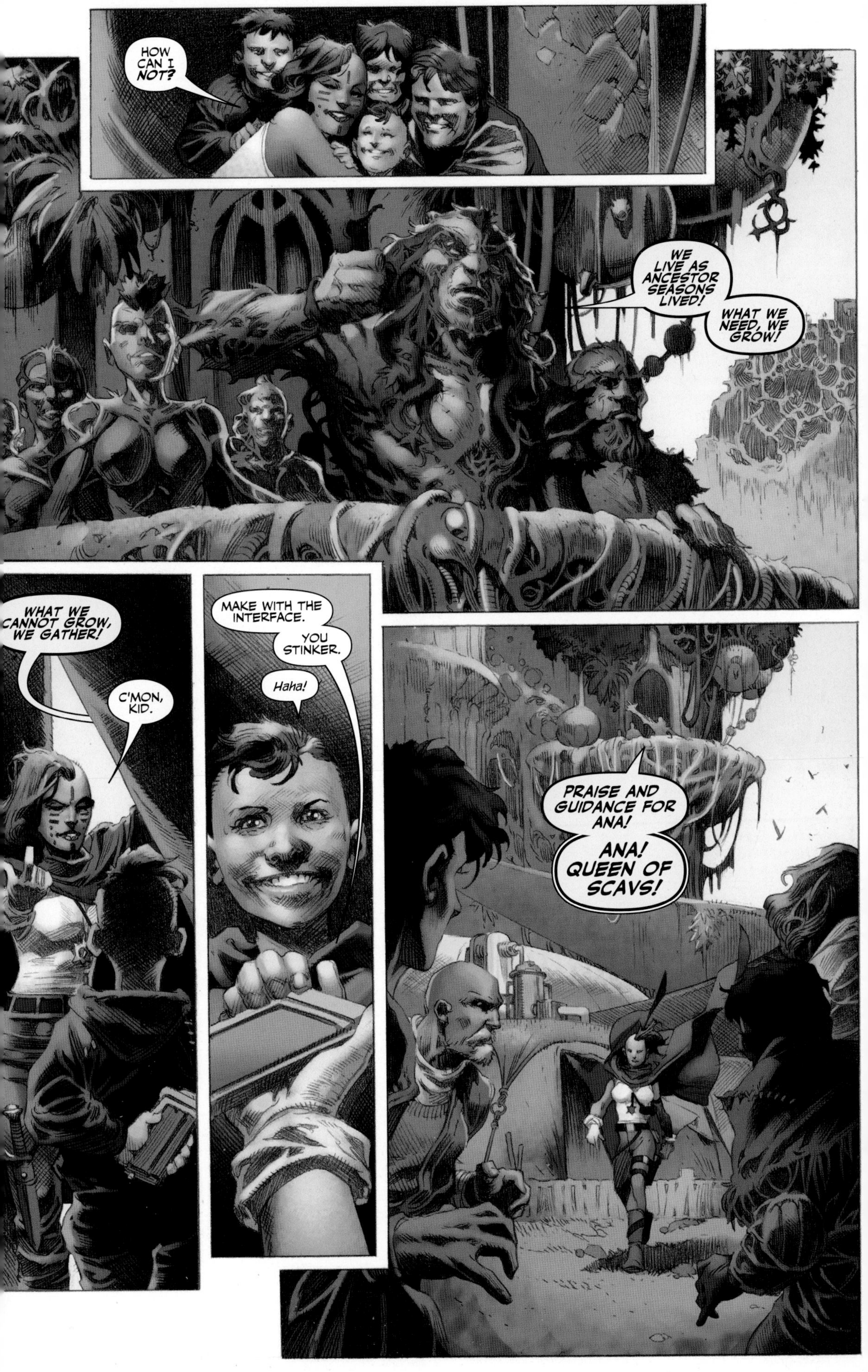
HOW CAN I NOT?
WE LIVE AS ANCESTOR SEASONS LIVED!
WHAT WE NEED, WE GROW!
WHAT WE CANNOT GROW, WE GATHER!
C'MON, KID.
MAKE WITH THE INTERFACE.
YOU STINKER.
Haha!
PRAISE AND GUIDANCE FOR ANA!
ANA! QUEEN OF SCAVS!

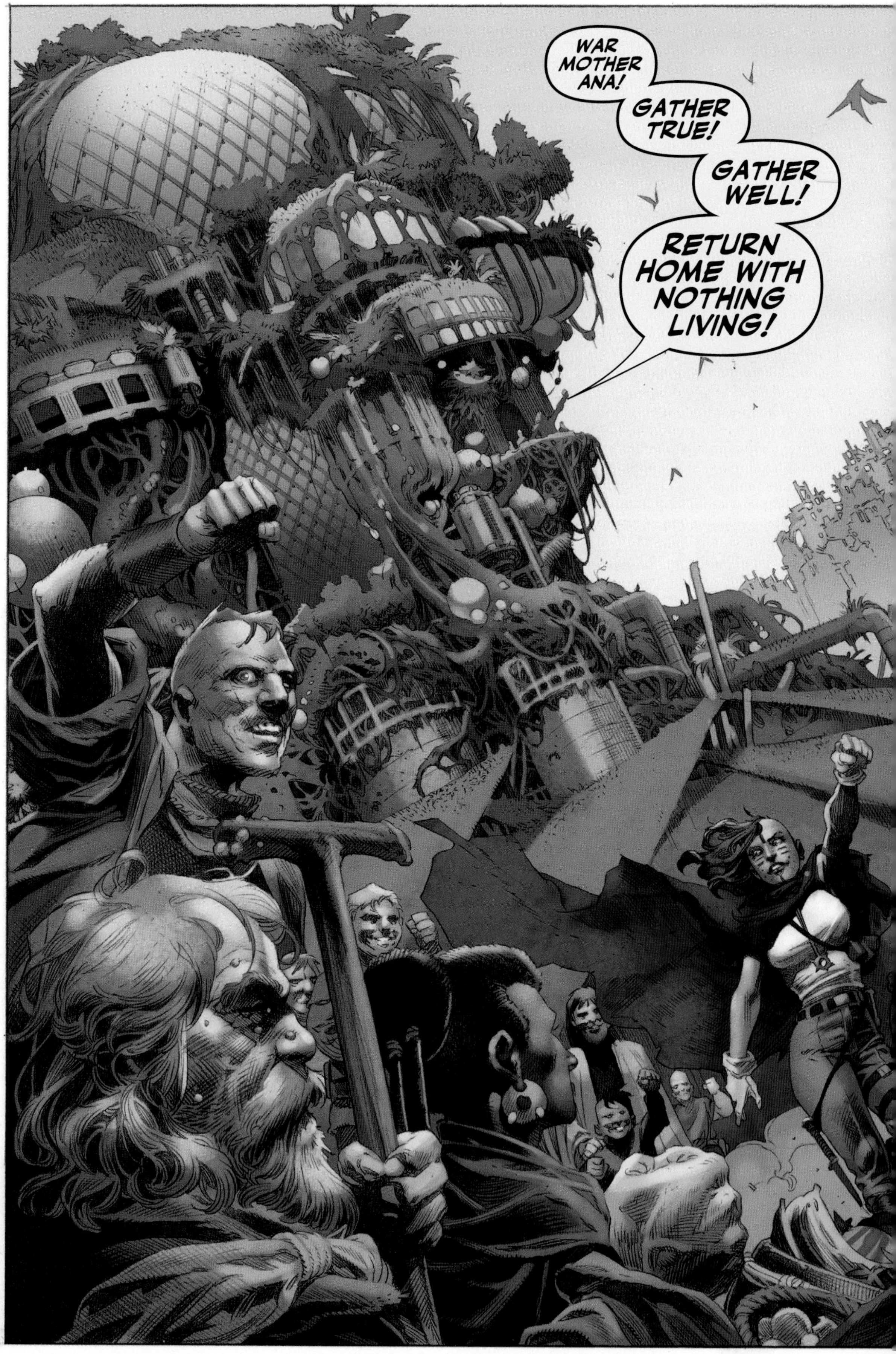
WAR MOTHER ANA!
GATHER TRUE!
GATHER WELL!
RETURN HOME WITH NOTHING LIVING!

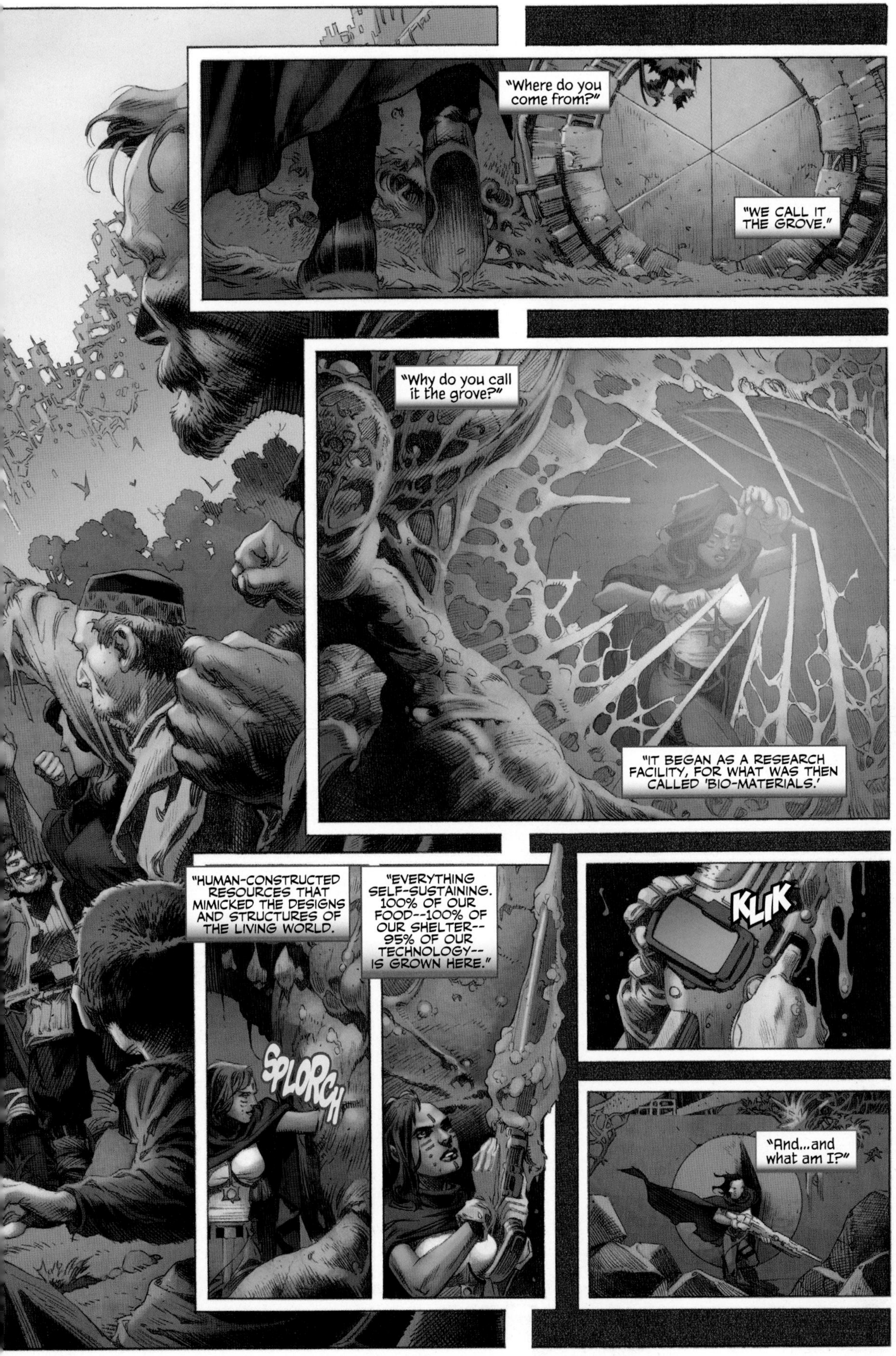
"Where do you come from?"
"WE CALL IT THE GROVE."
"Why do you call it the grove?"
"IT BEGAN AS A RESEARCH FACILITY, FOR WHAT WAS THEN CALLED 'BIO-MATERIALS.'
"HUMAN-CONSTRUCTED RESOURCES THAT MIMICKED THE DESIGNS AND STRUCTURES OF THE LIVING WORLD.
SPLORCH
"EVERYTHING SELF-SUSTAINING. 100% OF OUR FOOD--100% OF OUR SHELTER--95% OF OUR TECHNOLOGY--IS GROWN HERE."
KLIK
"And...and what am I?"

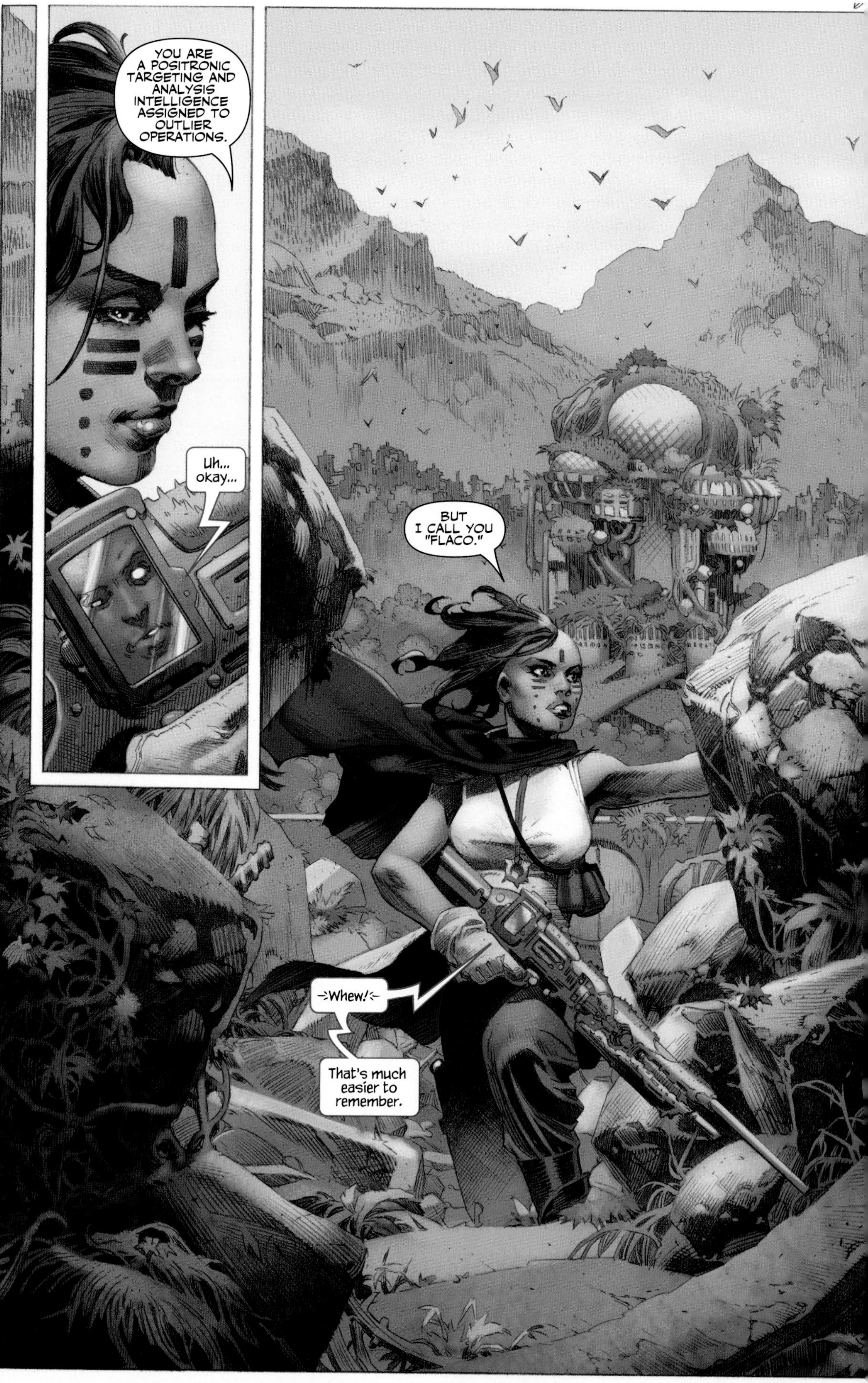
YOU ARE A POSITRONIC TARGETING AND ANALYSIS INTELLIGENCE ASSIGNED TO OUTLIER OPERATIONS.
Uh... okay...
BUT I CALL YOU "FLACO."
-Whew!-
That's much easier to remember.

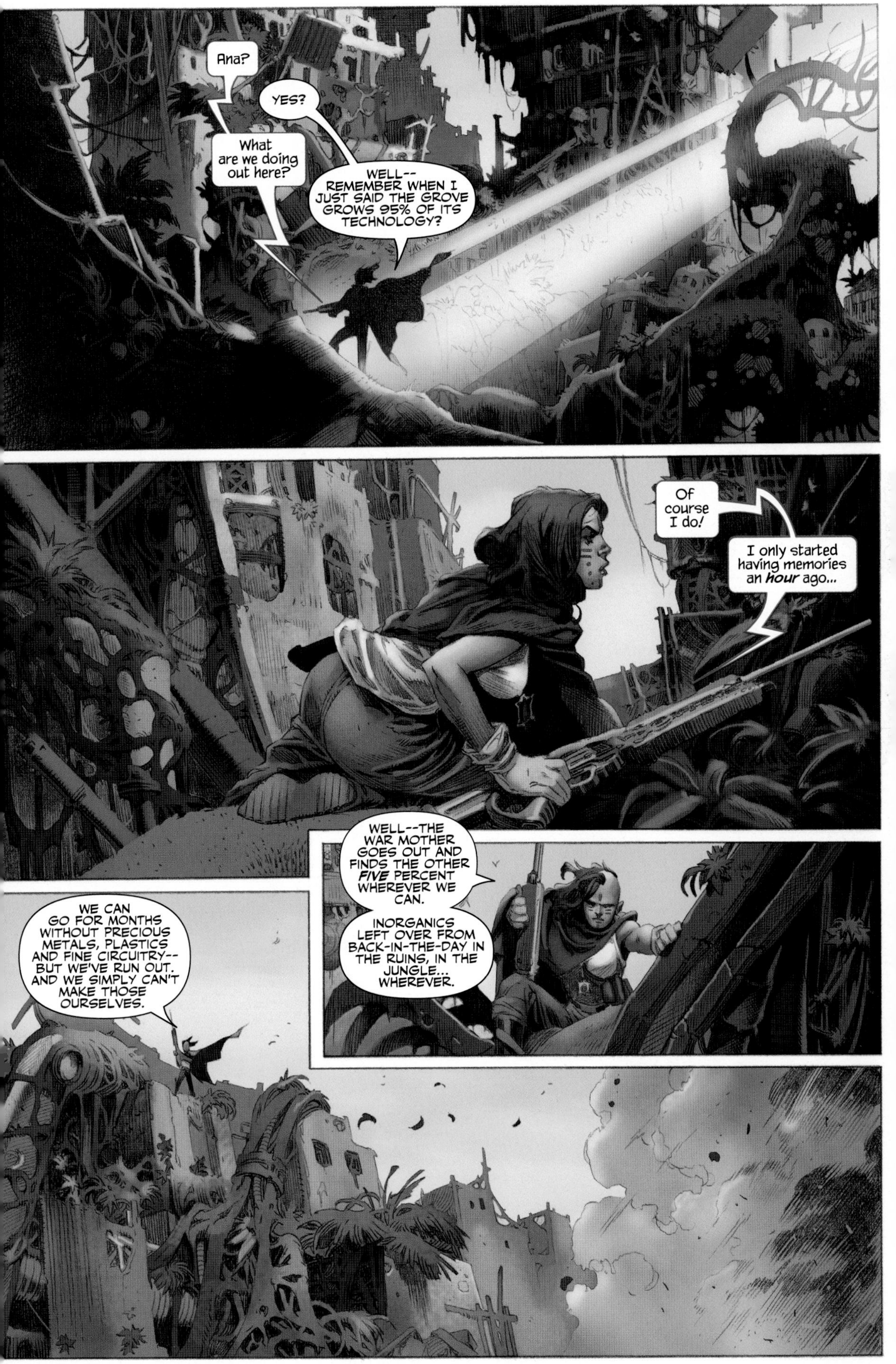
Ana?
YES?
What are we doing out here?
WELL-- REMEMBER WHEN I JUST SAID THE GROVE GROWS 95% OF ITS TECHNOLOGY?
Of course I do!
I only started having memories an *hour* ago...
WELL--THE WAR MOTHER GOES OUT AND FINDS THE OTHER *FIVE* PERCENT WHEREVER WE CAN.
INORGANICS LEFT OVER FROM BACK-IN-THE-DAY IN THE RUINS, IN THE JUNGLE... WHEREVER.
WE CAN GO FOR MONTHS WITHOUT PRECIOUS METALS, PLASTICS AND FINE CIRCUITRY-- BUT WE'VE RUN OUT. AND WE SIMPLY CAN'T MAKE THOSE OURSELVES.

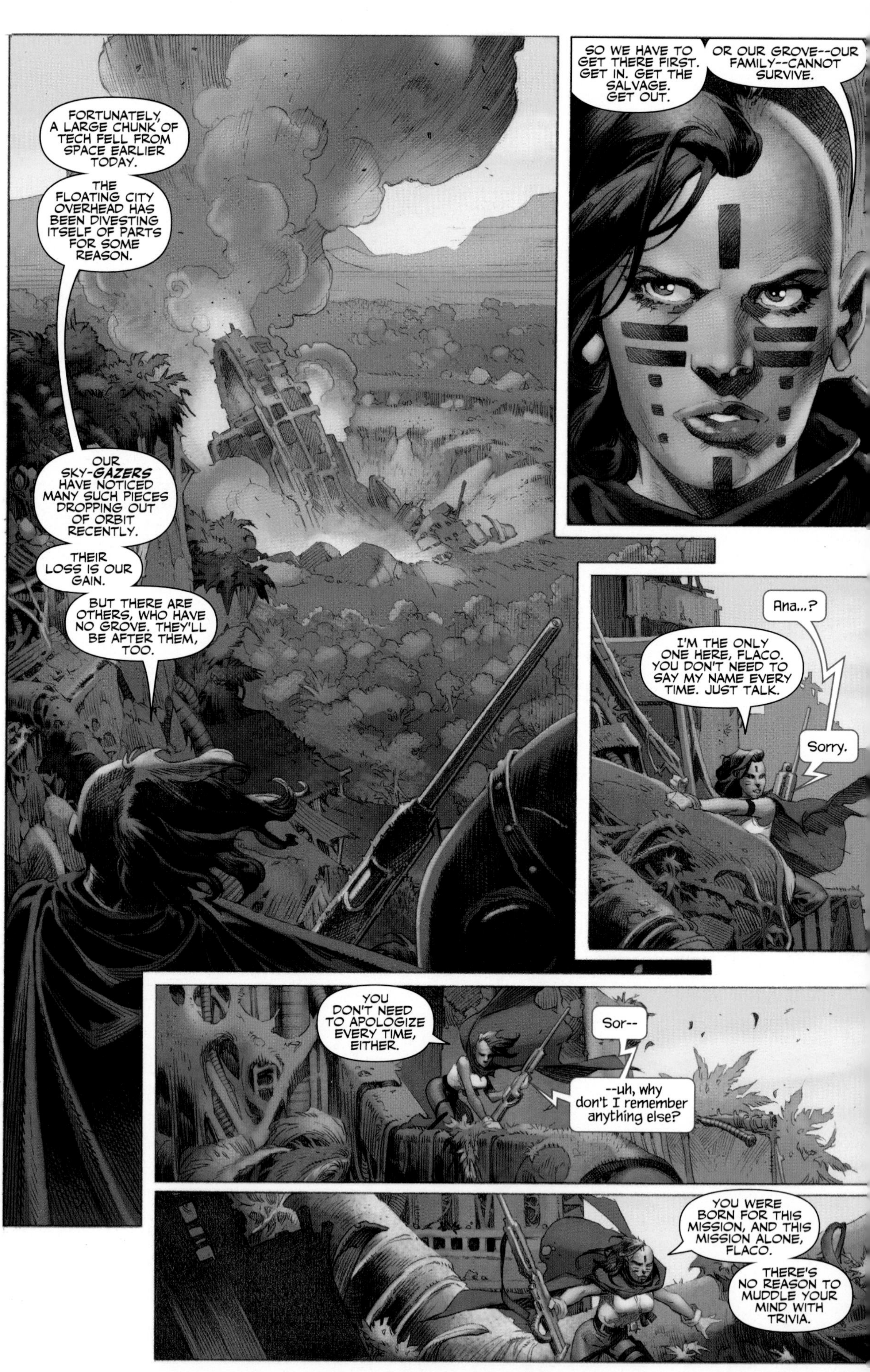
FORTUNATELY, A LARGE CHUNK OF TECH FELL FROM SPACE EARLIER TODAY.
THE FLOATING CITY OVERHEAD HAS BEEN DIVESTING ITSELF OF PARTS FOR SOME REASON.
OUR SKY-GAZERS HAVE NOTICED MANY SUCH PIECES DROPPING OUT OF ORBIT RECENTLY.
THEIR LOSS IS OUR GAIN.
BUT THERE ARE OTHERS, WHO HAVE NO GROVE. THEY'LL BE AFTER THEM, TOO.
SO WE HAVE TO GET THERE FIRST. GET IN. GET THE SALVAGE. GET OUT.
OR OUR GROVE--OUR FAMILY--CANNOT SURVIVE.
Ana...?
I'M THE ONLY ONE HERE, FLACO. YOU DON'T NEED TO SAY MY NAME EVERY TIME. JUST TALK.
Sorry.
YOU DON'T NEED TO APOLOGIZE EVERY TIME, EITHER.
Sor--
--uh, why don't I remember anything else?
YOU WERE BORN FOR THIS MISSION, AND THIS MISSION ALONE, FLACO.
THERE'S NO REASON TO MUDDLE YOUR MIND WITH TRIVIA.

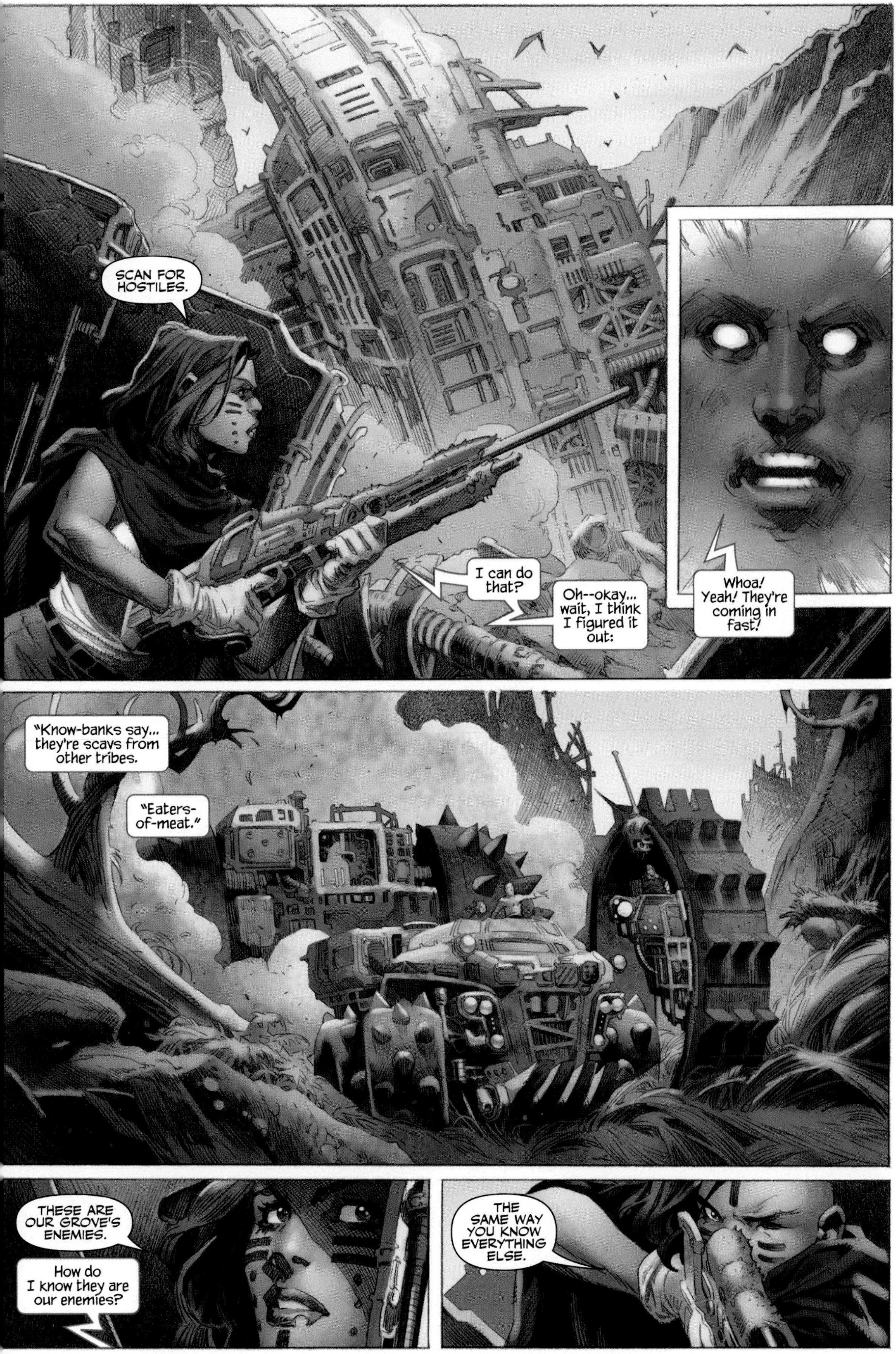
SCAN FOR HOSTILES.
I can do that?
Oh--okay... wait, I think I figured it out:
Whoa! Yeah! They're coming in fast!
"Know-banks say... they're scavs from other tribes.
"Eaters-of-meat."
THESE ARE OUR GROVE'S ENEMIES.
How do I know they are our enemies?
THE SAME WAY YOU KNOW EVERYTHING ELSE.

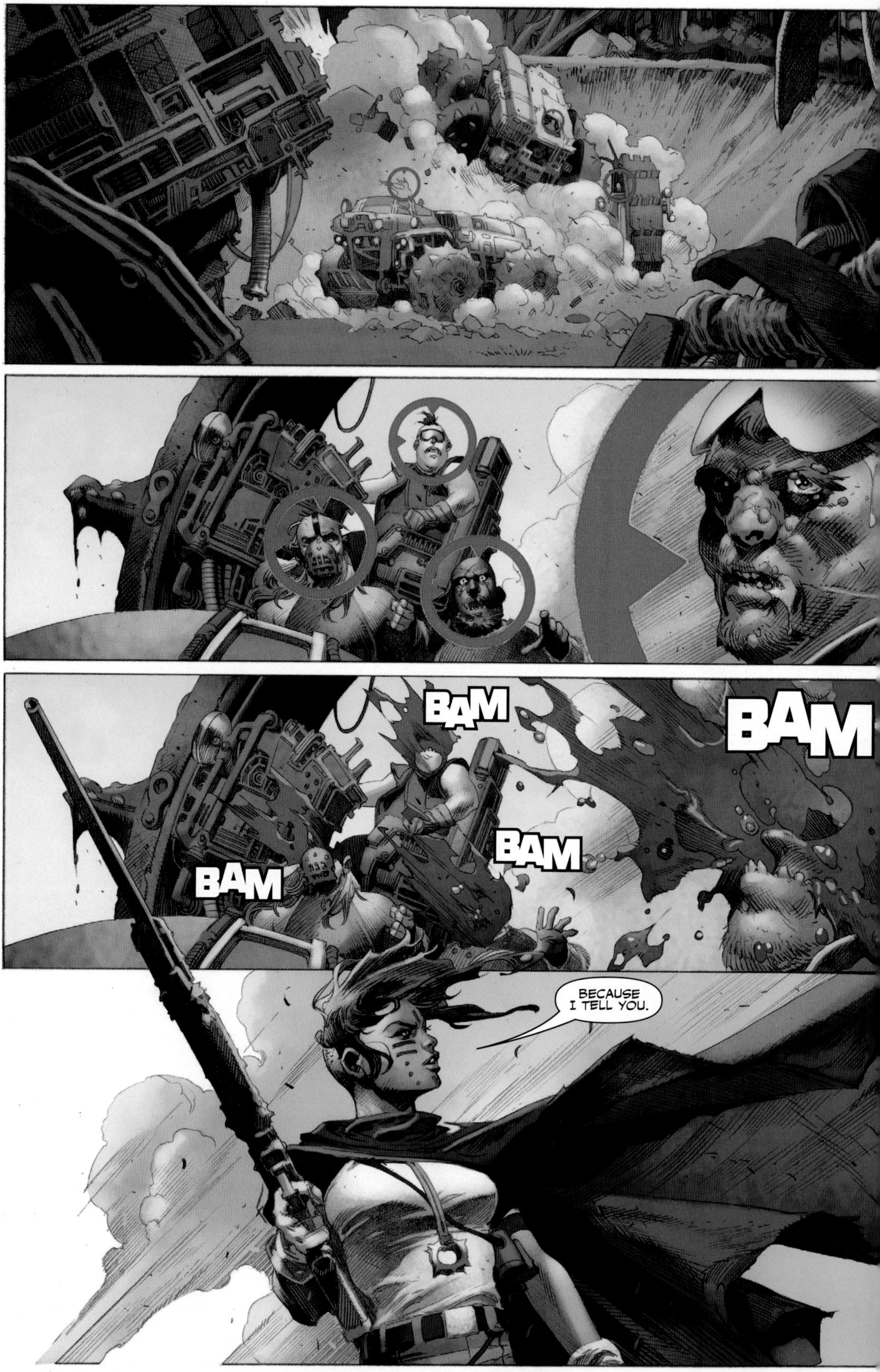
BAM
BAM
BAM
BAM
BECAUSE I TELL YOU.

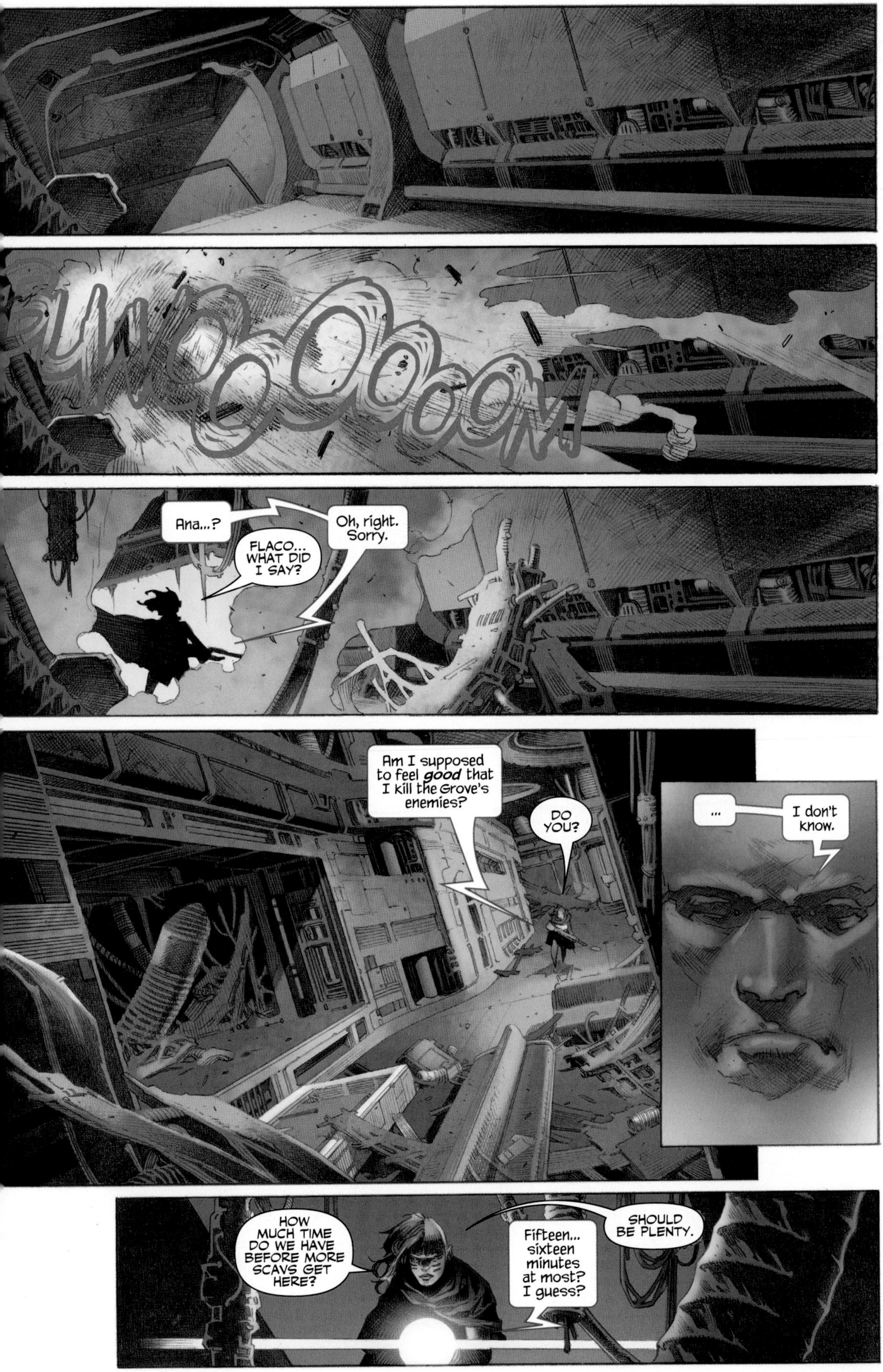

BWOOOOOOOM
Ana...?
FLACO... WHAT DID I SAY?
Oh, right. Sorry.
Am I supposed to feel **good** that I kill the Grove's enemies?
DO YOU?
...
I don't know.
HOW MUCH TIME DO WE HAVE BEFORE MORE SCAVS GET HERE?
Fifteen... sixteen minutes at most? I guess?
SHOULD BE PLENTY.

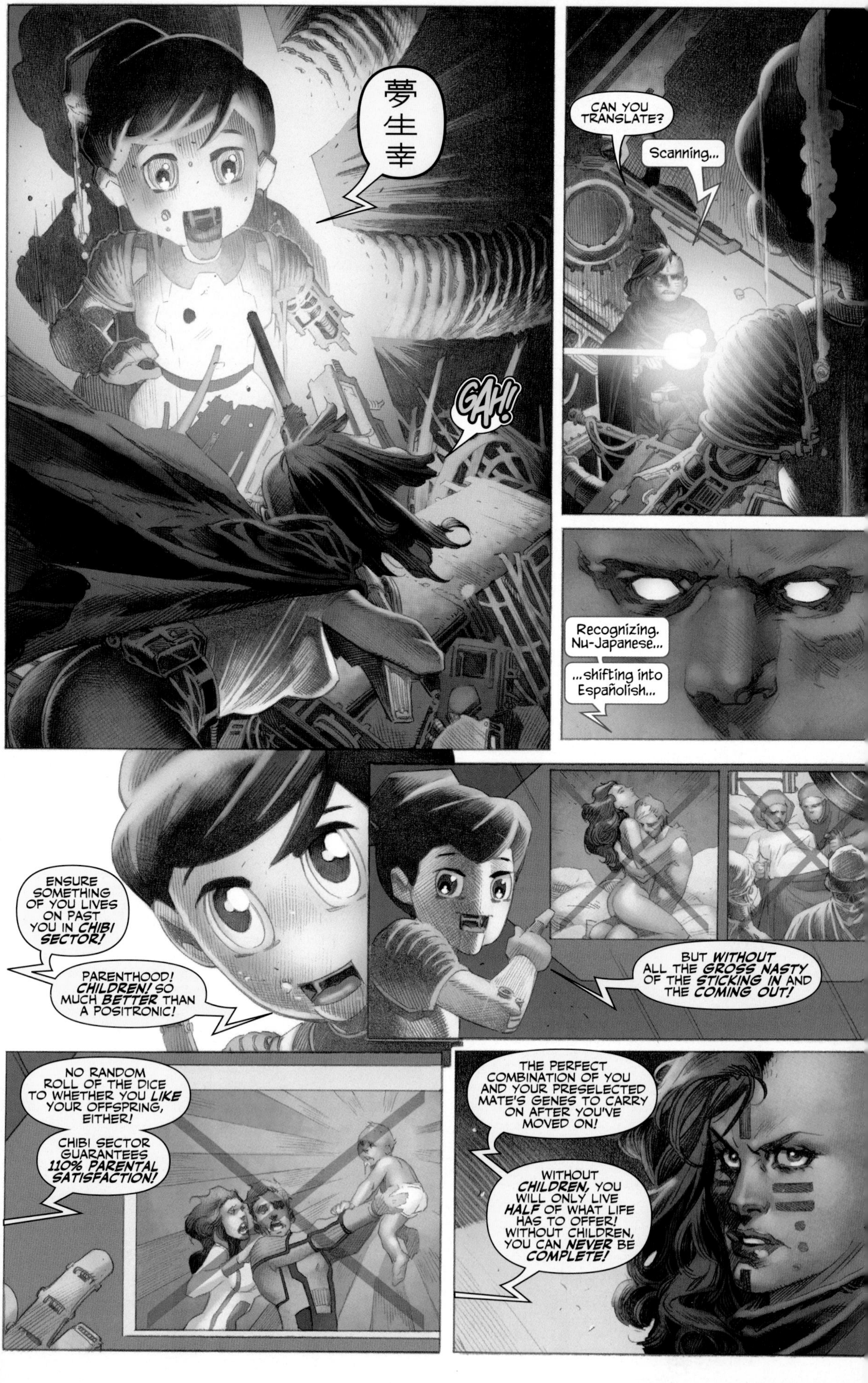
夢生幸
GAH!
CAN YOU TRANSLATE?
Scanning...
Recognizing. Nu-Japanese...
...shifting into Españolish...
ENSURE SOMETHING OF YOU LIVES ON PAST YOU IN CHIBI SECTOR!
PARENTHOOD! CHILDREN! SO MUCH BETTER THAN A POSITRONIC!
BUT WITHOUT ALL THE GROSS NASTY OF THE STICKING IN AND THE COMING OUT!
NO RANDOM ROLL OF THE DICE TO WHETHER YOU LIKE YOUR OFFSPRING, EITHER!
CHIBI SECTOR GUARANTEES 110% PARENTAL SATISFACTION!
THE PERFECT COMBINATION OF YOU AND YOUR PRESELECTED MATE'S GENES TO CARRY ON AFTER YOU'VE MOVED ON!
WITHOUT CHILDREN, YOU WILL ONLY LIVE HALF OF WHAT LIFE HAS TO OFFER! WITHOUT CHILDREN, YOU CAN NEVER BE COMPLETE!

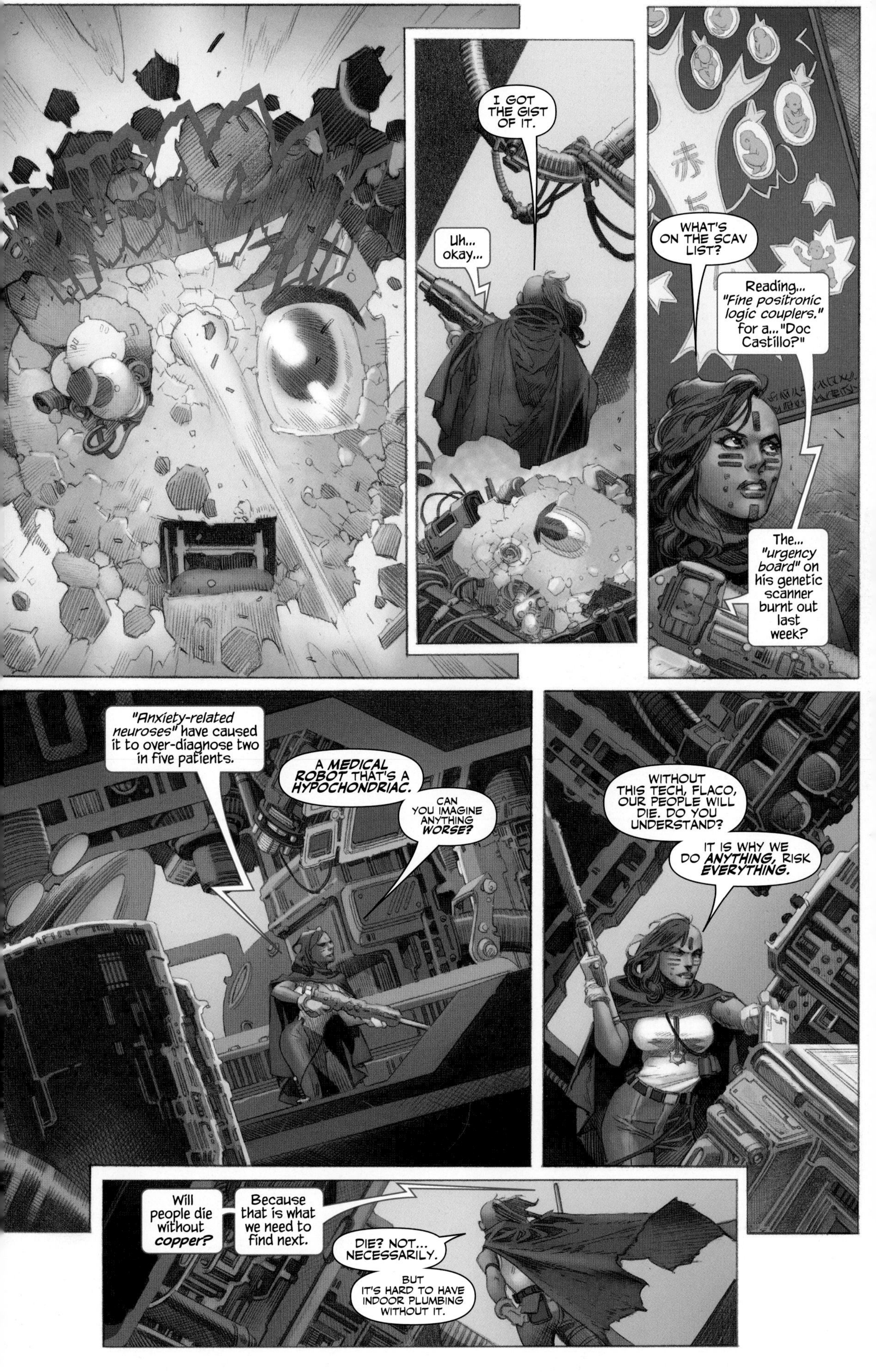
I GOT THE GIST OF IT.
Uh... okay...
WHAT'S ON THE SCAV LIST?
Reading... "Fine positronic logic couplers." for a... "Doc Castillo?"
The... "urgency board" on his genetic scanner burnt out last week?
"Anxiety-related neuroses" have caused it to over-diagnose two in five patients.
A MEDICAL ROBOT THAT'S A HYPOCHONDRIAC.
CAN YOU IMAGINE ANYTHING WORSE?
WITHOUT THIS TECH, FLACO, OUR PEOPLE WILL DIE. DO YOU UNDERSTAND?
IT IS WHY WE DO ANYTHING, RISK EVERYTHING.
Will people die without copper?
Because that is what we need to find next.
DIE? NOT... NECESSARILY.
BUT IT'S HARD TO HAVE INDOOR PLUMBING WITHOUT IT.

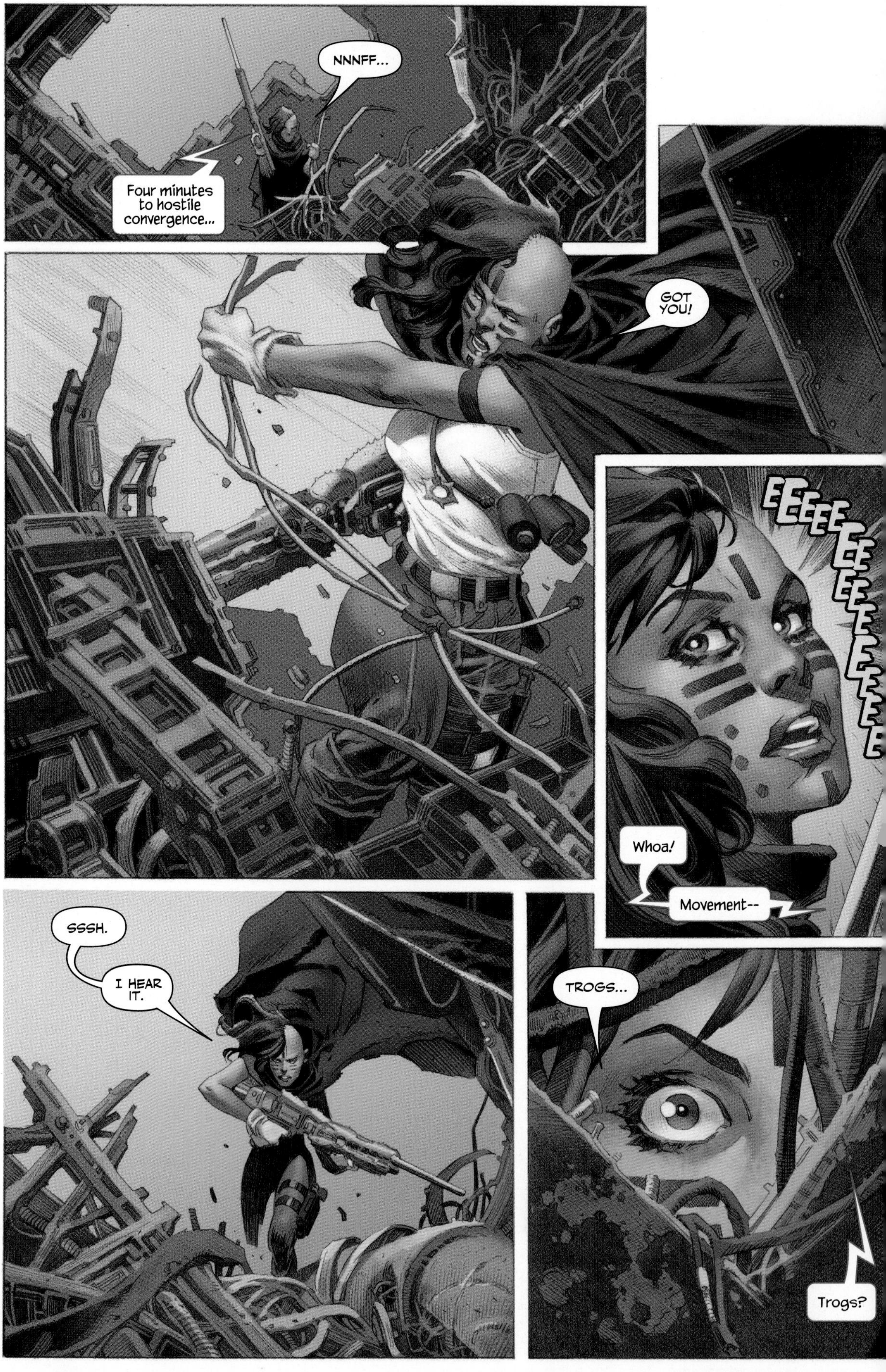
NNNFF...
Four minutes to hostile convergence...
GOT YOU!
EEEEEEEEEEEEEE
Whoa!
Movement--
SSSH.
I HEAR IT.
TROGS...
Trogs?

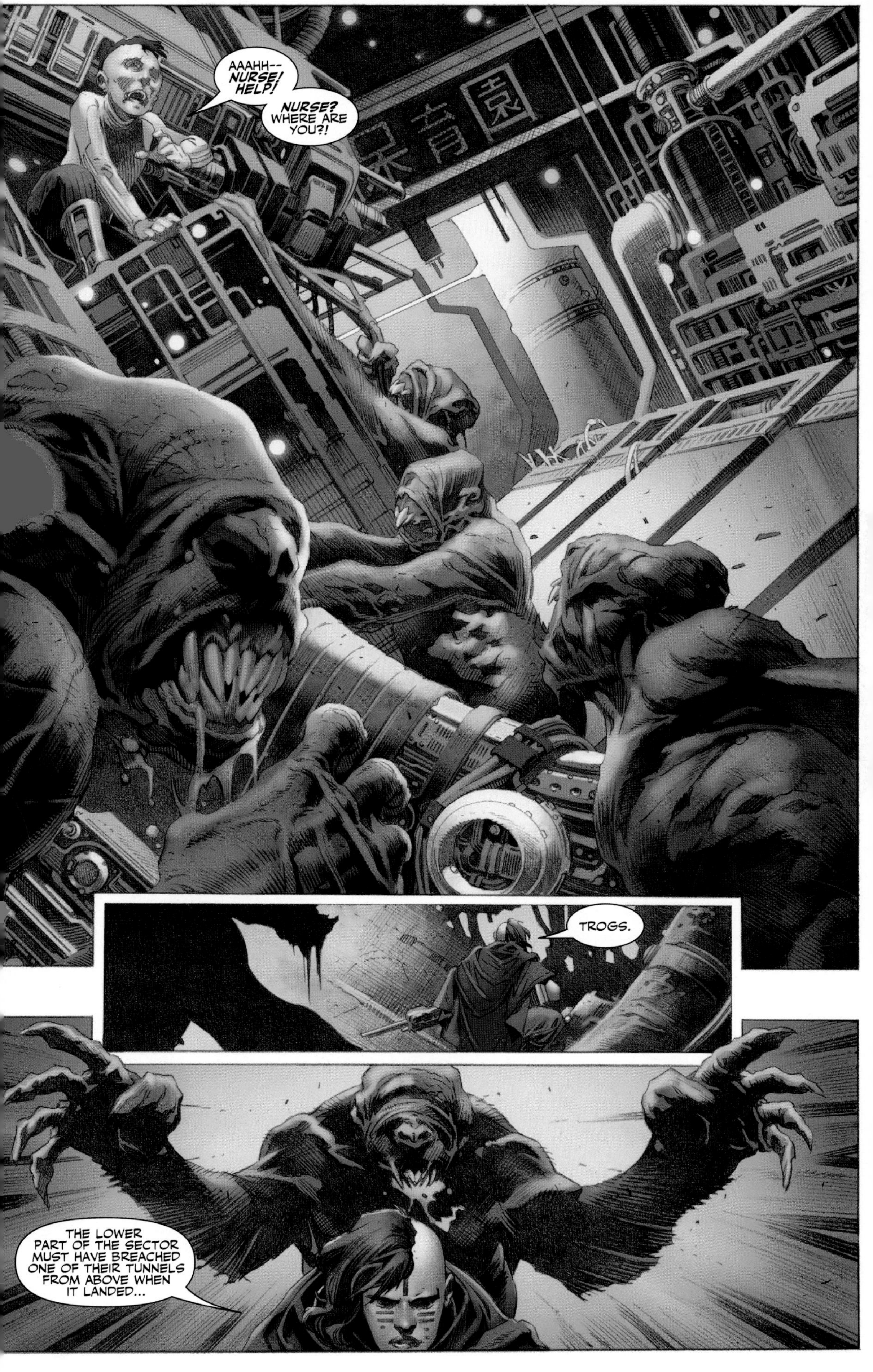
AAAHH-- NURSE! HELP!
NURSE? WHERE ARE YOU?!
TROGS.
THE LOWER PART OF THE SECTOR MUST HAVE BREACHED ONE OF THEIR TUNNELS FROM ABOVE WHEN IT LANDED...

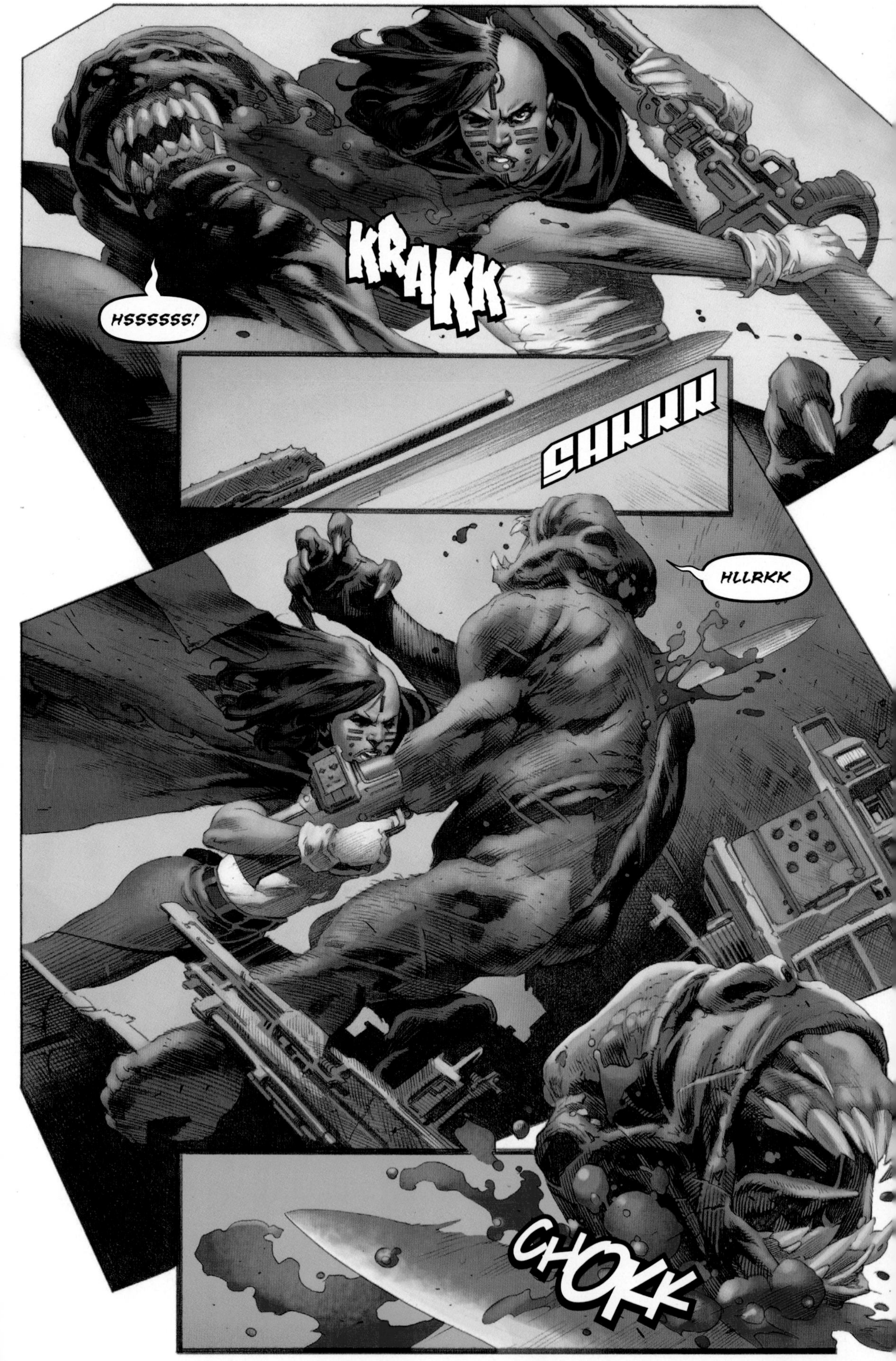
KRAKK
HSSSSSS!
SHKKK
HLLRKK
CHOKK

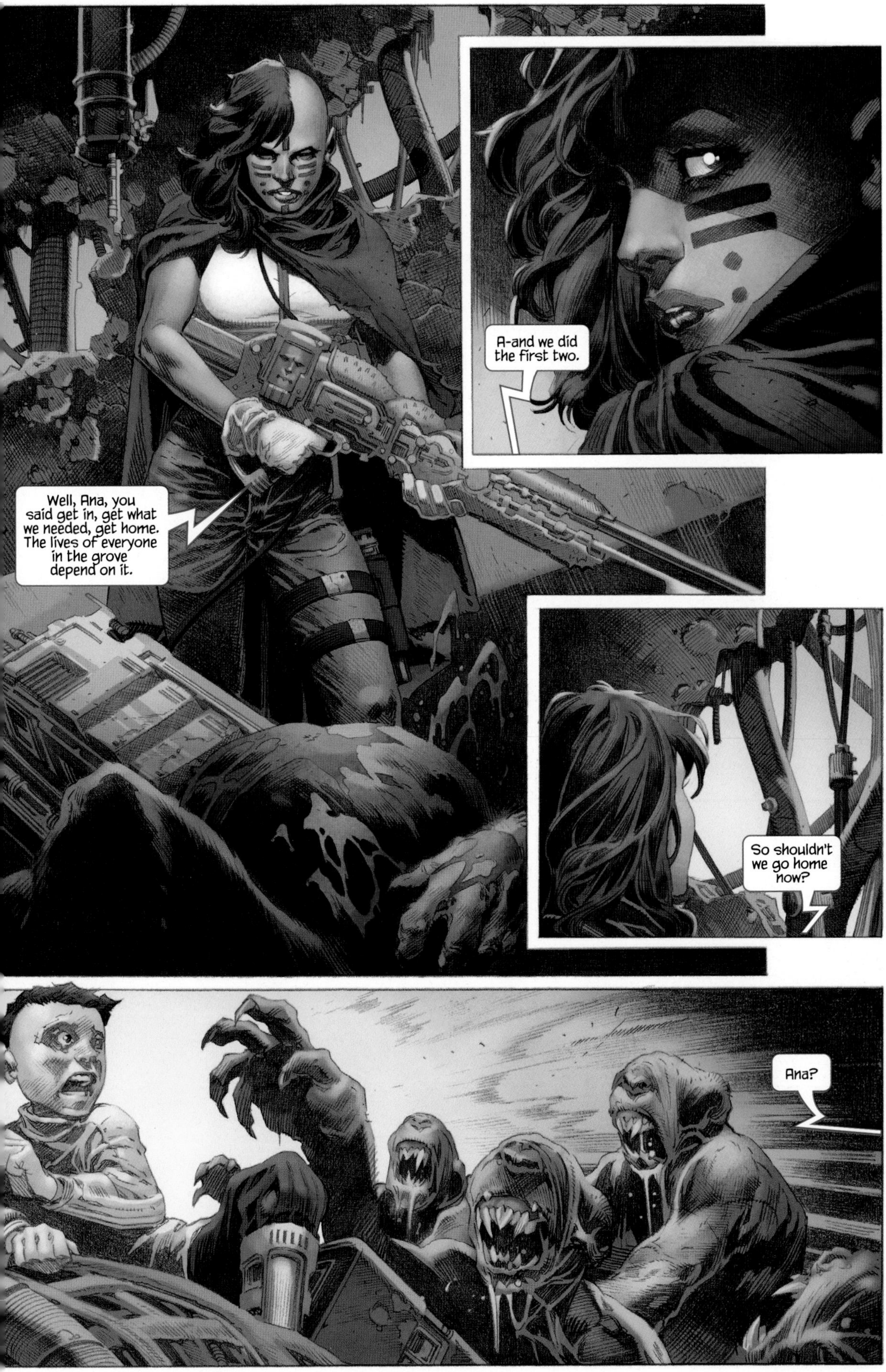
A-and we did the first two.
Well, Ana, you said get in, get what we needed, get home. The lives of everyone in the grove depend on it.
So shouldn't we go home now?
Ana?

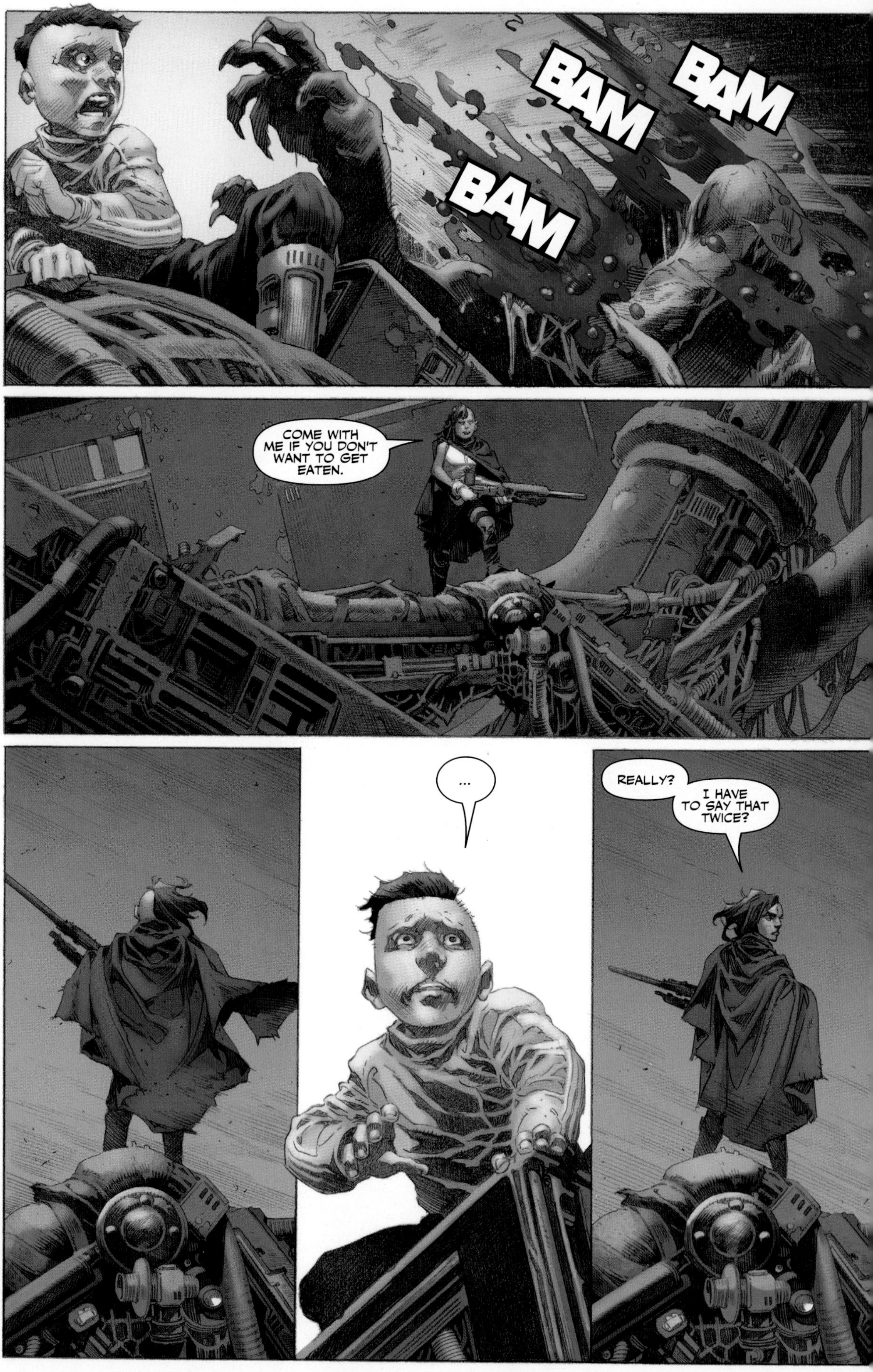
BAM
BAM
BAM
COME WITH ME IF YOU DON'T WANT TO GET EATEN.
...
REALLY?
I HAVE TO SAY THAT TWICE?

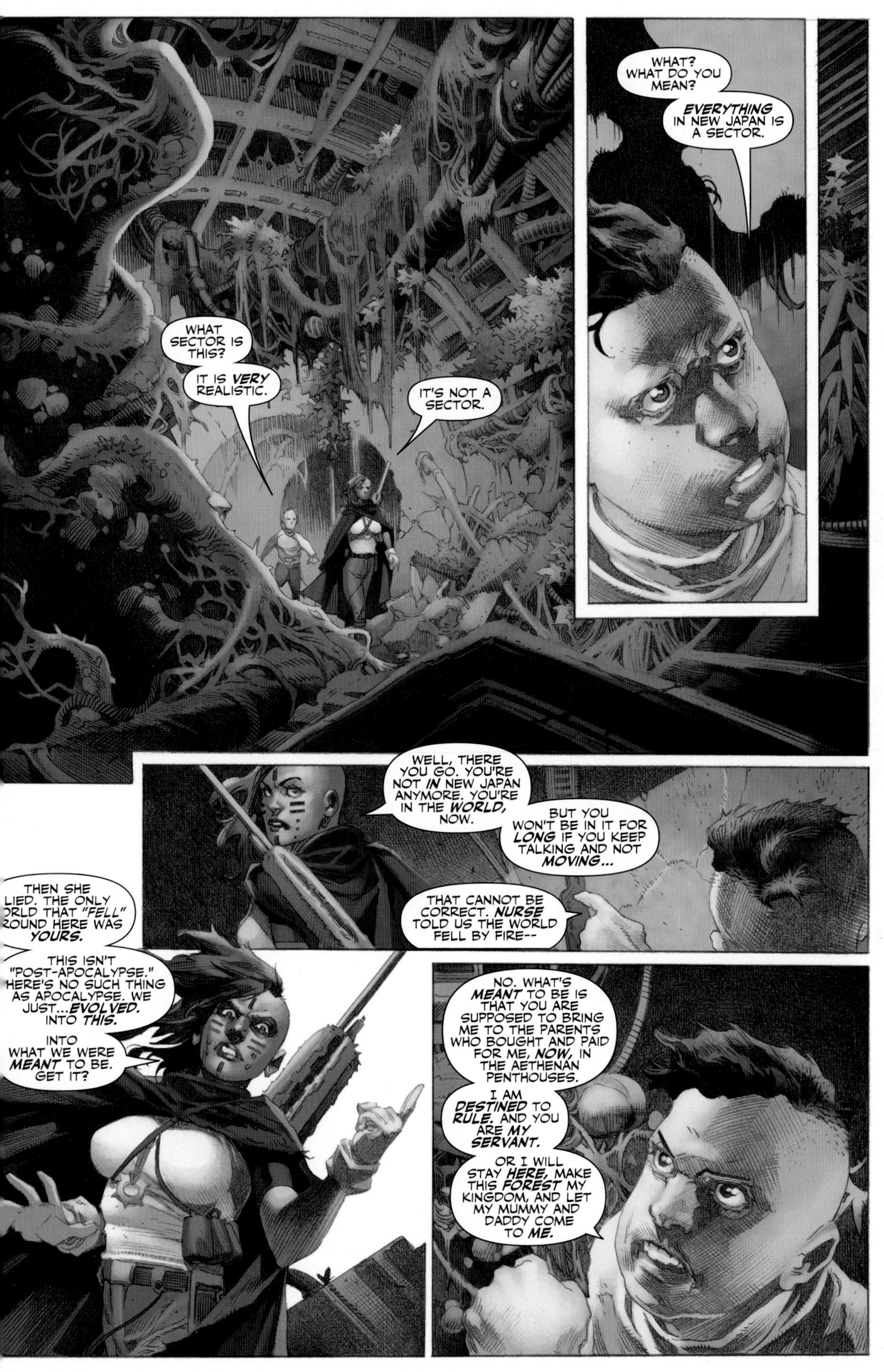
WHAT SECTOR IS THIS?
IT IS VERY REALISTIC.
IT'S NOT A SECTOR.
WHAT? WHAT DO YOU MEAN?
EVERYTHING IN NEW JAPAN IS A SECTOR.
WELL, THERE YOU GO. YOU'RE NOT IN NEW JAPAN ANYMORE. YOU'RE IN THE WORLD, NOW.
BUT YOU WON'T BE IN IT FOR LONG IF YOU KEEP TALKING AND NOT MOVING...
THAT CANNOT BE CORRECT. NURSE TOLD US THE WORLD FELL BY FIRE--
THEN SHE LIED. THE ONLY ORLD THAT "FELL" ROUND HERE WAS YOURS.
THIS ISN'T "POST-APOCALYPSE." HERE'S NO SUCH THING AS APOCALYPSE. WE JUST...EVOLVED. INTO THIS.
INTO WHAT WE WERE MEANT TO BE. GET IT?
NO. WHAT'S MEANT TO BE IS THAT YOU ARE SUPPOSED TO BRING ME TO THE PARENTS WHO BOUGHT AND PAID FOR ME, NOW, IN THE AETHENAN PENTHOUSES.
I AM DESTINED TO RULE. AND YOU ARE MY SERVANT.
OR I WILL STAY HERE, MAKE THIS FOREST MY KINGDOM, AND LET MY MUMMY AND DADDY COME TO ME.

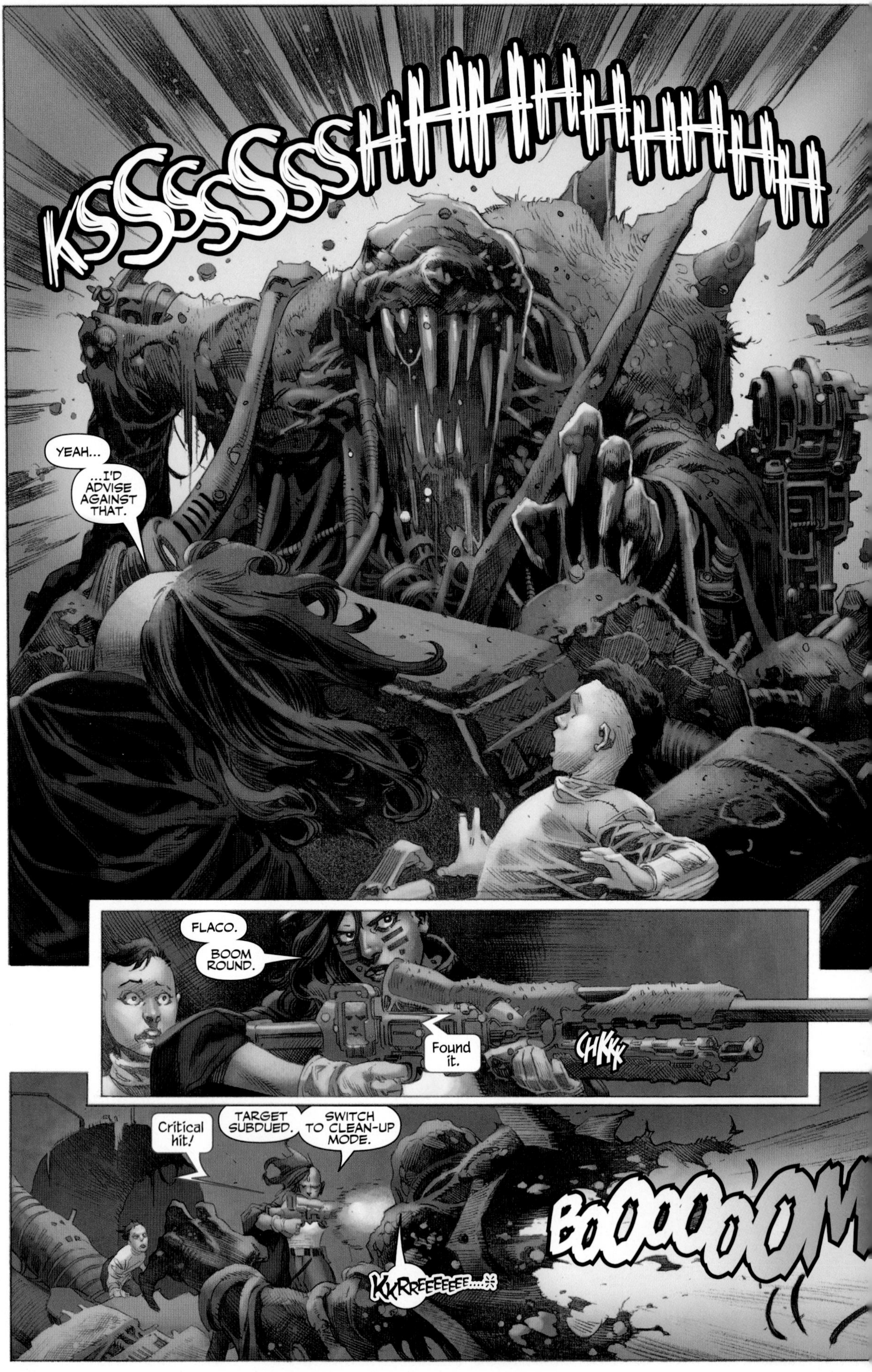
KSSSSSSSHHHHHHHHHHHH
YEAH...
...I'D ADVISE AGAINST THAT.
FLACO.
BOOM ROUND.
Found it.
CHKKK
Critical hit!
TARGET SUBDUED.
SWITCH TO CLEAN-UP MODE.
BOOOOOOM
KKRREEEEEEE...

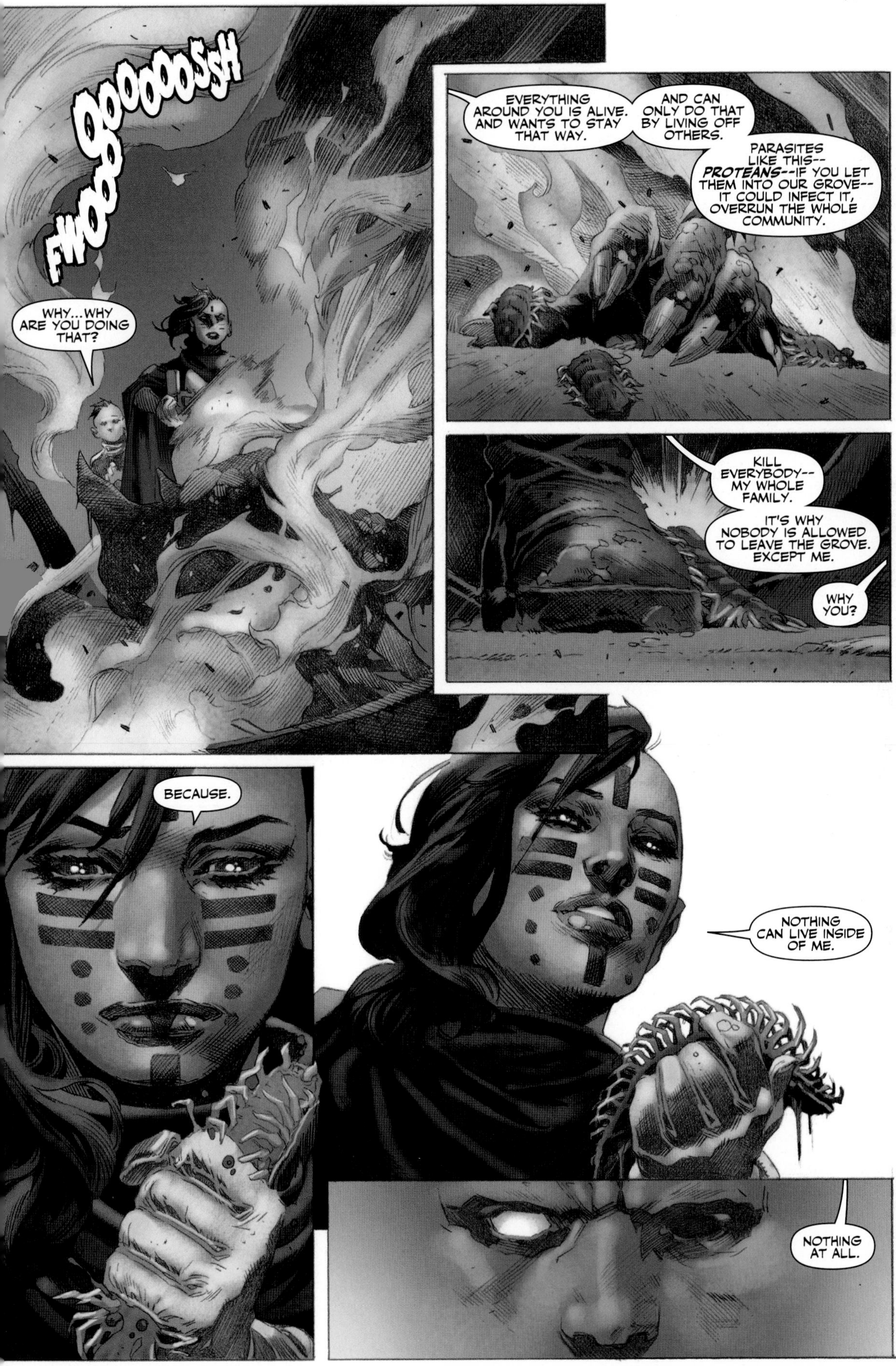
FWOOOOOOOOSH
WHY...WHY ARE YOU DOING THAT?
EVERYTHING AROUND YOU IS ALIVE. AND WANTS TO STAY THAT WAY.
AND CAN ONLY DO THAT BY LIVING OFF OTHERS.
PARASITES LIKE THIS--PROTEANS--IF YOU LET THEM INTO OUR GROVE--IT COULD INFECT IT, OVERRUN THE WHOLE COMMUNITY.
KILL EVERYBODY--MY WHOLE FAMILY.
IT'S WHY NOBODY IS ALLOWED TO LEAVE THE GROVE. EXCEPT ME.
WHY YOU?
BECAUSE.
NOTHING CAN LIVE INSIDE OF ME.
NOTHING AT ALL.

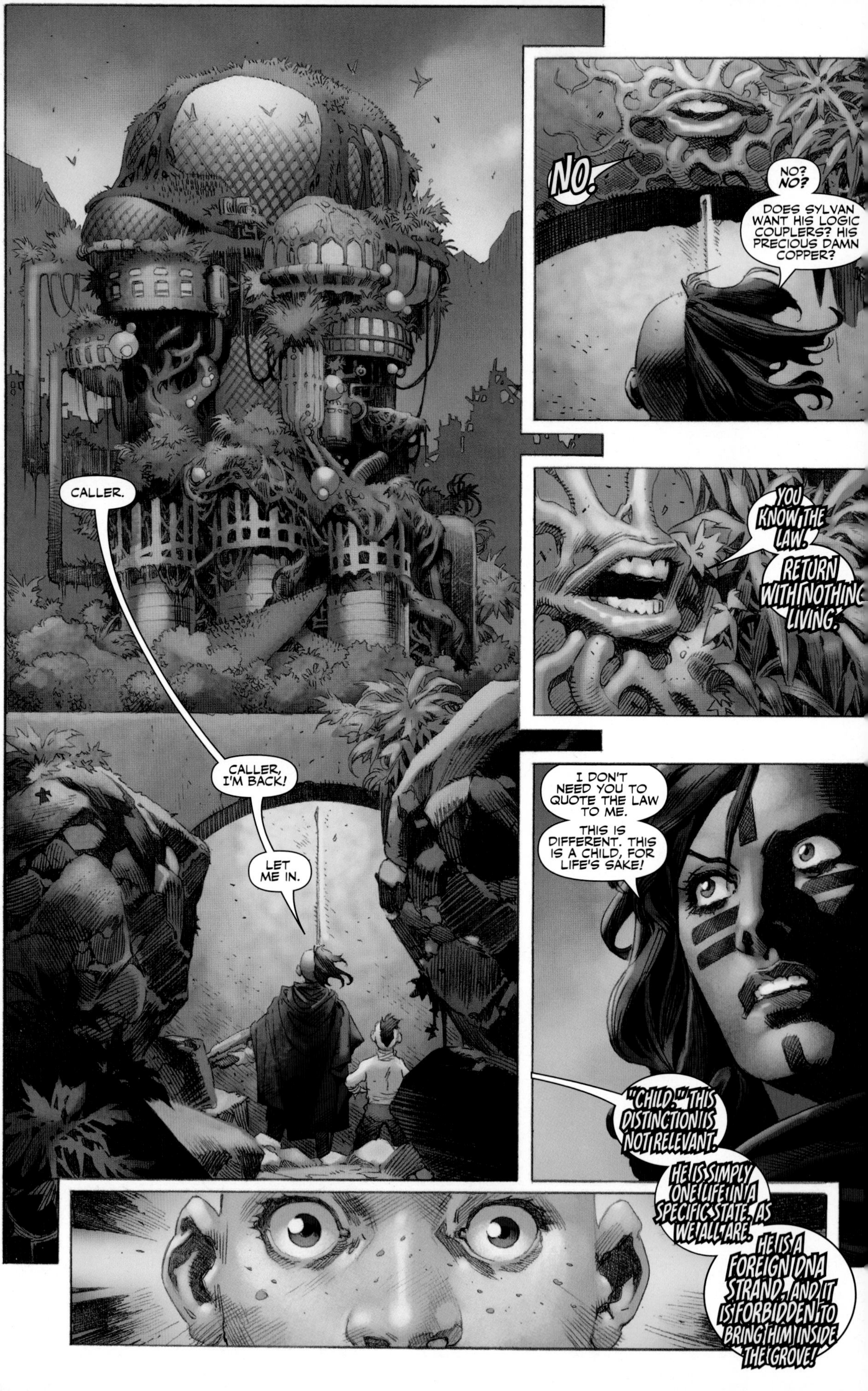
CALLER.
CALLER, I'M BACK!
LET ME IN.
NO.
NO? NO?
DOES SYLVAN WANT HIS LOGIC COUPLERS? HIS PRECIOUS DAMN COPPER?
YOU KNOW THE LAW.
RETURN WITH NOTHING LIVING.
I DON'T NEED YOU TO QUOTE THE LAW TO ME.
THIS IS DIFFERENT. THIS IS A CHILD, FOR LIFE'S SAKE!
"CHILD." THIS DISTINCTION IS NOT RELEVANT.
HE IS SIMPLY ONE LIFE IN A SPECIFIC STATE, AS WE ALL ARE.
HE IS A FOREIGN DNA STRAND, AND IT IS FORBIDDEN TO BRING HIM INSIDE THE GROVE!

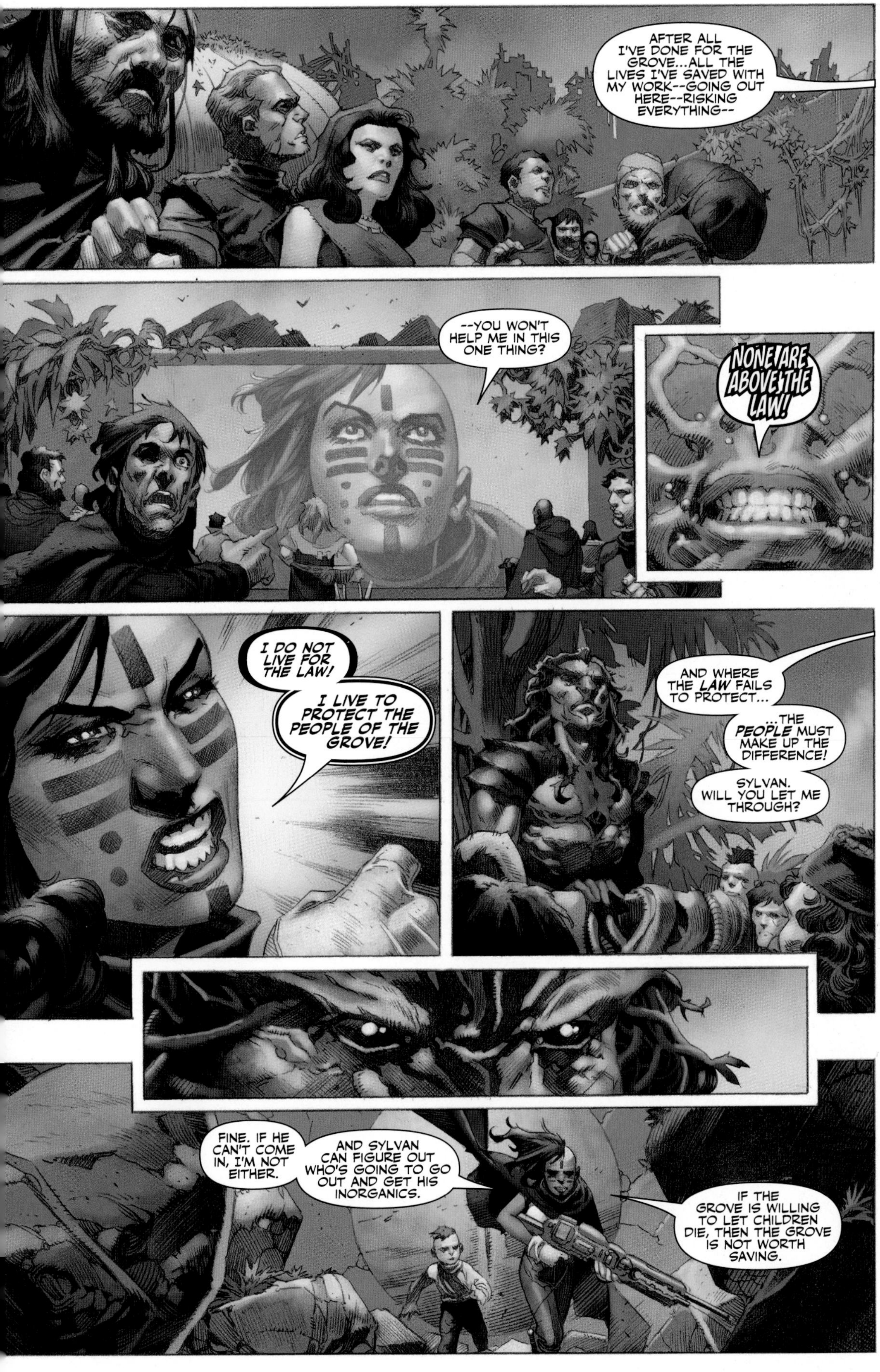

AFTER ALL I'VE DONE FOR THE GROVE...ALL THE LIVES I'VE SAVED WITH MY WORK--GOING OUT HERE--RISKING EVERYTHING--
--YOU WON'T HELP ME IN THIS ONE THING?
NONE ARE ABOVE THE LAW!
I DO NOT LIVE FOR THE LAW!
I LIVE TO PROTECT THE PEOPLE OF THE GROVE!
AND WHERE THE LAW FAILS TO PROTECT...
...THE PEOPLE MUST MAKE UP THE DIFFERENCE!
SYLVAN. WILL YOU LET ME THROUGH?
FINE. IF HE CAN'T COME IN, I'M NOT EITHER.
AND SYLVAN CAN FIGURE OUT WHO'S GOING TO GO OUT AND GET HIS INORGANICS.
IF THE GROVE IS WILLING TO LET CHILDREN DIE, THEN THE GROVE IS NOT WORTH SAVING.

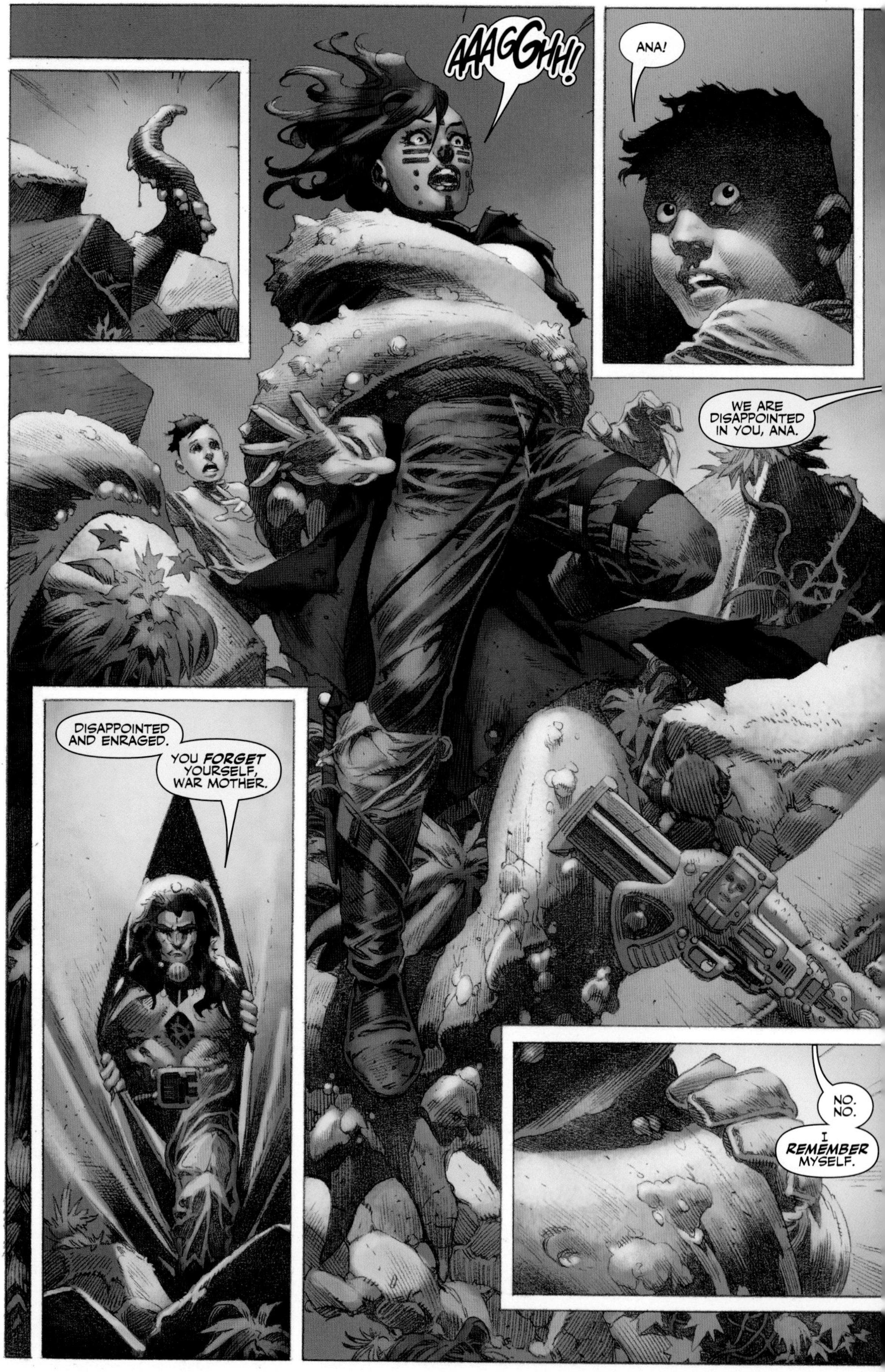
AAAGGHH!
ANA!
WE ARE DISAPPOINTED IN YOU, ANA.
DISAPPOINTED AND ENRAGED.
YOU FORGET YOURSELF, WAR MOTHER.
NO. NO.
I REMEMBER MYSELF.

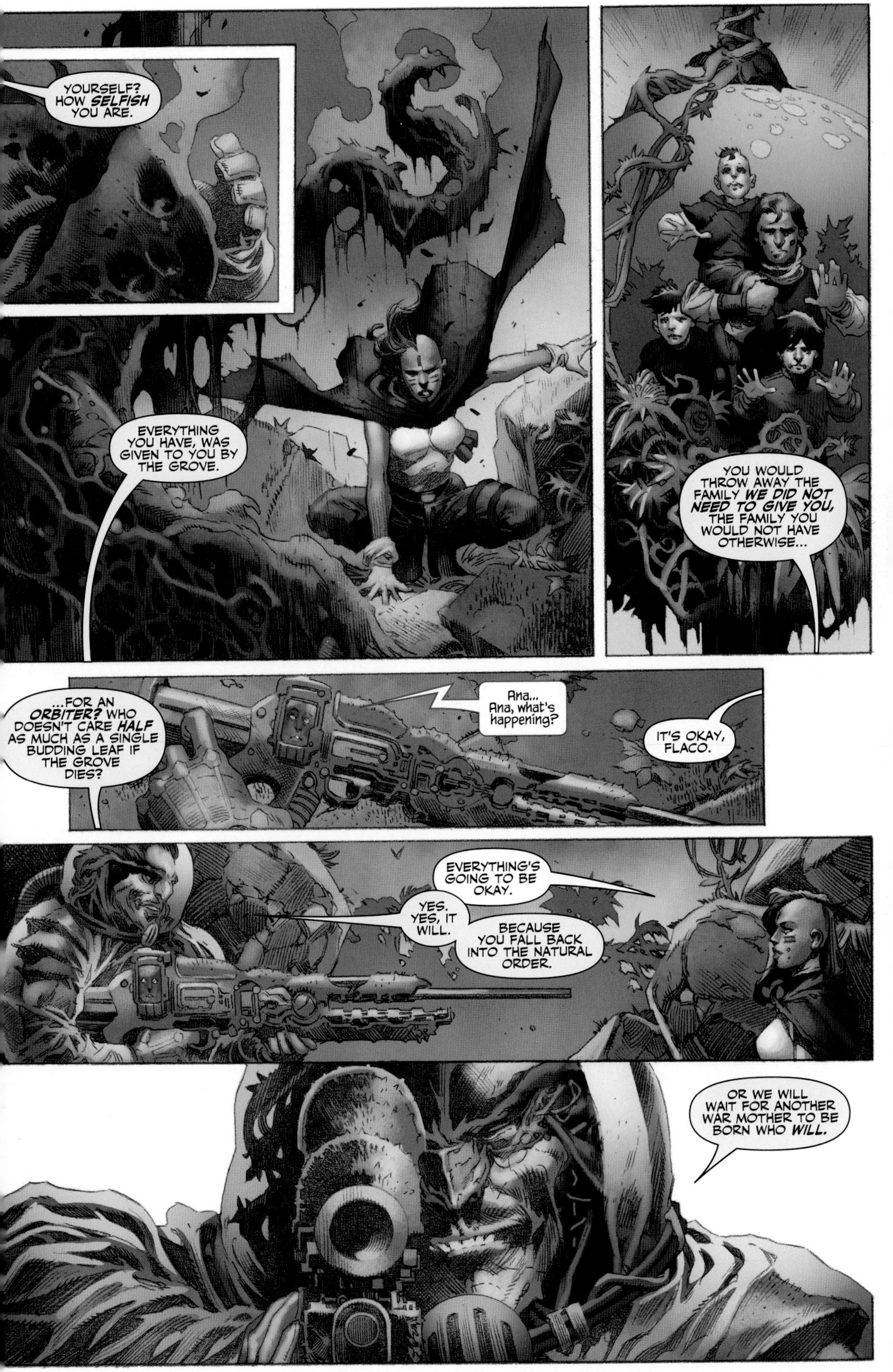
YOURSELF? HOW SELFISH YOU ARE.
EVERYTHING YOU HAVE, WAS GIVEN TO YOU BY THE GROVE.
YOU WOULD THROW AWAY THE FAMILY WE DID NOT NEED TO GIVE YOU, THE FAMILY YOU WOULD NOT HAVE OTHERWISE...
...FOR AN ORBITER? WHO DOESN'T CARE HALF AS MUCH AS A SINGLE BUDDING LEAF IF THE GROVE DIES?
Ana... Ana, what's happening?
IT'S OKAY, FLACO.
EVERYTHING'S GOING TO BE OKAY.
YES. YES, IT WILL.
BECAUSE YOU FALL BACK INTO THE NATURAL ORDER.
OR WE WILL WAIT FOR ANOTHER WAR MOTHER TO BE BORN WHO WILL.

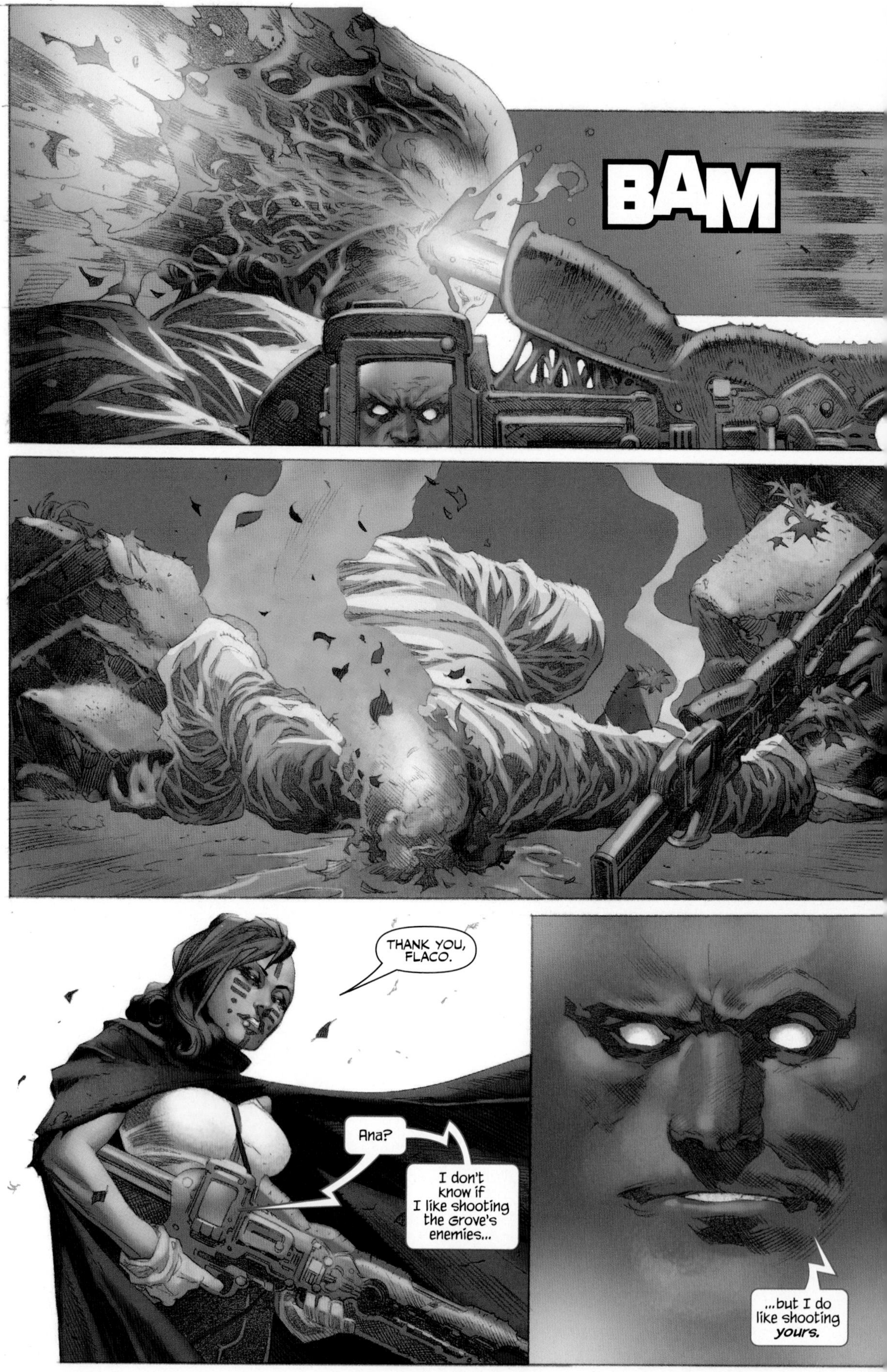
BAM
THANK YOU, FLACO.
Ana?
I don't know if I like shooting the Grove's enemies...
...but I do like shooting *yours.*

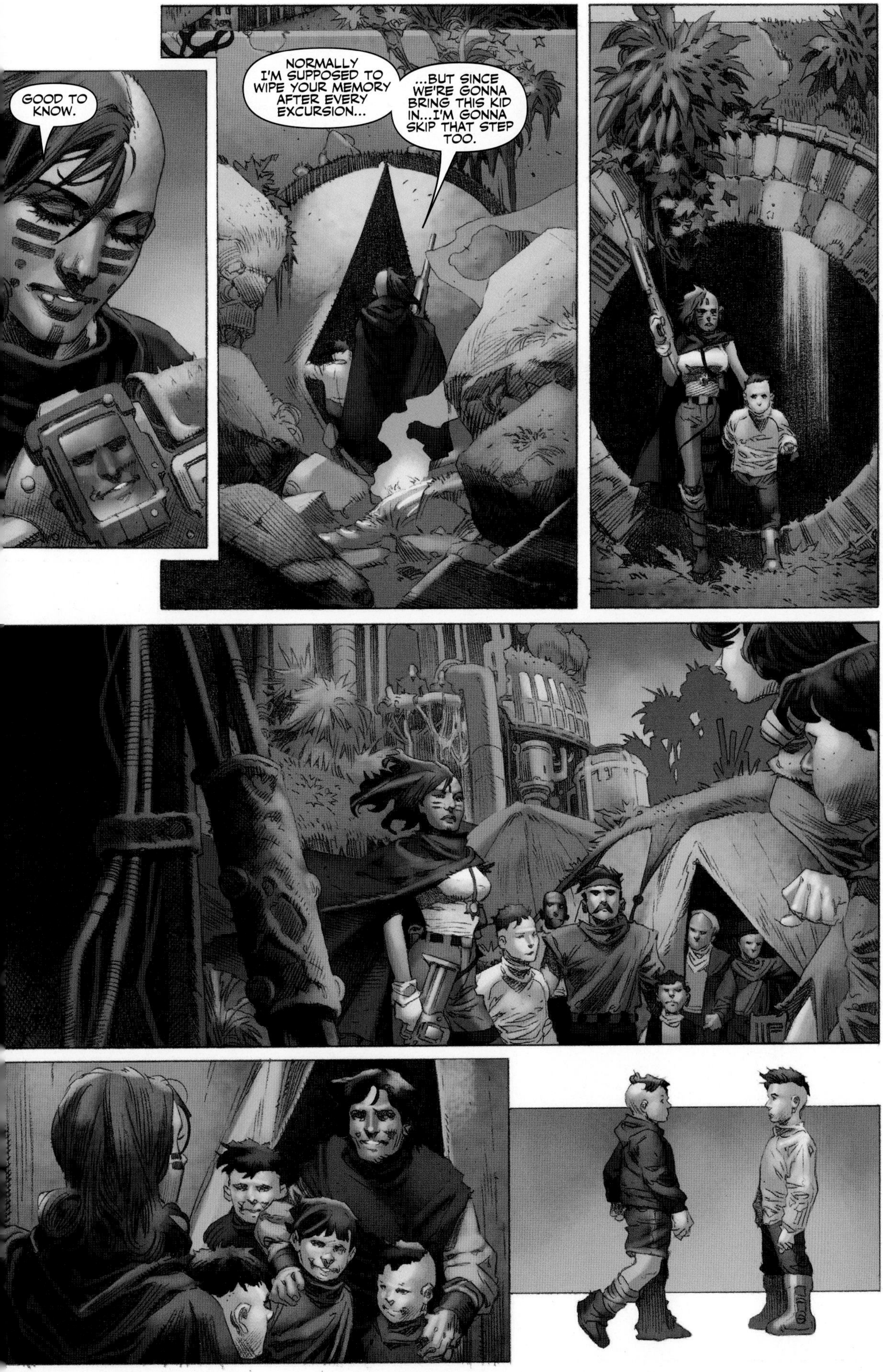
GOOD TO KNOW.
NORMALLY I'M SUPPOSED TO WIPE YOUR MEMORY AFTER EVERY EXCURSION...
...BUT SINCE WE'RE GONNA BRING THIS KID IN...I'M GONNA SKIP THAT STEP TOO.

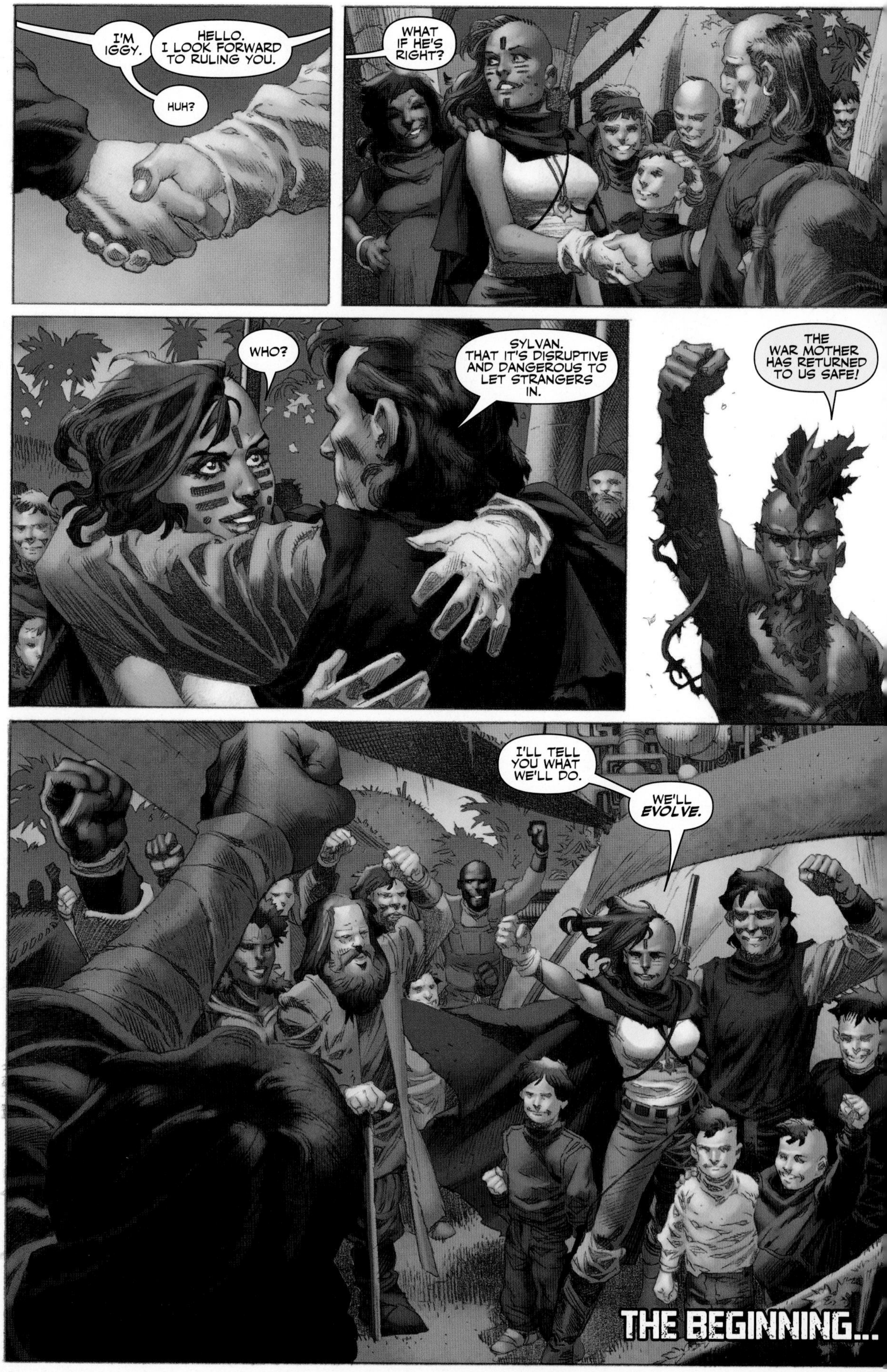
I'M IGGY.
HELLO. I LOOK FORWARD TO RULING YOU.
HUH?
WHAT IF HE'S RIGHT?
WHO?
SYLVAN. THAT IT'S DISRUPTIVE AND DANGEROUS TO LET STRANGERS IN.
THE WAR MOTHER HAS RETURNED TO US SAFE!
I'LL TELL YOU WHAT WE'LL DO.
WE'LL EVOLVE.
THE BEGINNING...

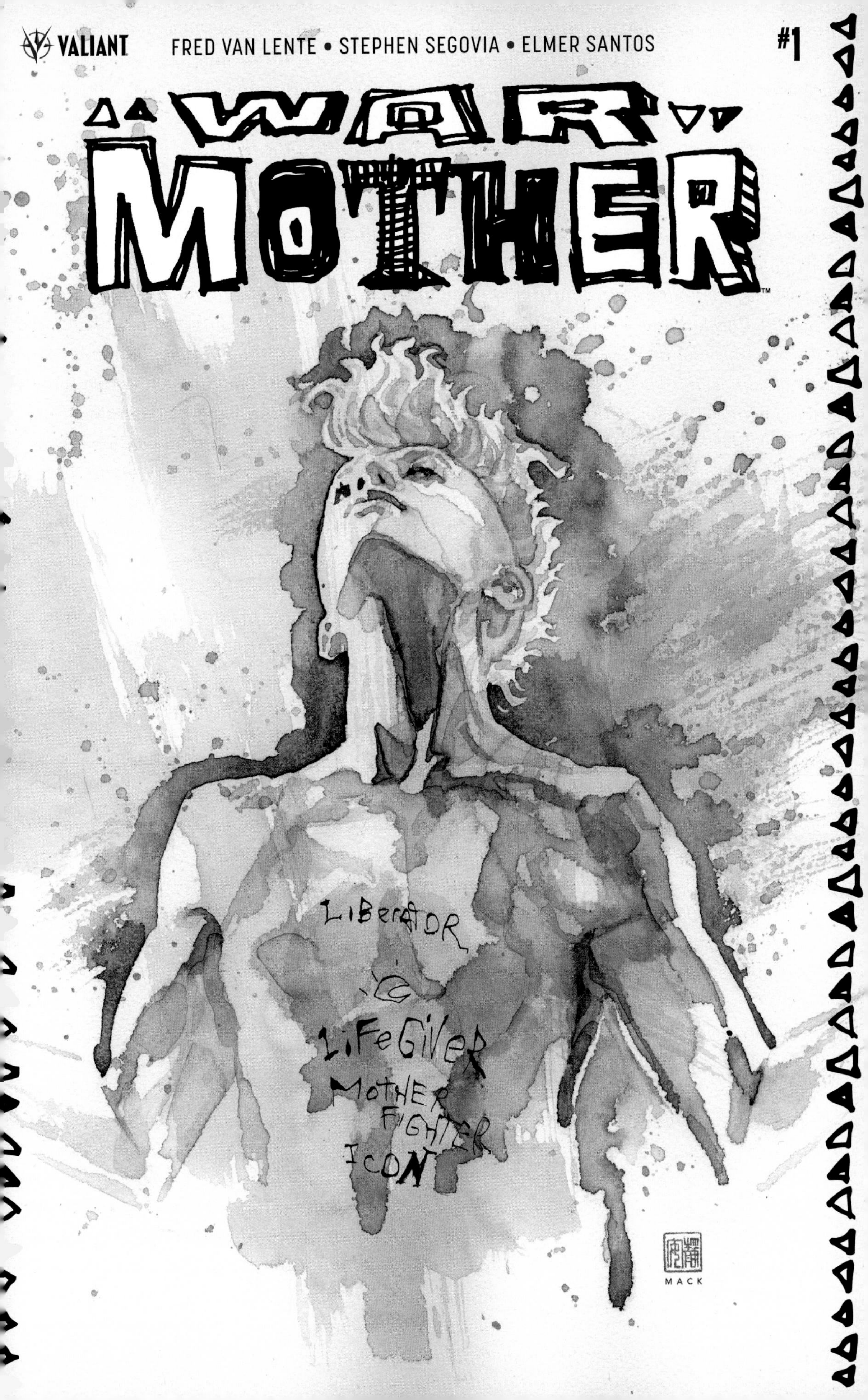
VALIANT
FRED VAN LENTE • STEPHEN SEGOVIA • ELMER SANTOS
#1
WAR MOTHER
LIBERATOR
LIFEGIVER
MOTHER
FIGHTER
ICON
MACK

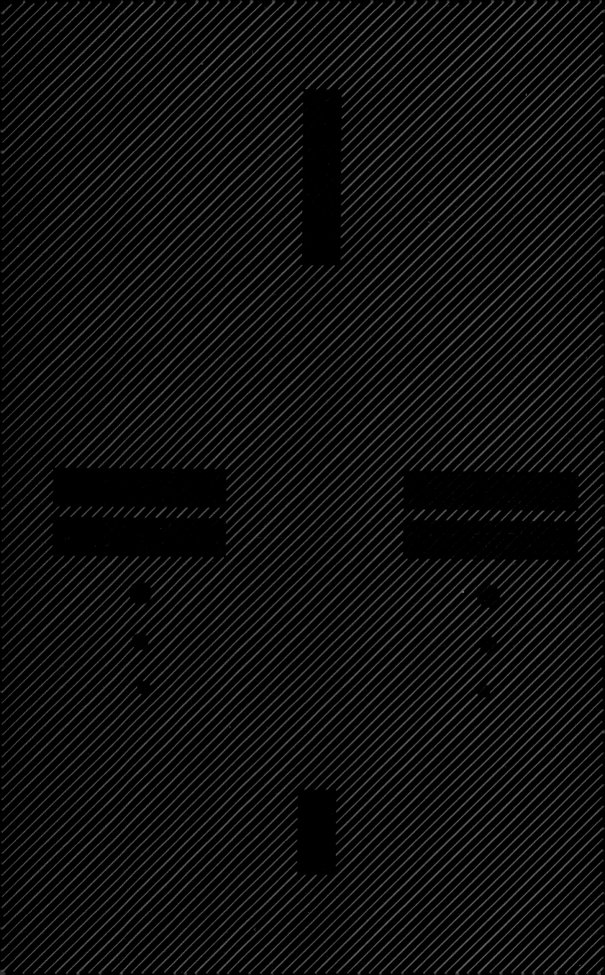

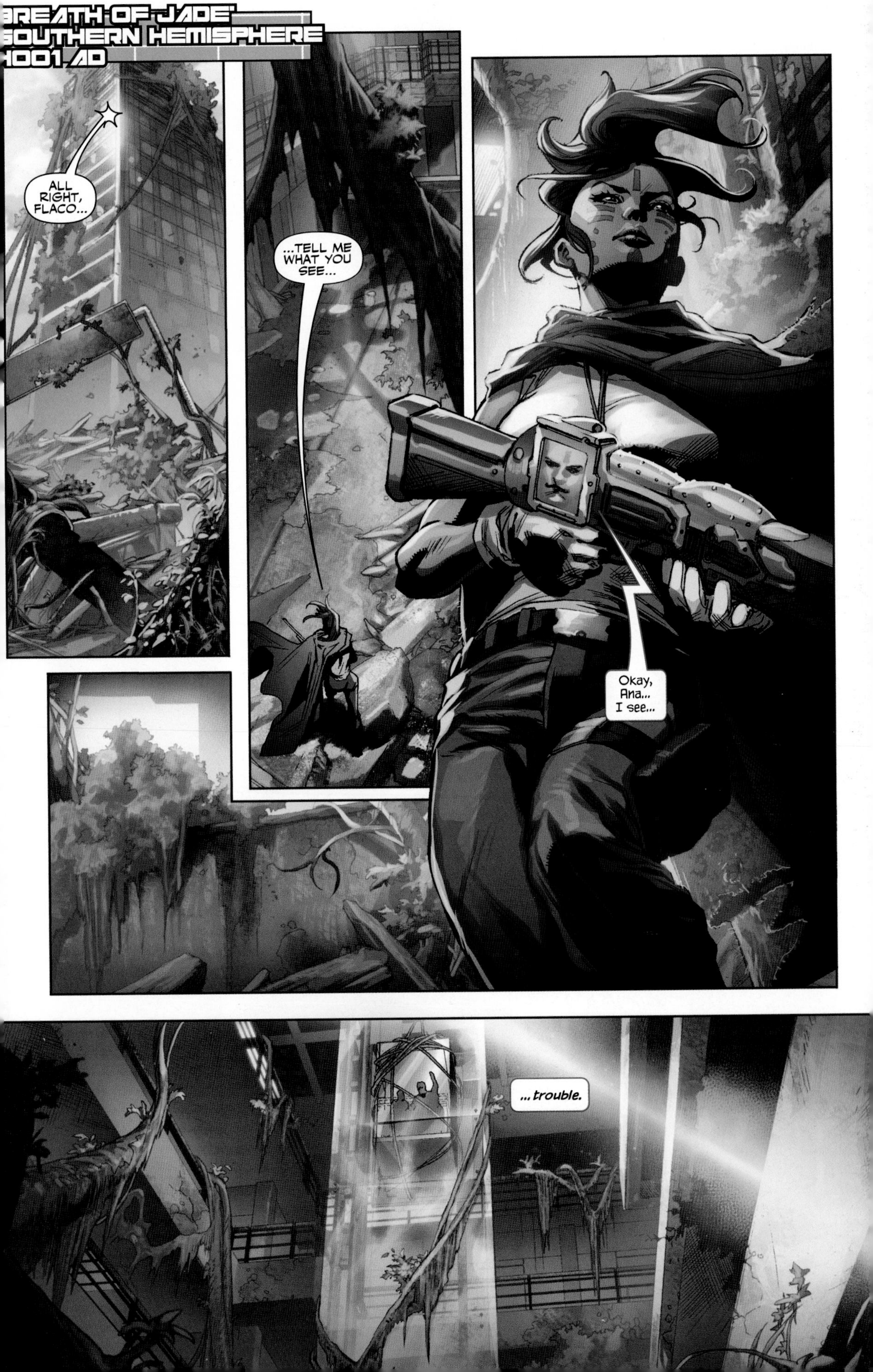
BREATH OF JADE' SOUTHERN HEMISPHERE 4001 AD
ALL RIGHT, FLACO...
...TELL ME WHAT YOU SEE...
Okay, Ana... I see...
...trouble.

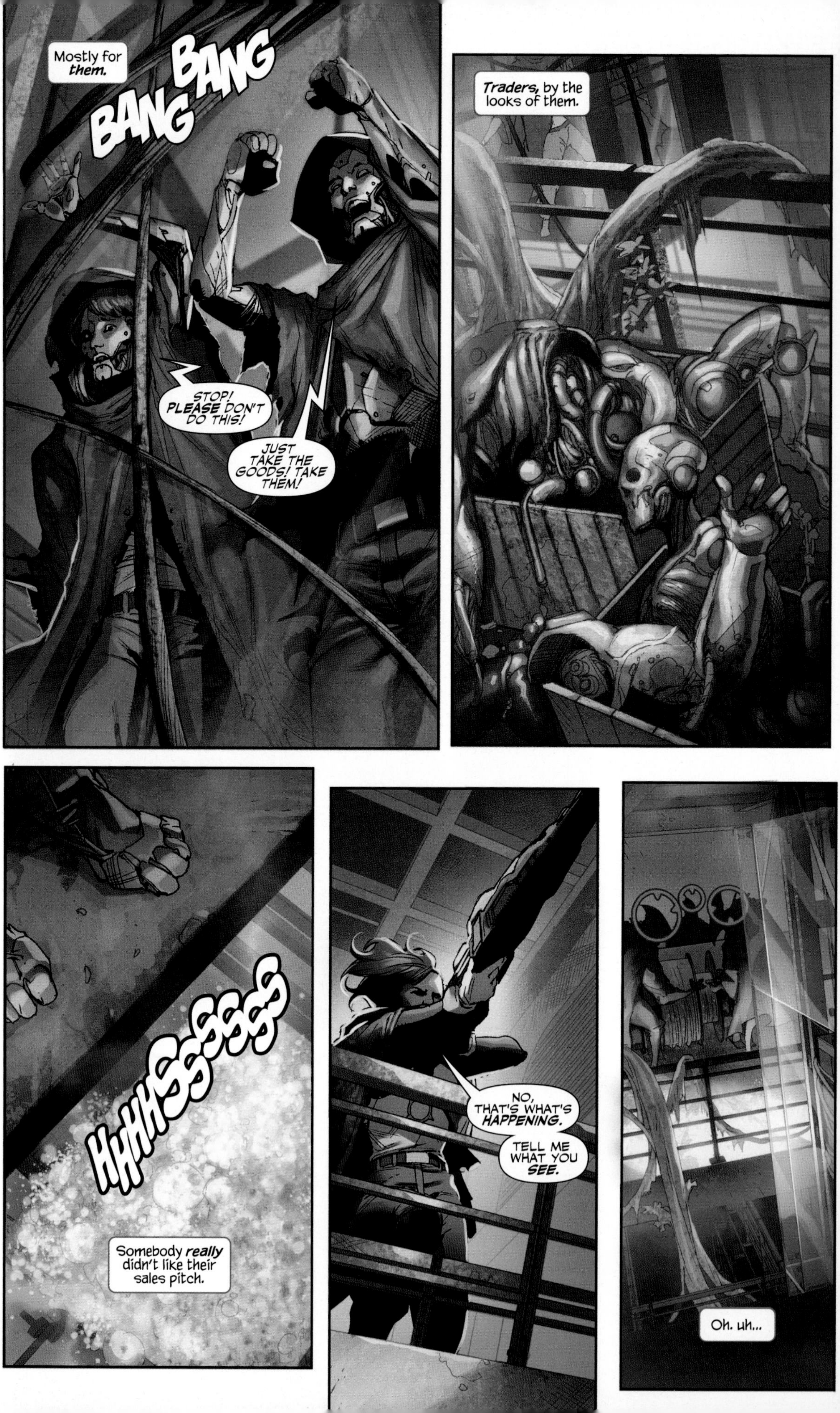
Mostly for *them.*
BANG BANG
STOP! *PLEASE* DON'T DO THIS!
JUST TAKE THE GOODS! TAKE THEM!
Traders, by the looks of them.
HHHHSSSSSSS
Somebody *really* didn't like their sales pitch.
NO, THAT'S WHAT'S *HAPPENING.*
TELL ME WHAT YOU *SEE.*
Oh. uh...

They've been captured by the Urbanites.

And...

...oh! I see! I see!

I see an old surplus *nova* grenade.

THAT'S MY BOY.

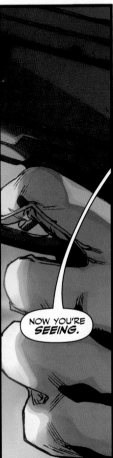

NOW YOU'RE *SEEING.*

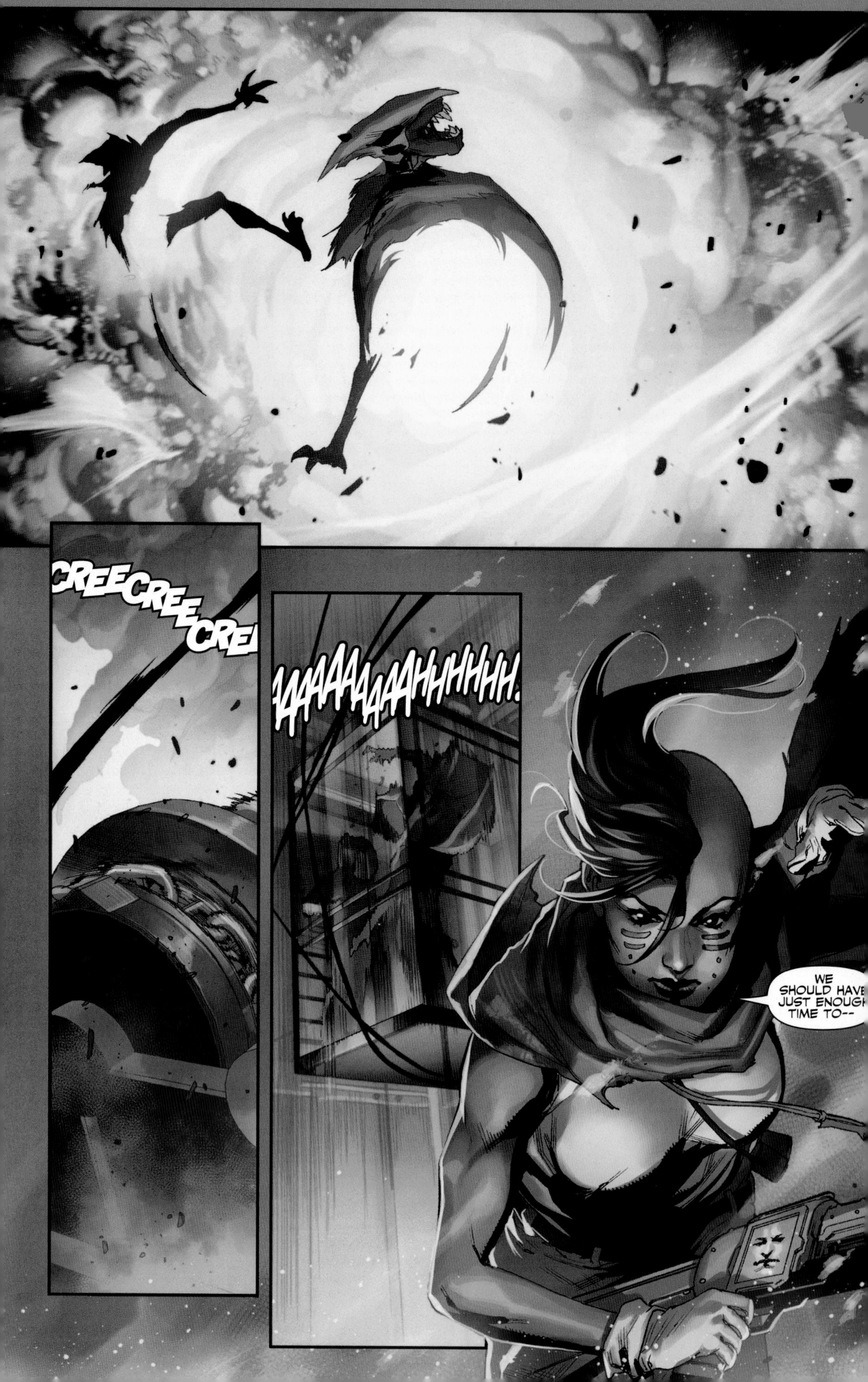
CREECREECRE
AAAAAAAAAAHHHHHH!
WE SHOULD HAVE JUST ENOUGH TIME TO--

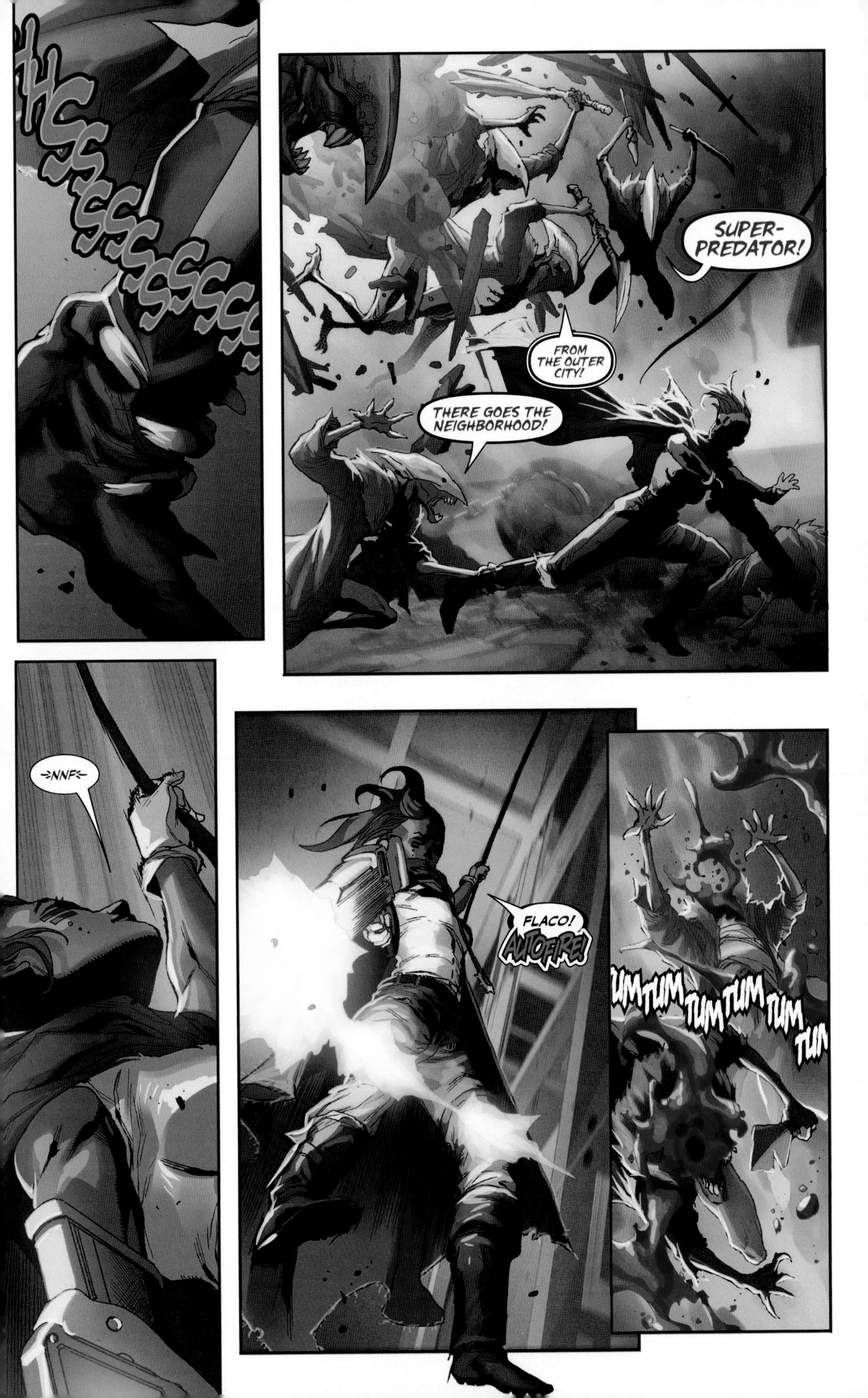
THSSSSSSSSSSS
SUPER-PREDATOR!
FROM THE OUTER CITY!
THERE GOES THE NEIGHBORHOOD!
NNF
FLACO! AUTOFIRE!
TUM TUM TUM TUM TUM TUM

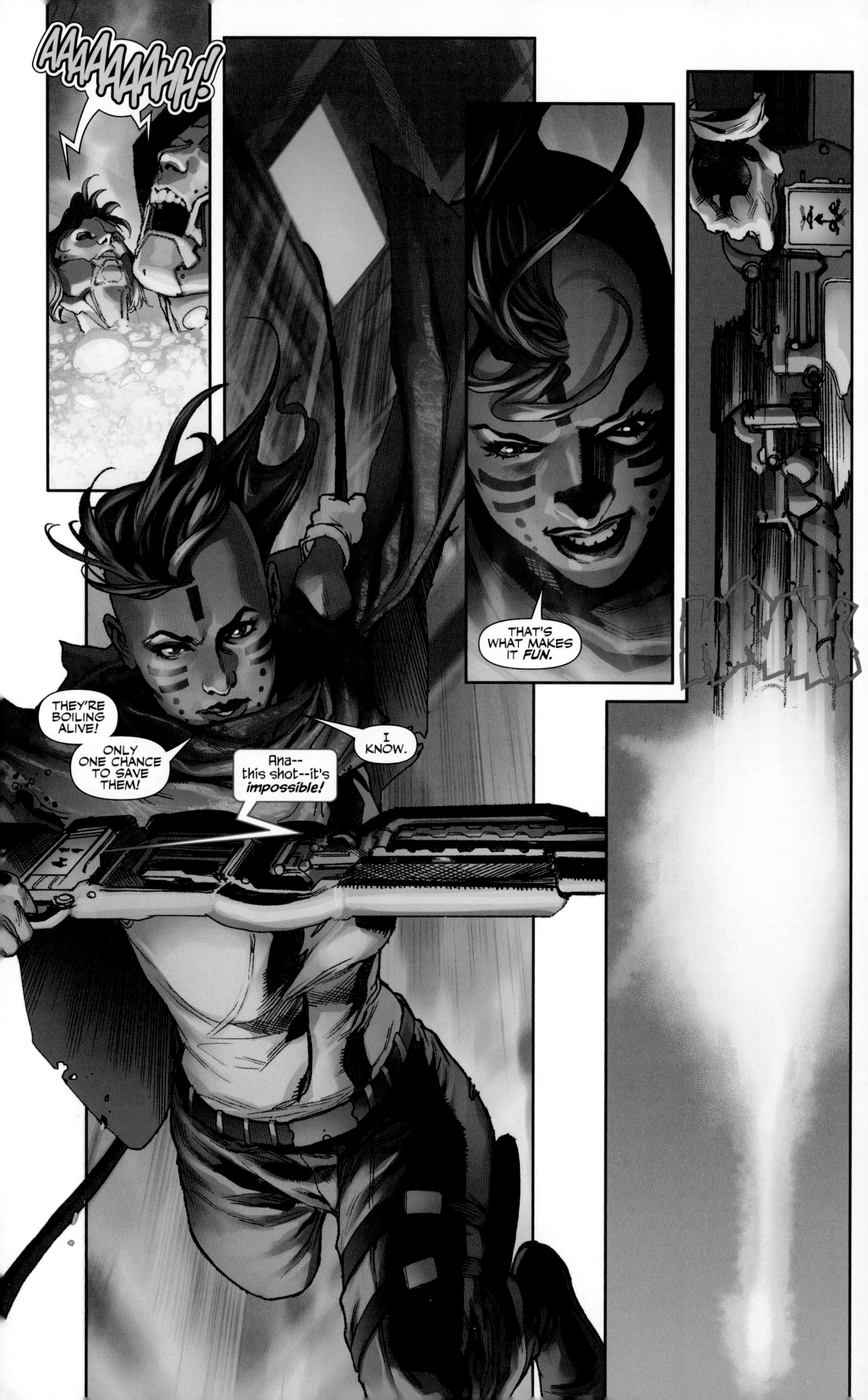
AAAAAAAHH!
THEY'RE BOILING ALIVE!
ONLY ONE CHANCE TO SAVE THEM!
I KNOW.
Ana-- this shot--it's *impossible!*
THAT'S WHAT MAKES IT *FUN.*

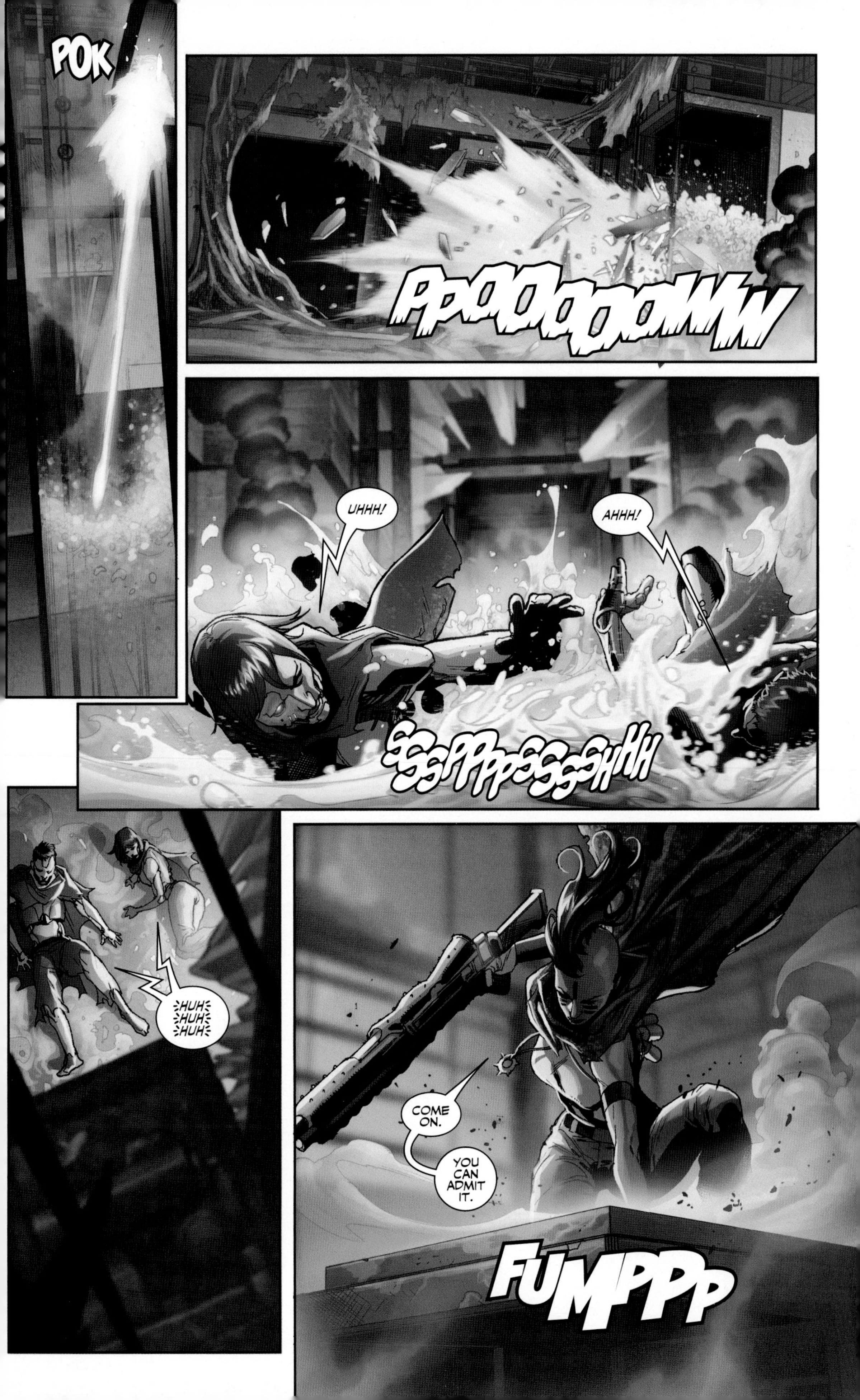
POK
PPOOOOOOMW
UHHH!
AHHH!
SSSPPPPSSSSHHH
HUH HUH HUH
COME ON.
YOU CAN ADMIT IT.
FUMPPP

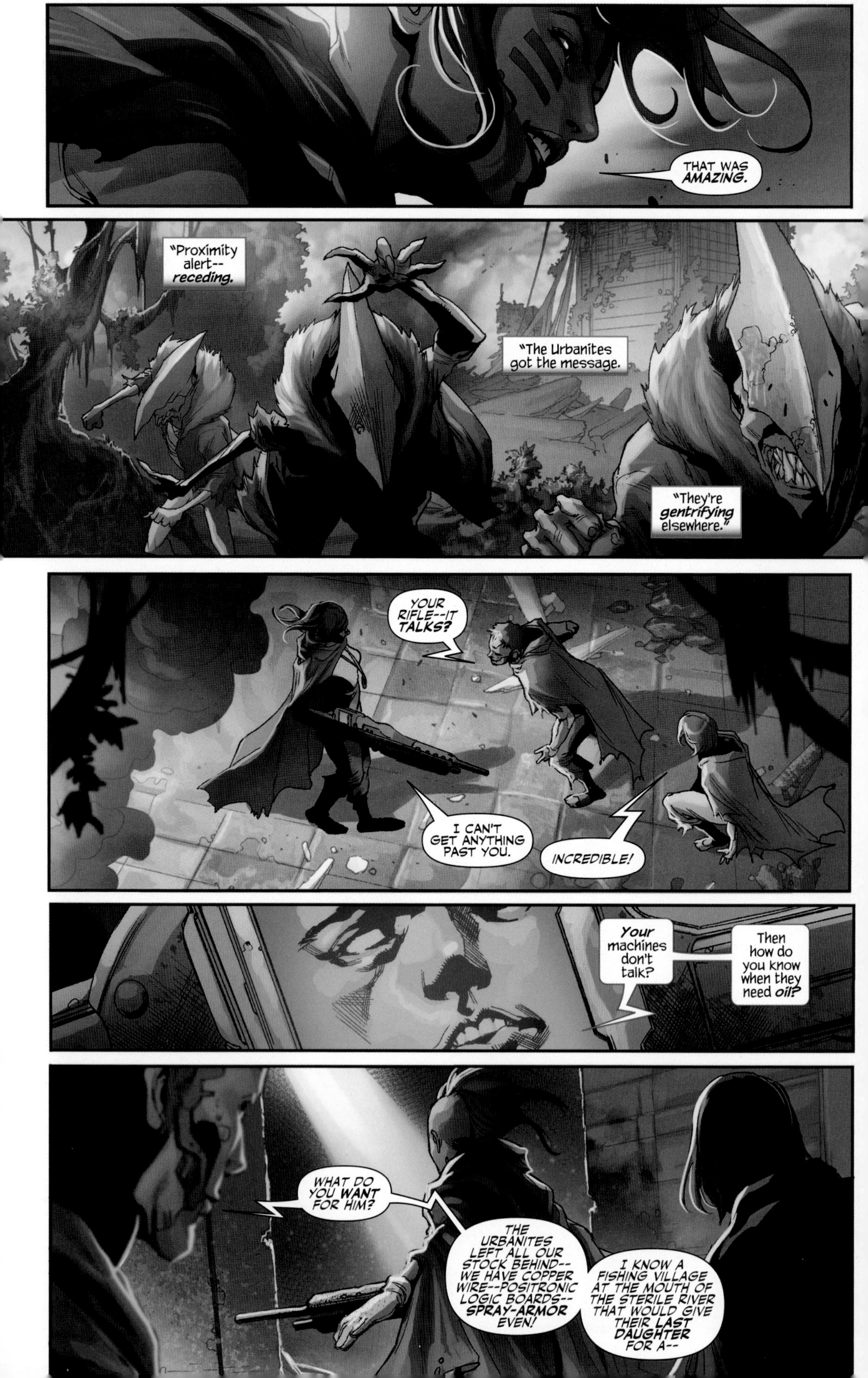
THAT WAS AMAZING.
"Proximity alert--receding.
"The Urbanites got the message.
"They're gentrifying elsewhere."
YOUR RIFLE--IT TALKS?
I CAN'T GET ANYTHING PAST YOU.
INCREDIBLE!
Your machines don't talk?
Then how do you know when they need oil?
WHAT DO YOU WANT FOR HIM?
THE URBANITES LEFT ALL OUR STOCK BEHIND--WE HAVE COPPER WIRE--POSITRONIC LOGIC BOARDS--SPRAY-ARMOR EVEN!
I KNOW A FISHING VILLAGE AT THE MOUTH OF THE STERILE RIVER THAT WOULD GIVE THEIR LAST DAUGHTER FOR A--

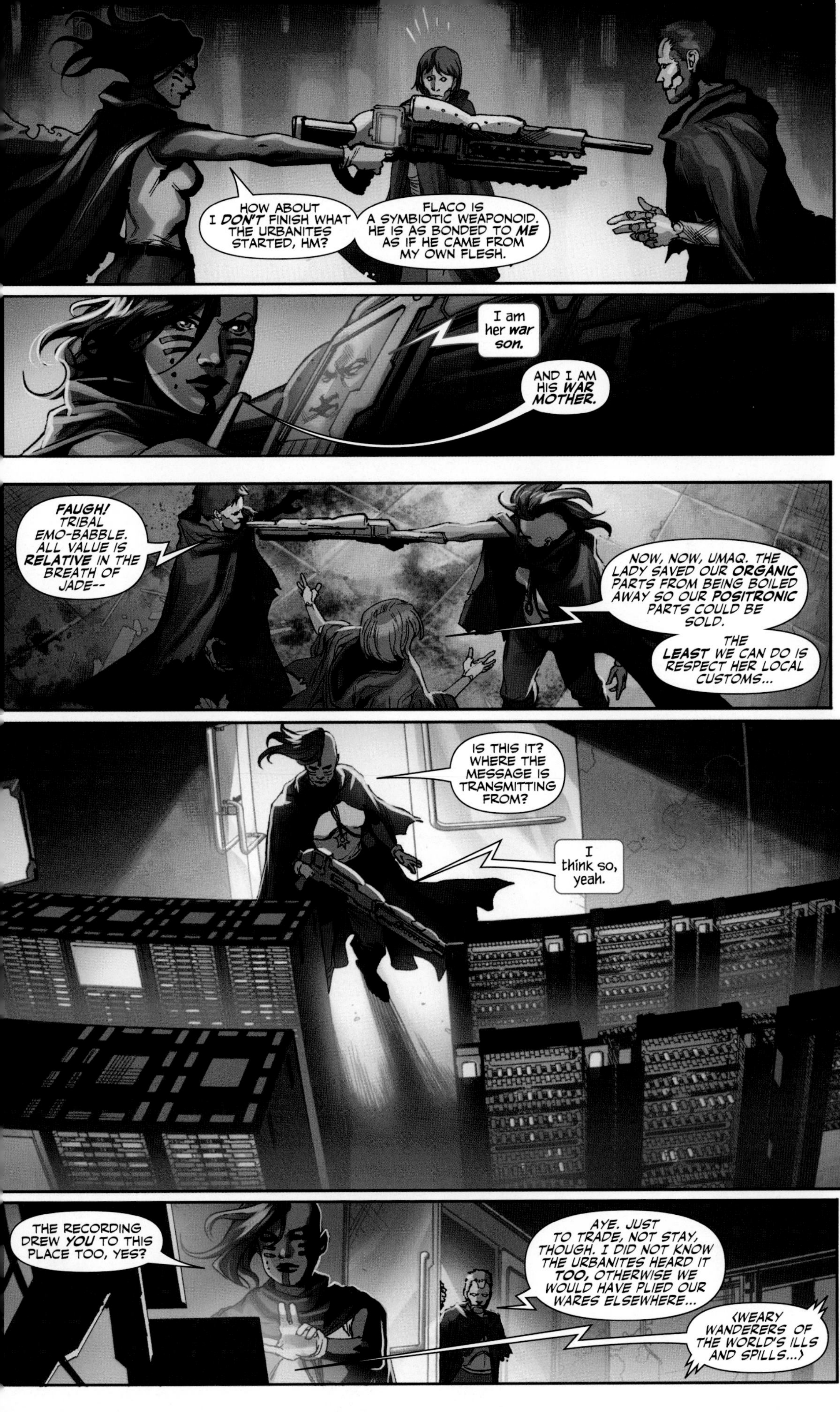
HOW ABOUT I *DON'T* FINISH WHAT THE URBANITES STARTED, HM?
FLACO IS A SYMBIOTIC WEAPONOID. HE IS AS BONDED TO *ME* AS IF HE CAME FROM MY OWN FLESH.
I am her *war son.*
AND I AM HIS *WAR MOTHER.*
FAUGH! TRIBAL EMO-BABBLE. ALL VALUE IS ***RELATIVE*** IN THE BREATH OF JADE--
NOW, NOW, UMAQ. THE LADY SAVED OUR **ORGANIC** PARTS FROM BEING BOILED AWAY SO OUR **POSITRONIC** PARTS COULD BE SOLD.
THE **LEAST** WE CAN DO IS RESPECT HER LOCAL CUSTOMS...
IS THIS IT? WHERE THE MESSAGE IS TRANSMITTING FROM?
I think so, yeah.
THE RECORDING DREW *YOU* TO THIS PLACE TOO, YES?
AYE. JUST TO TRADE, NOT STAY, THOUGH. I DID NOT KNOW THE URBANITES HEARD IT *TOO*, OTHERWISE WE WOULD HAVE PLIED OUR WARES ELSEWHERE...
‹WEARY WANDERERS OF THE WORLD'S ILLS AND SPILLS...›

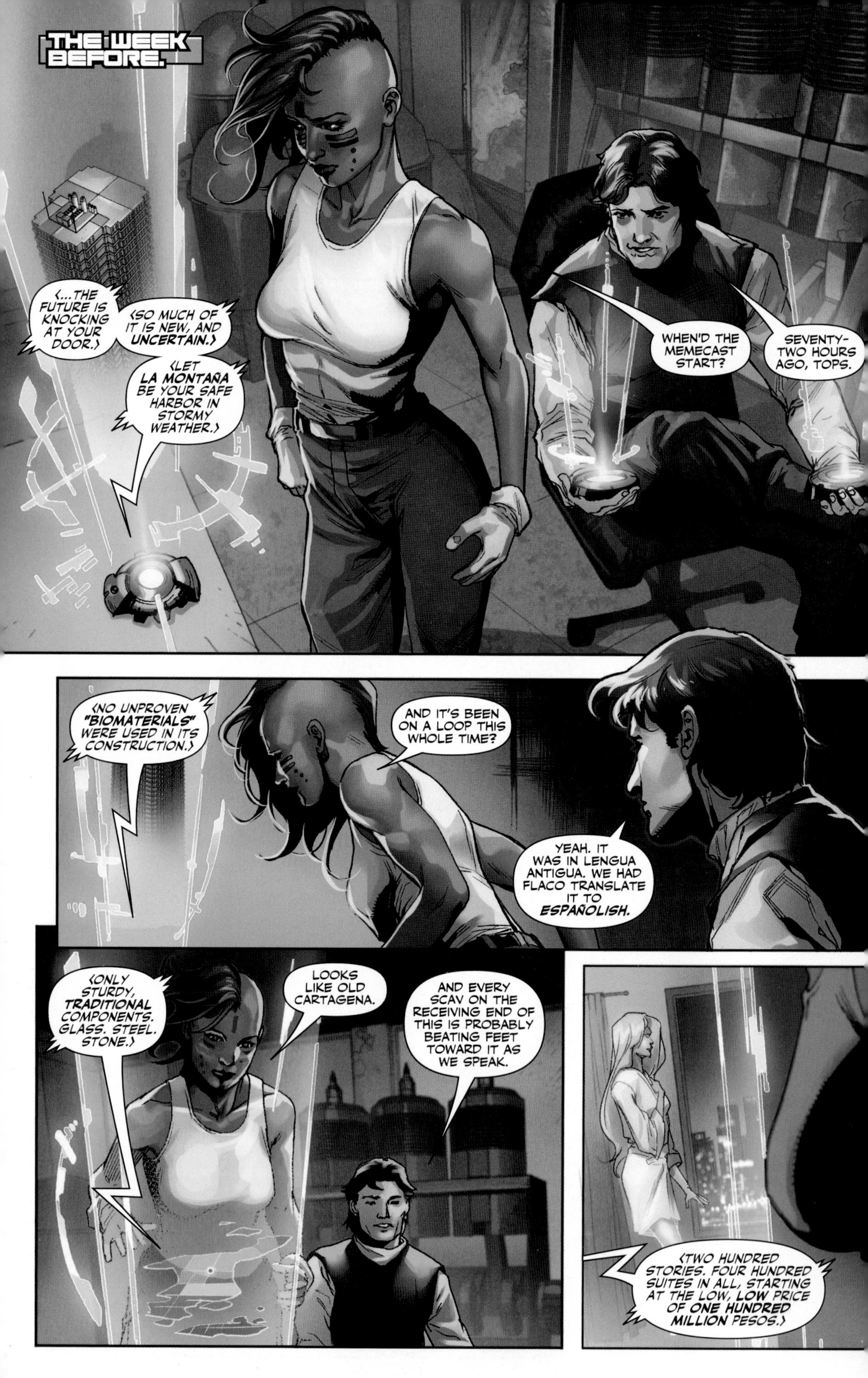
THE WEEK BEFORE.
‹...THE FUTURE IS KNOCKING AT YOUR DOOR.›
‹SO MUCH OF IT IS NEW, AND UNCERTAIN.›
‹LET LA MONTAÑA BE YOUR SAFE HARBOR IN STORMY WEATHER.›
WHEN'D THE MEMECAST START?
SEVENTY-TWO HOURS AGO, TOPS.
‹NO UNPROVEN "BIOMATERIALS" WERE USED IN ITS CONSTRUCTION.›
AND IT'S BEEN ON A LOOP THIS WHOLE TIME?
YEAH. IT WAS IN LENGUA ANTIGUA. WE HAD FLACO TRANSLATE IT TO ESPAÑOLISH.
‹ONLY STURDY, TRADITIONAL COMPONENTS. GLASS. STEEL. STONE.›
LOOKS LIKE OLD CARTAGENA.
AND EVERY SCAV ON THE RECEIVING END OF THIS IS PROBABLY BEATING FEET TOWARD IT AS WE SPEAK.
‹TWO HUNDRED STORIES. FOUR HUNDRED SUITES IN ALL, STARTING AT THE LOW, LOW PRICE OF ONE HUNDRED MILLION PESOS.›

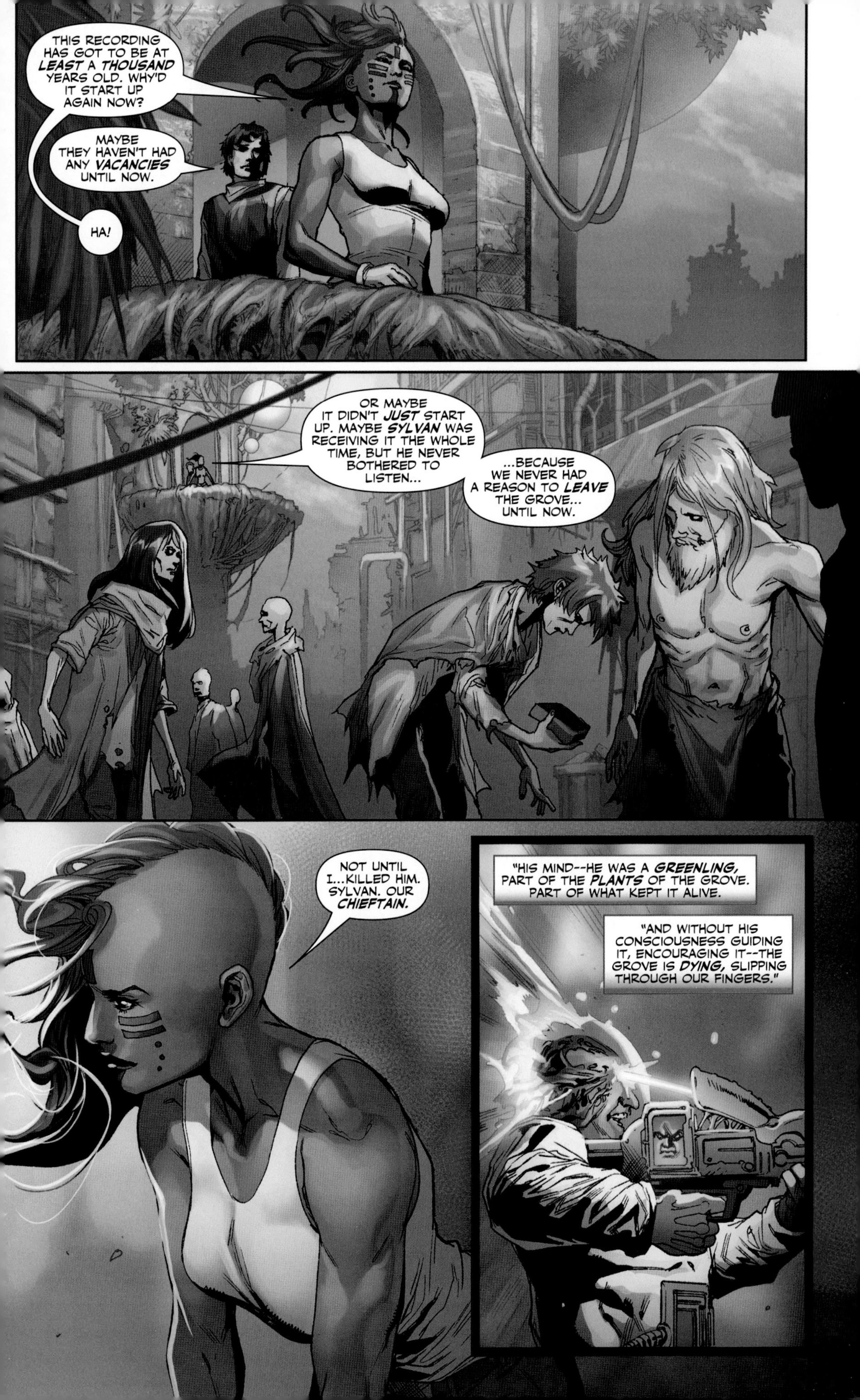
THIS RECORDING HAS GOT TO BE AT LEAST A THOUSAND YEARS OLD. WHY'D IT START UP AGAIN NOW?
MAYBE THEY HAVEN'T HAD ANY VACANCIES UNTIL NOW.
HA!
OR MAYBE IT DIDN'T JUST START UP. MAYBE SYLVAN WAS RECEIVING IT THE WHOLE TIME, BUT HE NEVER BOTHERED TO LISTEN...
...BECAUSE WE NEVER HAD A REASON TO LEAVE THE GROVE... UNTIL NOW.
NOT UNTIL I...KILLED HIM. SYLVAN. OUR CHIEFTAIN.
"HIS MIND--HE WAS A GREENLING, PART OF THE PLANTS OF THE GROVE. PART OF WHAT KEPT IT ALIVE.
"AND WITHOUT HIS CONSCIOUSNESS GUIDING IT, ENCOURAGING IT--THE GROVE IS DYING, SLIPPING THROUGH OUR FINGERS."

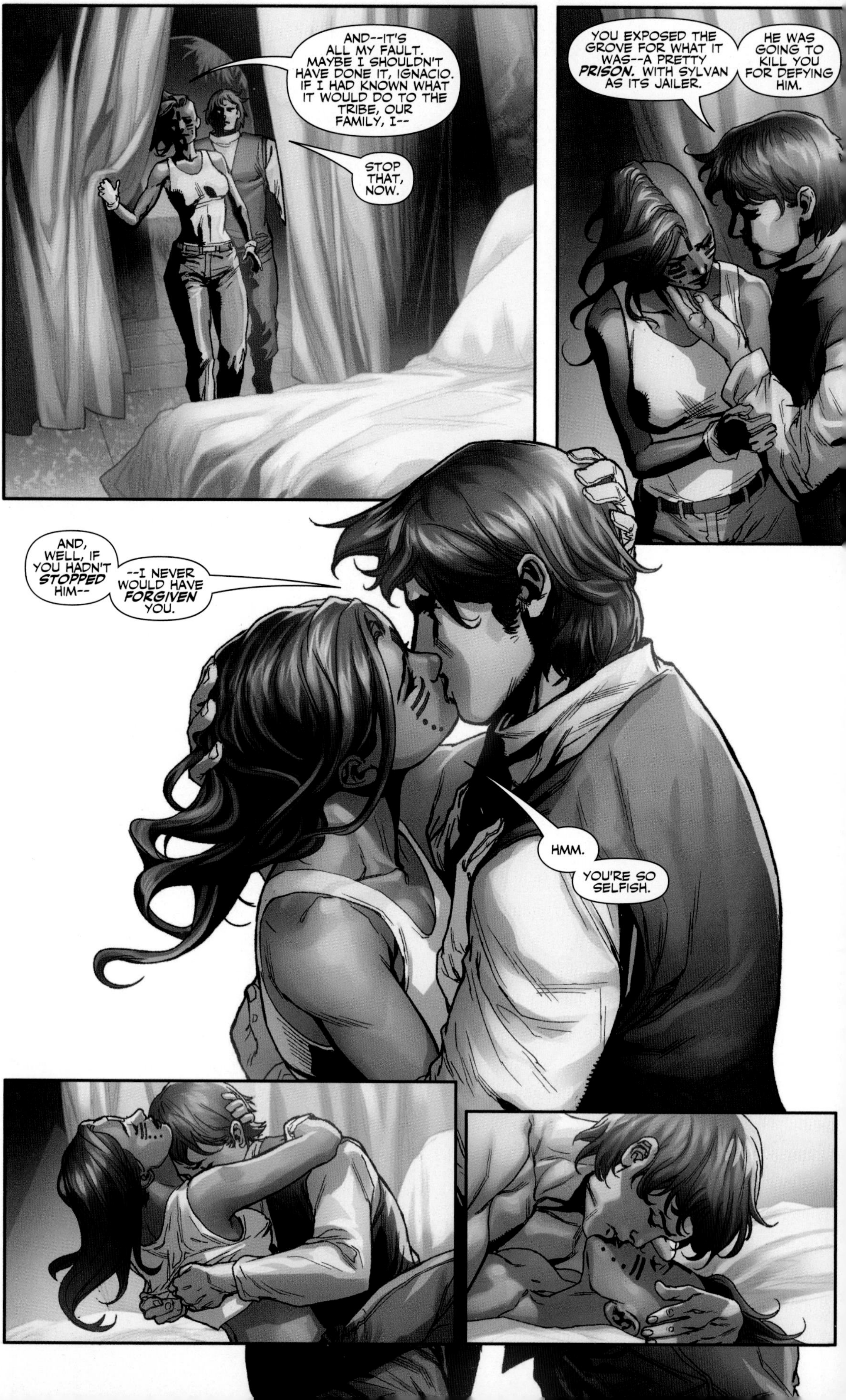
AND--IT'S ALL MY FAULT. MAYBE I SHOULDN'T HAVE DONE IT, IGNACIO. IF I HAD KNOWN WHAT IT WOULD DO TO THE TRIBE, OUR FAMILY, I--
STOP THAT, NOW.
YOU EXPOSED THE GROVE FOR WHAT IT WAS--A PRETTY **PRISON.** WITH SYLVAN AS ITS JAILER.
HE WAS GOING TO KILL YOU FOR DEFYING HIM.
AND, WELL, IF YOU HADN'T ***STOPPED*** HIM--
--I NEVER WOULD HAVE ***FORGIVEN*** YOU.
HMM.
YOU'RE SO SELFISH.

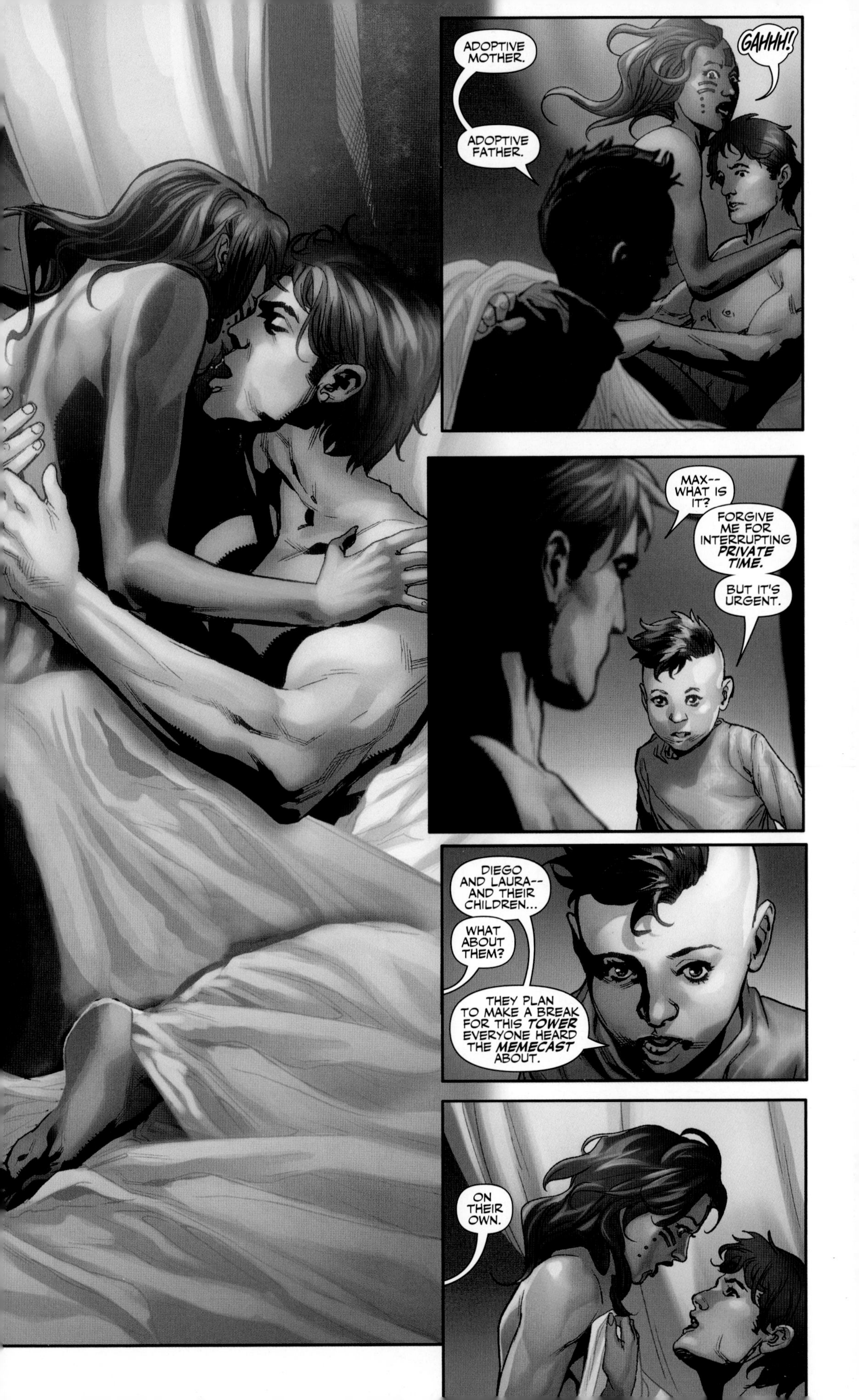
ADOPTIVE MOTHER.
ADOPTIVE FATHER.
GAHHH!
MAX-- WHAT IS IT?
FORGIVE ME FOR INTERRUPTING *PRIVATE TIME.*
BUT IT'S URGENT.
DIEGO AND LAURA-- AND THEIR CHILDREN...
WHAT ABOUT THEM?
THEY PLAN TO MAKE A BREAK FOR THIS *TOWER* EVERYONE HEARD THE *MEMECAST* ABOUT.
ON THEIR OWN.

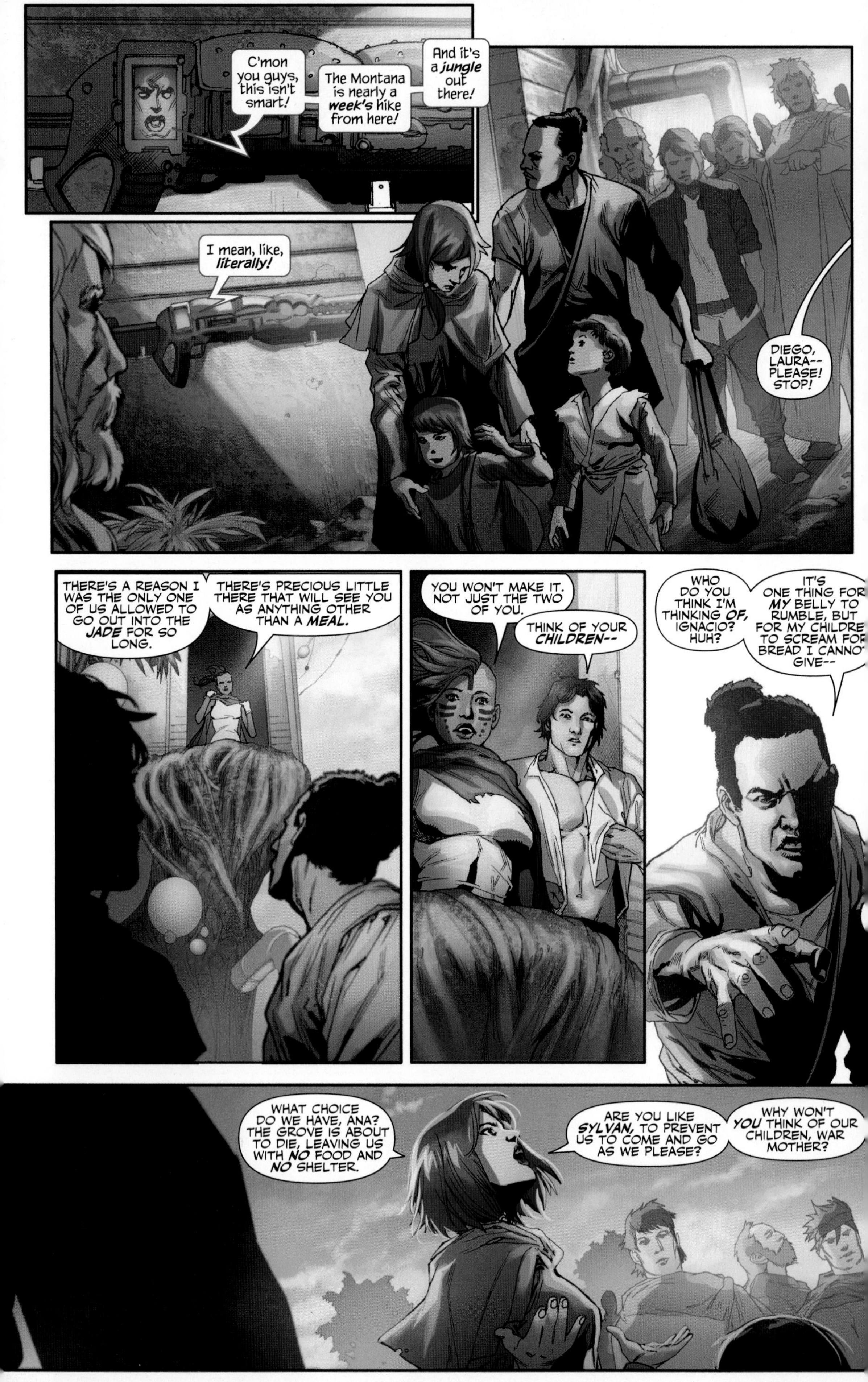

C'mon you guys, this isn't smart!
The Montana is nearly a week's hike from here!
And it's a jungle out there!
I mean, like, literally!
DIEGO, LAURA-- PLEASE! STOP!
THERE'S A REASON I WAS THE ONLY ONE OF US ALLOWED TO GO OUT INTO THE JADE FOR SO LONG.
THERE'S PRECIOUS LITTLE THERE THAT WILL SEE YOU AS ANYTHING OTHER THAN A MEAL.
YOU WON'T MAKE IT. NOT JUST THE TWO OF YOU.
THINK OF YOUR CHILDREN--
WHO DO YOU THINK I'M THINKING OF, IGNACIO? HUH?
IT'S ONE THING FOR MY BELLY TO RUMBLE, BUT FOR MY CHILDRE TO SCREAM FOR BREAD I CANNO GIVE--
WHAT CHOICE DO WE HAVE, ANA? THE GROVE IS ABOUT TO DIE, LEAVING US WITH NO FOOD AND NO SHELTER.
ARE YOU LIKE SYLVAN, TO PREVENT US TO COME AND GO AS WE PLEASE?
WHY WON'T YOU THINK OF OUR CHILDREN, WAR MOTHER?

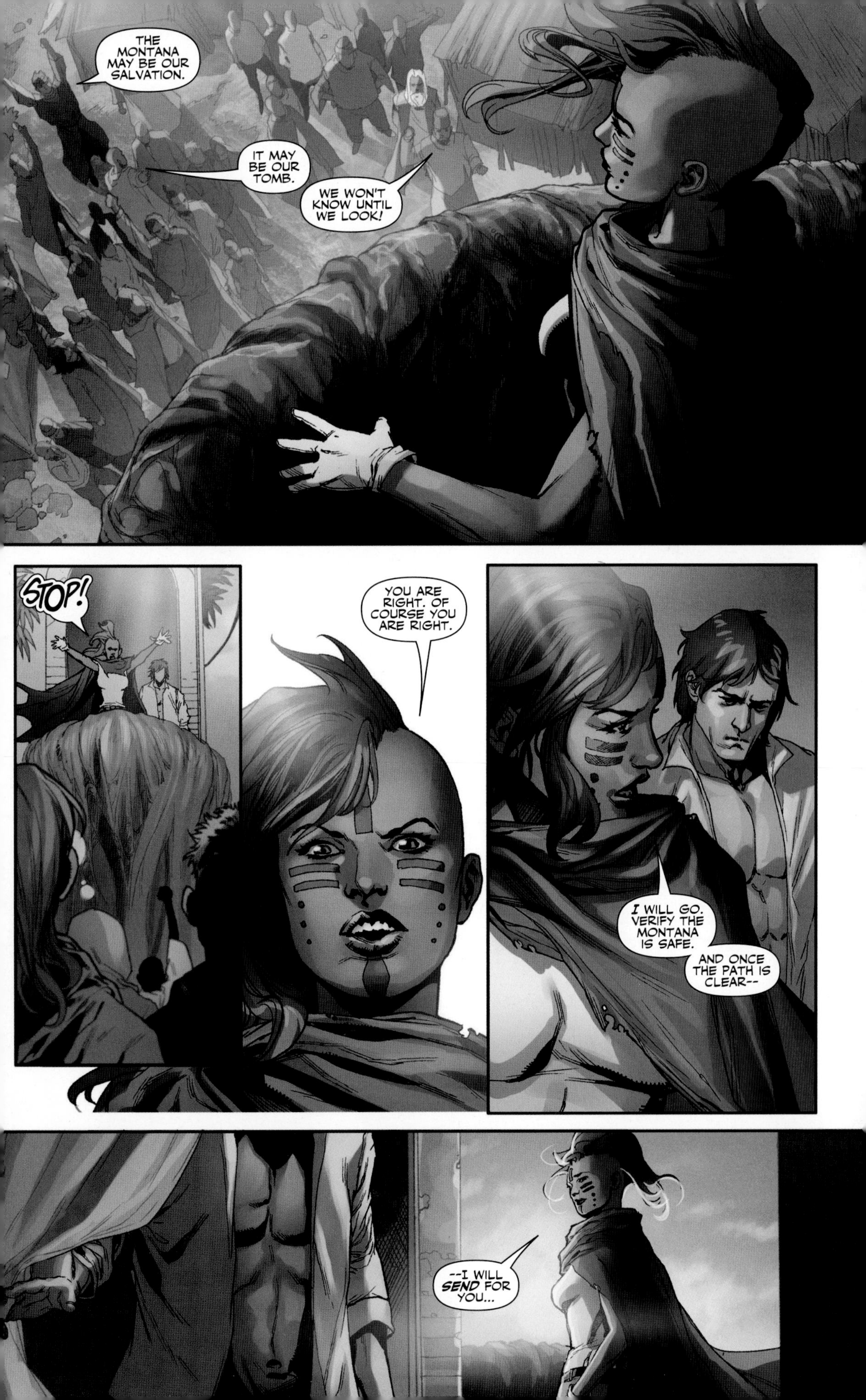
THE MONTANA MAY BE OUR SALVATION.
IT MAY BE OUR TOMB.
WE WON'T KNOW UNTIL WE LOOK!
STOP!
YOU ARE RIGHT. OF COURSE YOU ARE RIGHT.
I WILL GO. VERIFY THE MONTANA IS SAFE.
AND ONCE THE PATH IS CLEAR--
--I WILL SEND FOR YOU...

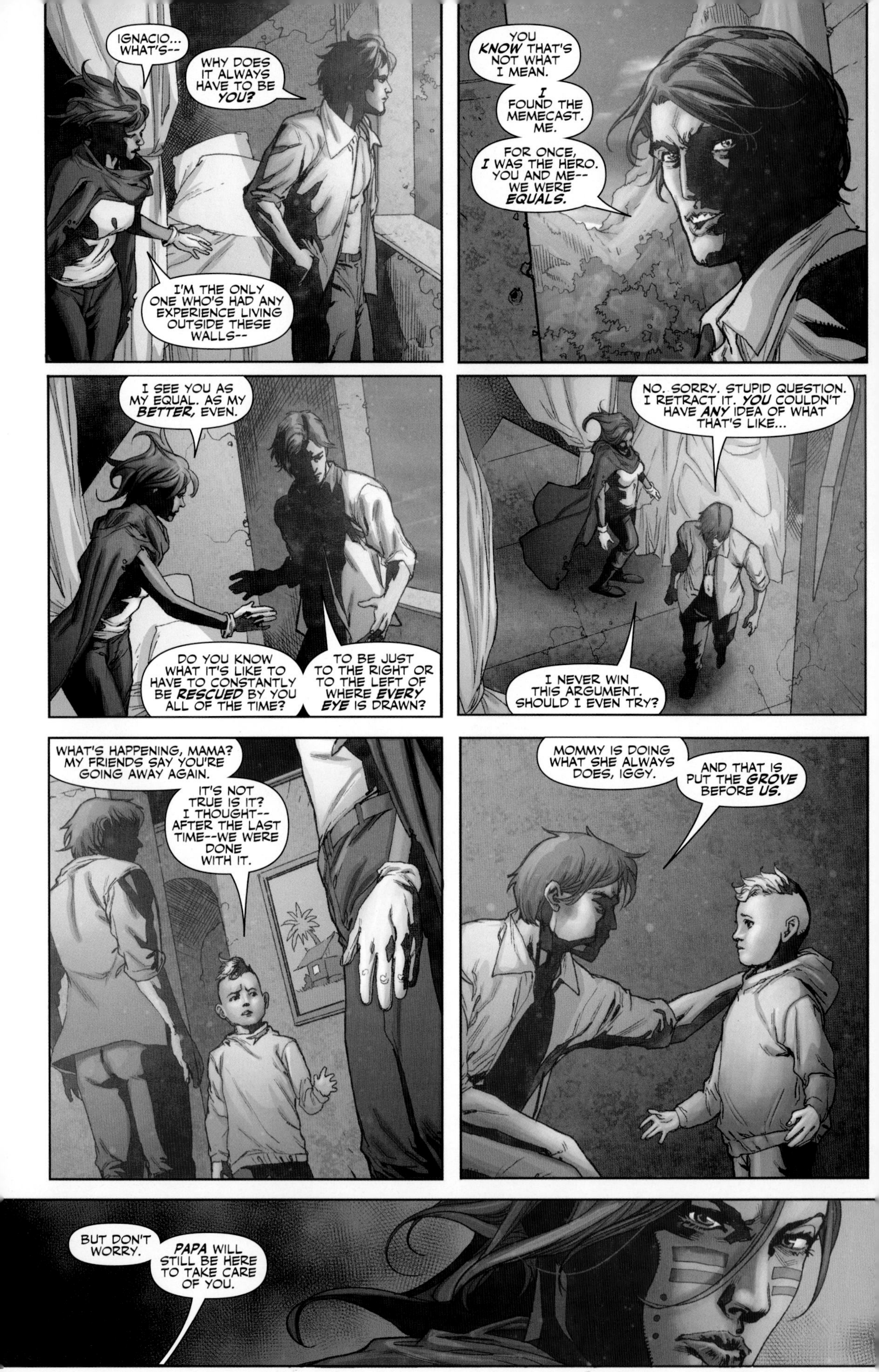
IGNACIO... WHAT'S--
WHY DOES IT ALWAYS HAVE TO BE *YOU?*
I'M THE ONLY ONE WHO'S HAD ANY EXPERIENCE LIVING OUTSIDE THESE WALLS--
YOU *KNOW* THAT'S NOT WHAT I MEAN.
I FOUND THE MEMECAST. ME.
FOR ONCE, *I* WAS THE HERO. YOU AND ME-- WE WERE *EQUALS.*
I SEE YOU AS MY EQUAL. AS MY *BETTER,* EVEN.
DO YOU KNOW WHAT IT'S LIKE TO HAVE TO CONSTANTLY BE *RESCUED* BY YOU ALL OF THE TIME?
TO BE JUST TO THE RIGHT OR TO THE LEFT OF WHERE *EVERY EYE* IS DRAWN?
NO. SORRY. STUPID QUESTION. I RETRACT IT. *YOU* COULDN'T HAVE *ANY* IDEA OF WHAT THAT'S LIKE...
I NEVER WIN THIS ARGUMENT. SHOULD I EVEN TRY?
WHAT'S HAPPENING, MAMA? MY FRIENDS SAY YOU'RE GOING AWAY AGAIN.
IT'S NOT TRUE IS IT? I THOUGHT-- AFTER THE LAST TIME--WE WERE DONE WITH IT.
MOMMY IS DOING WHAT SHE ALWAYS DOES, IGGY.
AND THAT IS PUT THE *GROVE* BEFORE *US.*
BUT DON'T WORRY.
PAPA WILL STILL BE HERE TO TAKE CARE OF YOU.

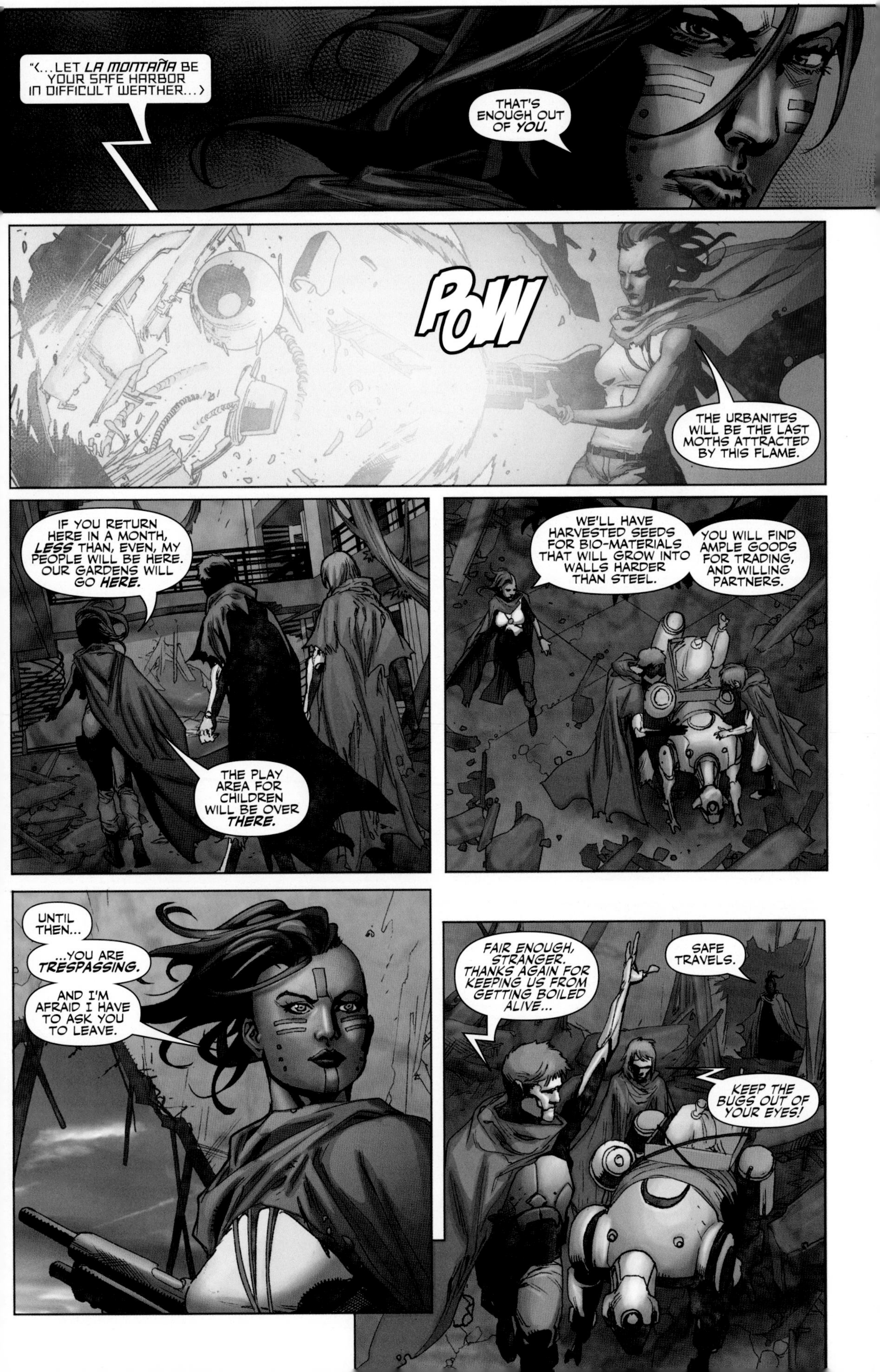
"<...LET LA MONTAÑA BE YOUR SAFE HARBOR IN DIFFICULT WEATHER...>
THAT'S ENOUGH OUT OF YOU.
POW
THE URBANITES WILL BE THE LAST MOTHS ATTRACTED BY THIS FLAME.
IF YOU RETURN HERE IN A MONTH, LESS THAN, EVEN, MY PEOPLE WILL BE HERE. OUR GARDENS WILL GO HERE.
THE PLAY AREA FOR CHILDREN WILL BE OVER THERE.
WE'LL HAVE HARVESTED SEEDS FOR BIO-MATERIALS THAT WILL GROW INTO WALLS HARDER THAN STEEL.
YOU WILL FIND AMPLE GOODS FOR TRADING, AND WILLING PARTNERS.
UNTIL THEN...
...YOU ARE TRESPASSING.
AND I'M AFRAID I HAVE TO ASK YOU TO LEAVE.
FAIR ENOUGH, STRANGER. THANKS AGAIN FOR KEEPING US FROM GETTING BOILED ALIVE...
SAFE TRAVELS.
KEEP THE BUGS OUT OF YOUR EYES!

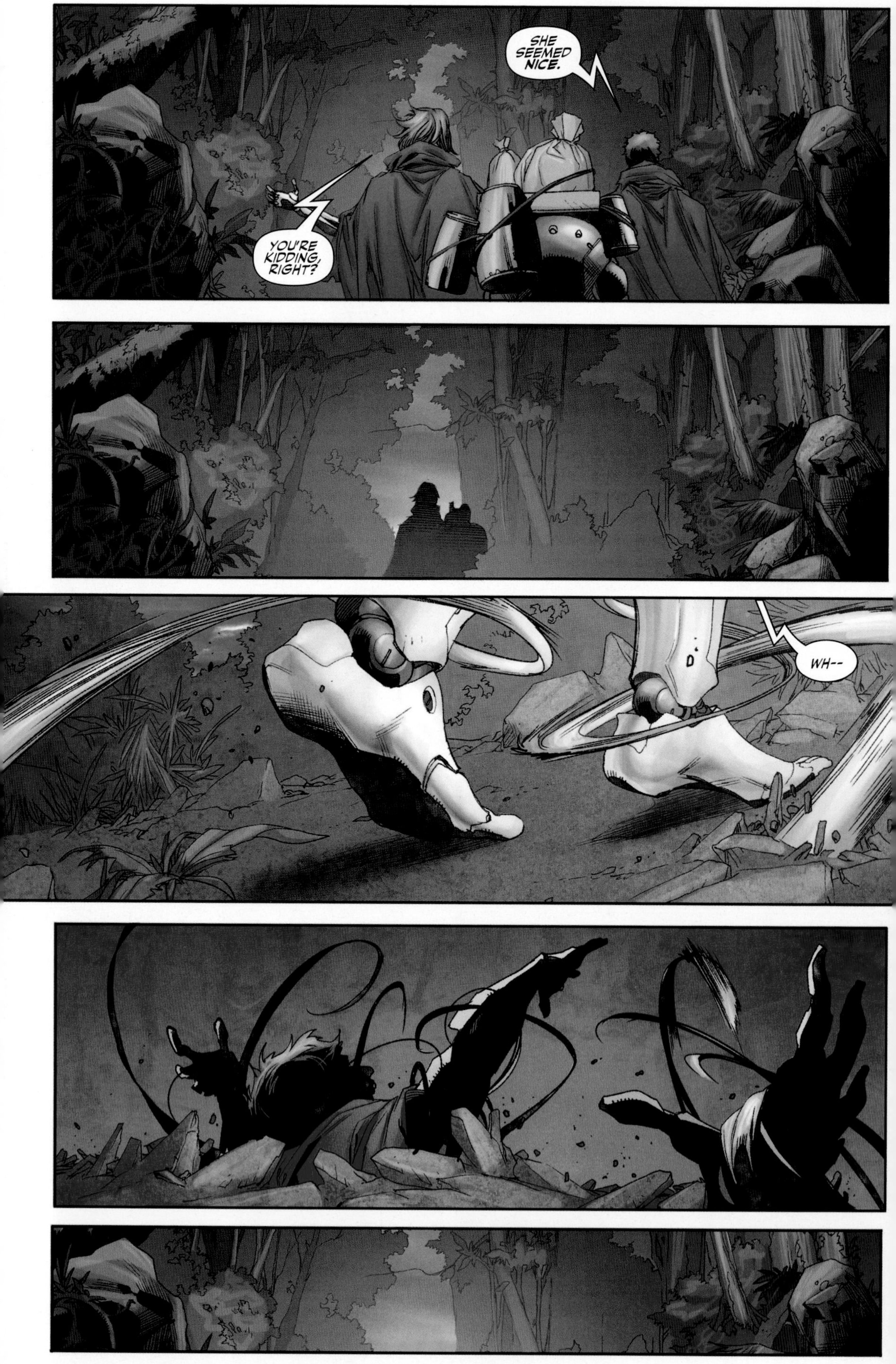
SHE SEEMED NICE.
YOU'RE KIDDING, RIGHT?
WH--

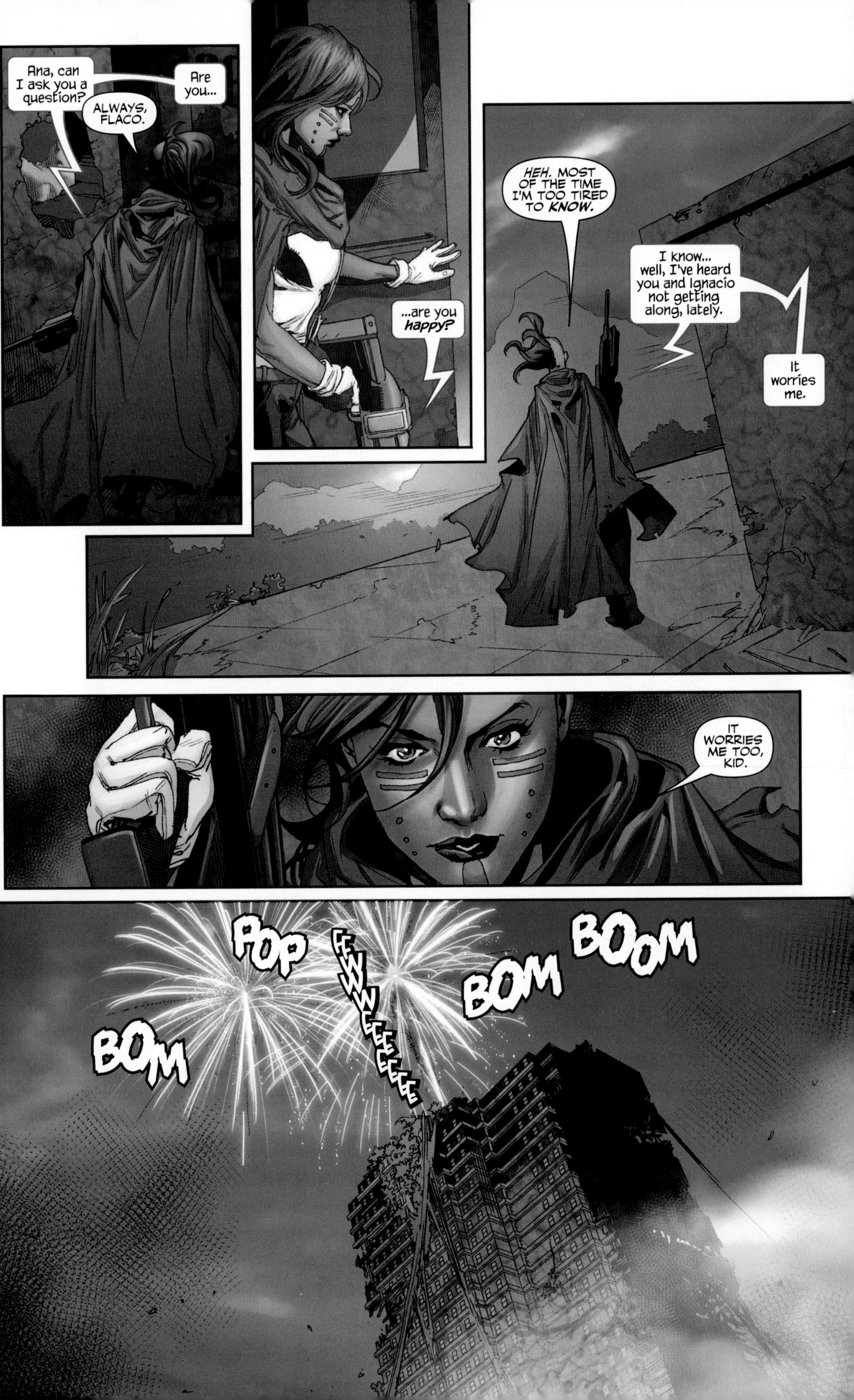
Ana, can I ask you a question?
ALWAYS, FLACO.
Are you...
...are you *happy?*
HEH. MOST OF THE TIME I'M TOO TIRED TO *KNOW.*
I know... well, I've heard you and Ignacio not getting along, lately.
It worries me.
IT WORRIES ME TOO, KID.
BOM
POP
FFWWEEEEEEEE
BOM
BOOM

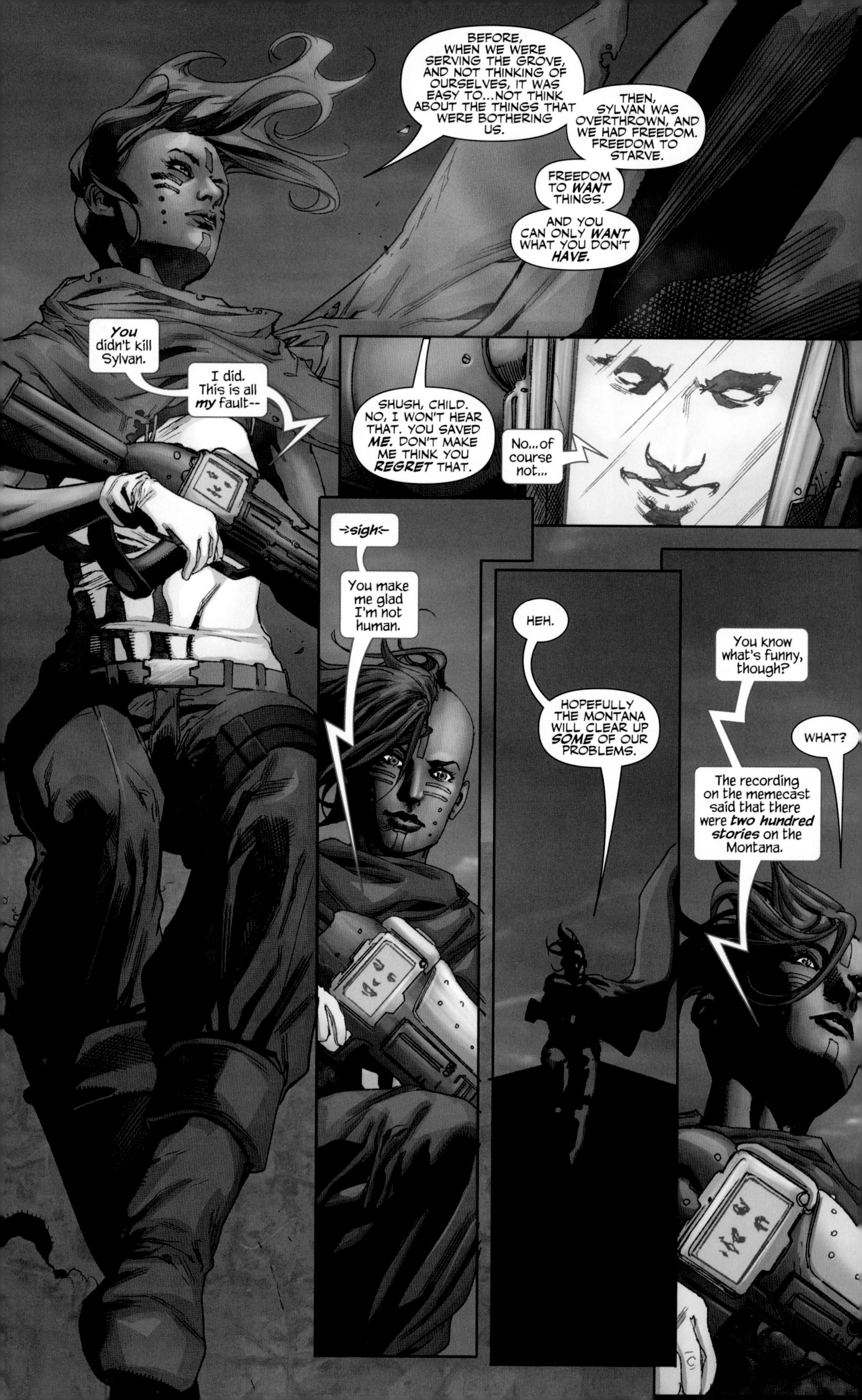
BEFORE, WHEN WE WERE SERVING THE GROVE, AND NOT THINKING OF OURSELVES, IT WAS EASY TO...NOT THINK ABOUT THE THINGS THAT WERE BOTHERING US.
THEN, SYLVAN WAS OVERTHROWN, AND WE HAD FREEDOM. FREEDOM TO STARVE.
FREEDOM TO *WANT* THINGS.
AND YOU CAN ONLY *WANT* WHAT YOU DON'T *HAVE.*
You didn't kill Sylvan.
I did. This is all *my* fault--
SHUSH, CHILD. NO, I WON'T HEAR THAT. YOU SAVED *ME.* DON'T MAKE ME THINK YOU *REGRET* THAT.
No...of course not...
-sigh-
You make me glad I'm not human.
HEH.
HOPEFULLY THE MONTANA WILL CLEAR UP *SOME* OF OUR PROBLEMS.
You know what's funny, though?
WHAT?
The recording on the memecast said that there were *two hundred stories* on the Montana.

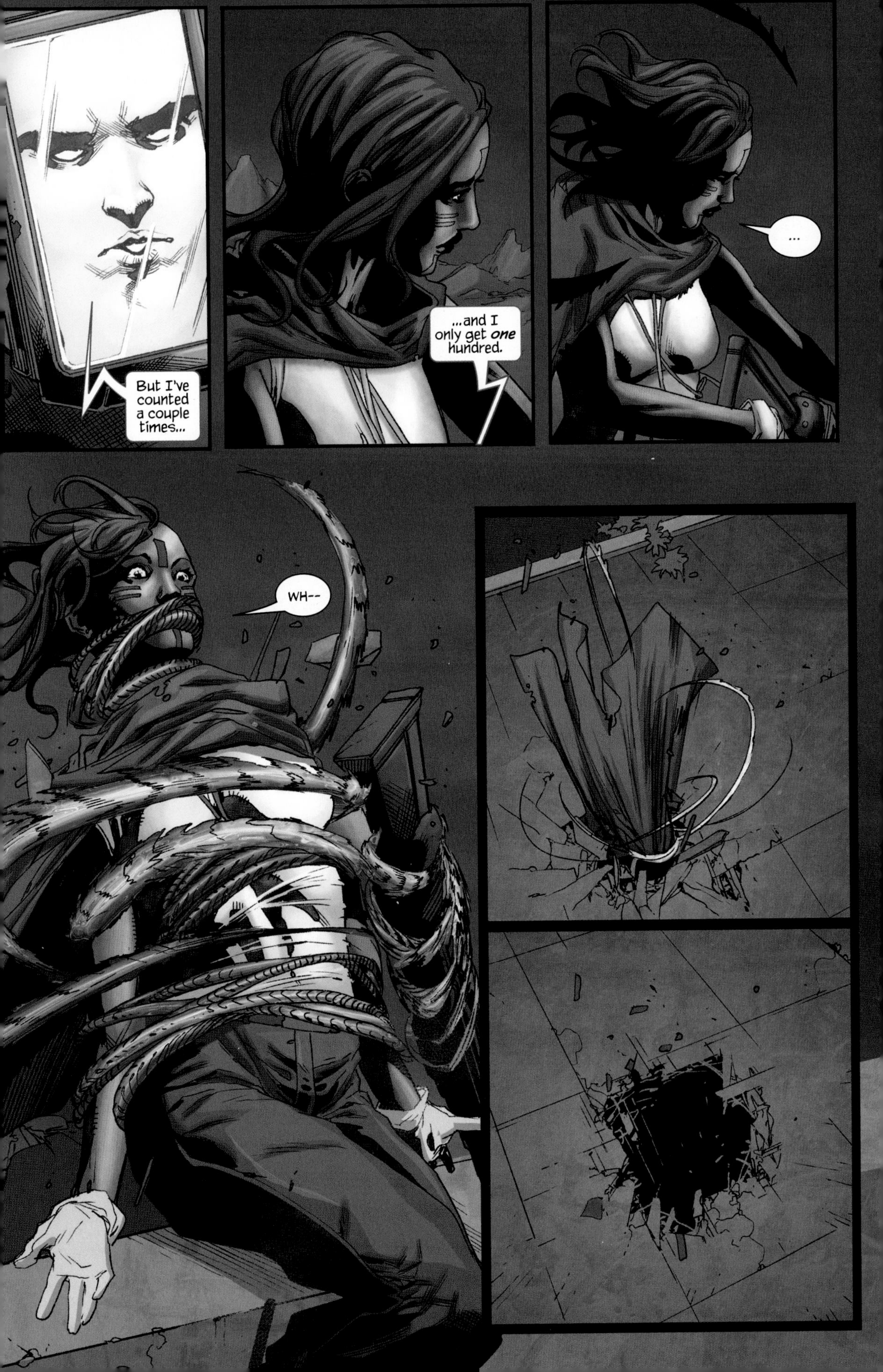
But I've counted a couple times...
...and I only get *one* hundred.
...
WH--

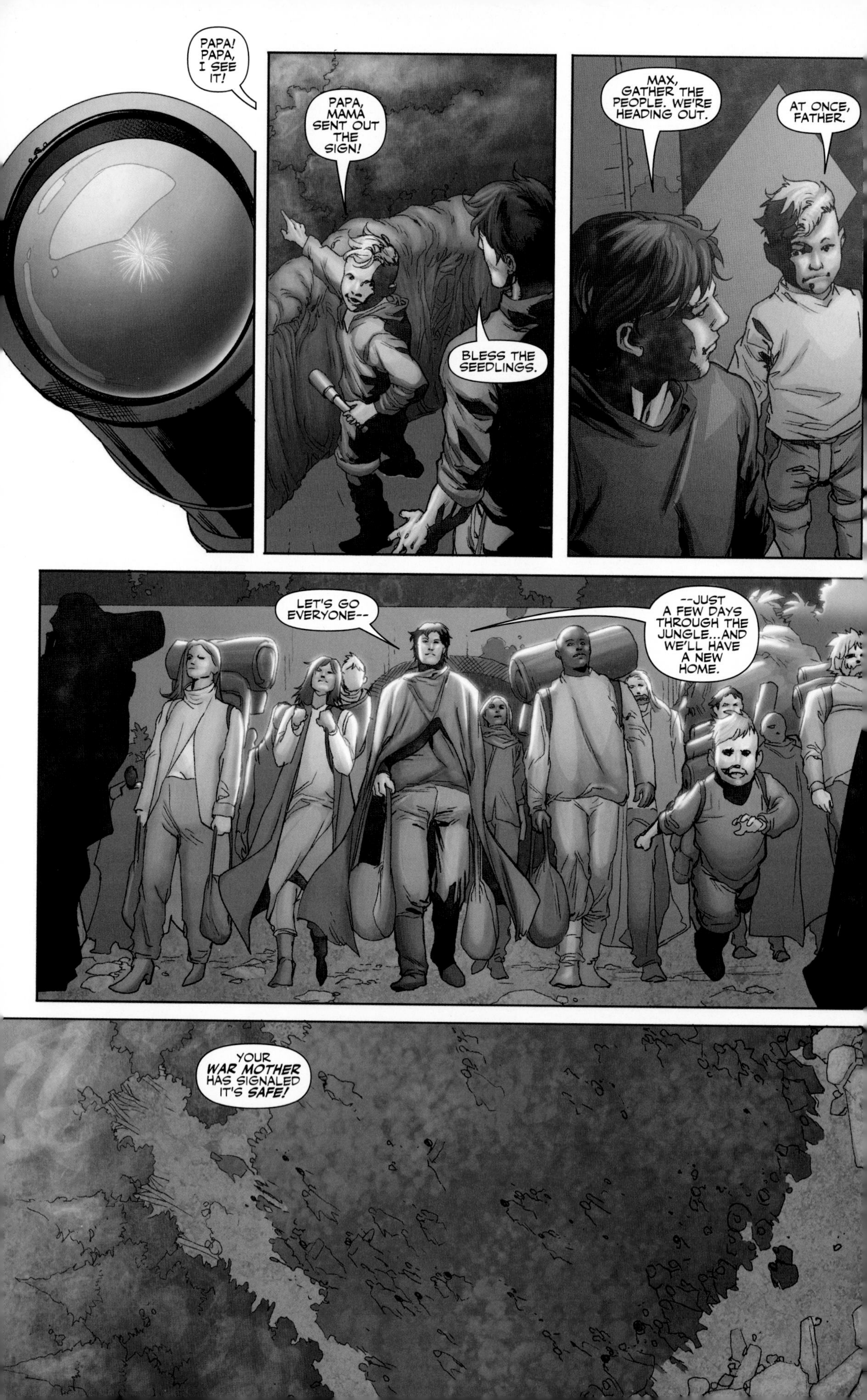
PAPA! PAPA, I SEE IT!
PAPA, MAMA SENT OUT THE SIGN!
BLESS THE SEEDLINGS.
MAX, GATHER THE PEOPLE. WE'RE HEADING OUT.
AT ONCE, FATHER.
LET'S GO EVERYONE--
--JUST A FEW DAYS THROUGH THE JUNGLE...AND WE'LL HAVE A NEW HOME.
YOUR WAR MOTHER HAS SIGNALED IT'S SAFE!

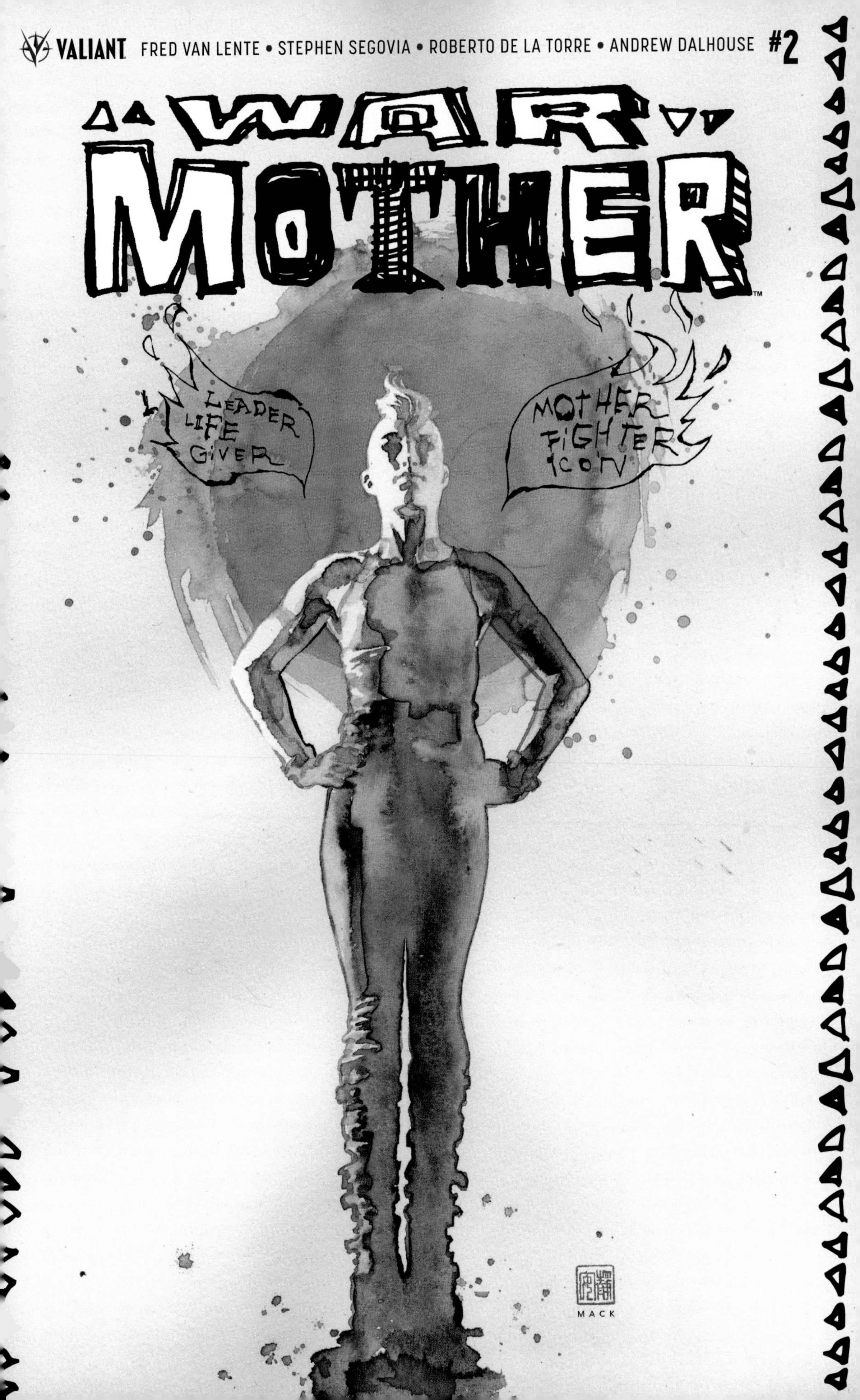
VALIANT
FRED VAN LENTE • STEPHEN SEGOVIA • ROBERTO DE LA TORRE • ANDREW DALHOUSE
#2
WAR MOTHER™
LEADER LIFE GIVER
MOTHER FIGHTER ICON
MACK

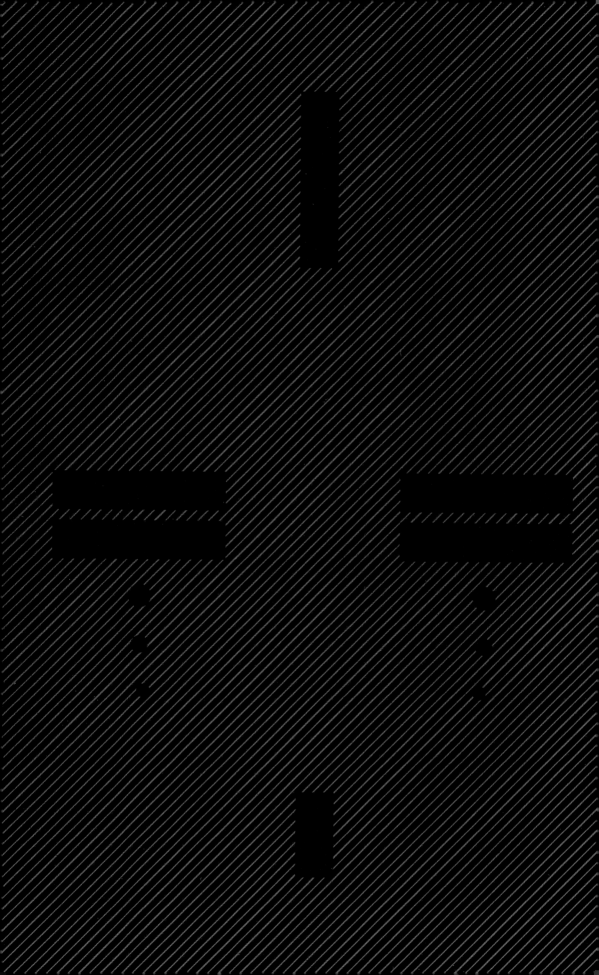

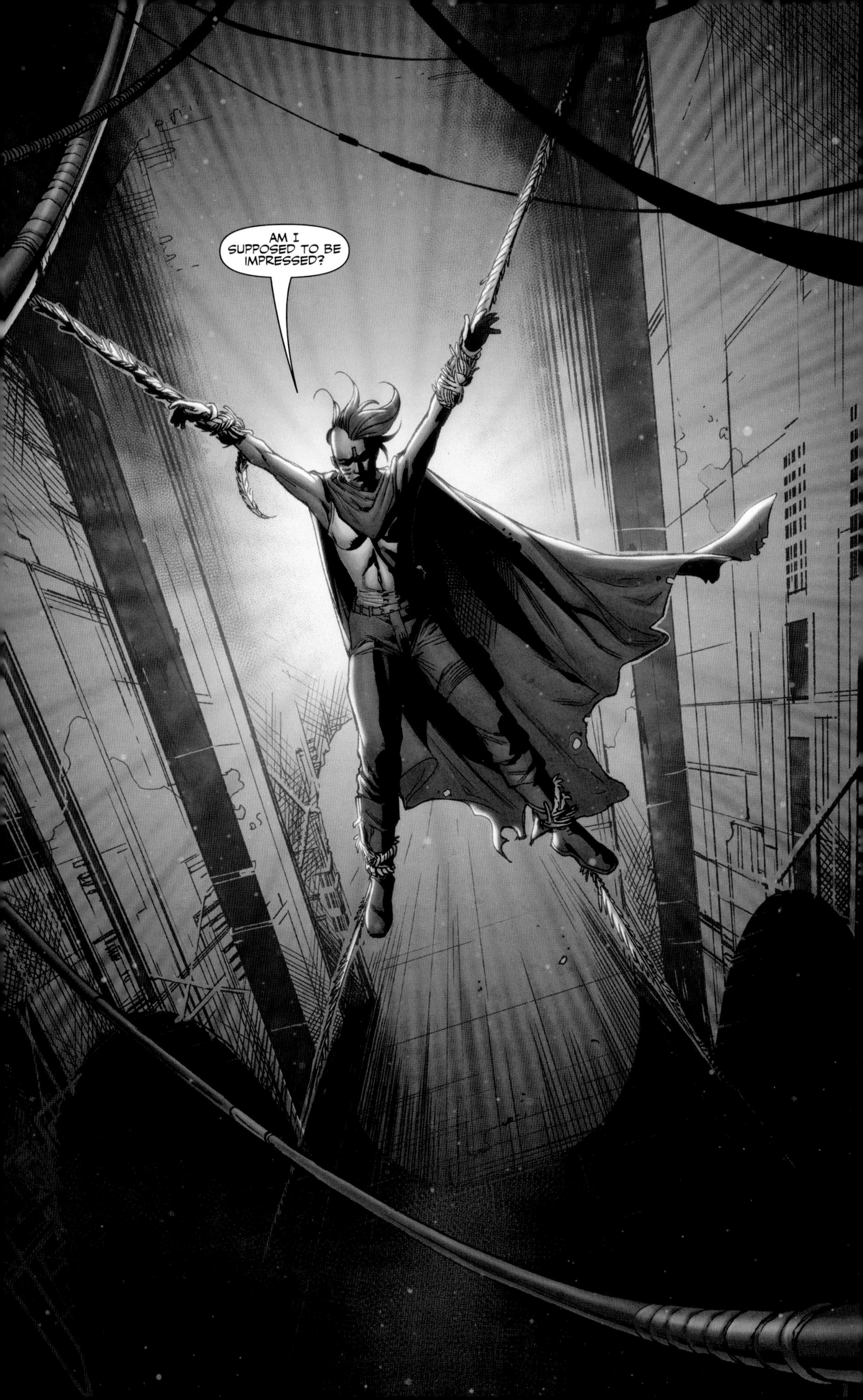
AM I SUPPOSED TO BE IMPRESSED?

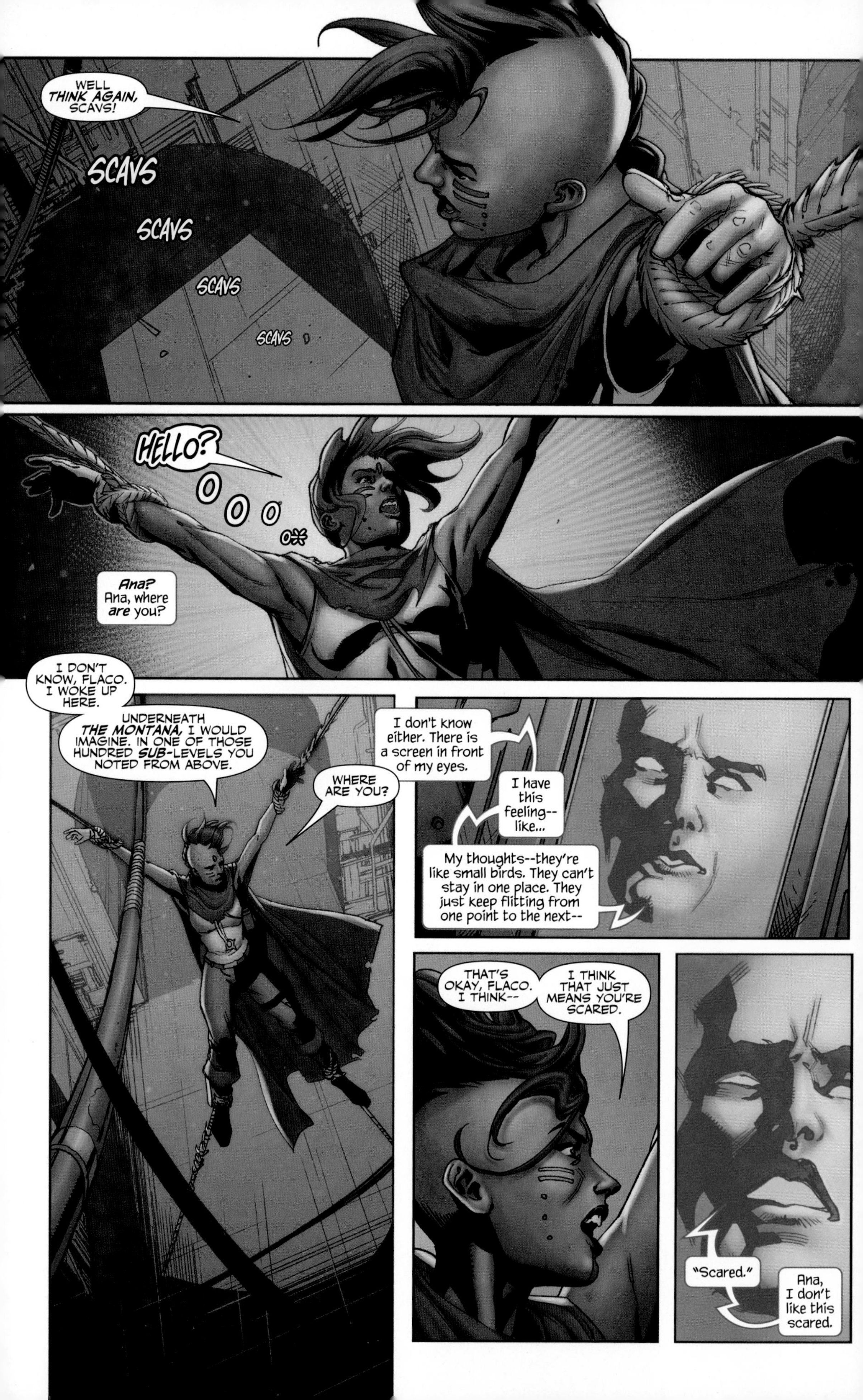
WELL THINK AGAIN, SCAVS!
SCAVS
SCAVS
SCAVS
SCAVS
HELLO?
O O O O
Ana? Ana, where are you?
I DON'T KNOW, FLACO. I WOKE UP HERE.
UNDERNEATH THE MONTANA, I WOULD IMAGINE. IN ONE OF THOSE HUNDRED SUB-LEVELS YOU NOTED FROM ABOVE.
WHERE ARE YOU?
I don't know either. There is a screen in front of my eyes.
I have this feeling-- like...
My thoughts--they're like small birds. They can't stay in one place. They just keep flitting from one point to the next--
THAT'S OKAY, FLACO. I THINK--
I THINK THAT JUST MEANS YOU'RE SCARED.
"Scared."
Ana, I don't like this scared.

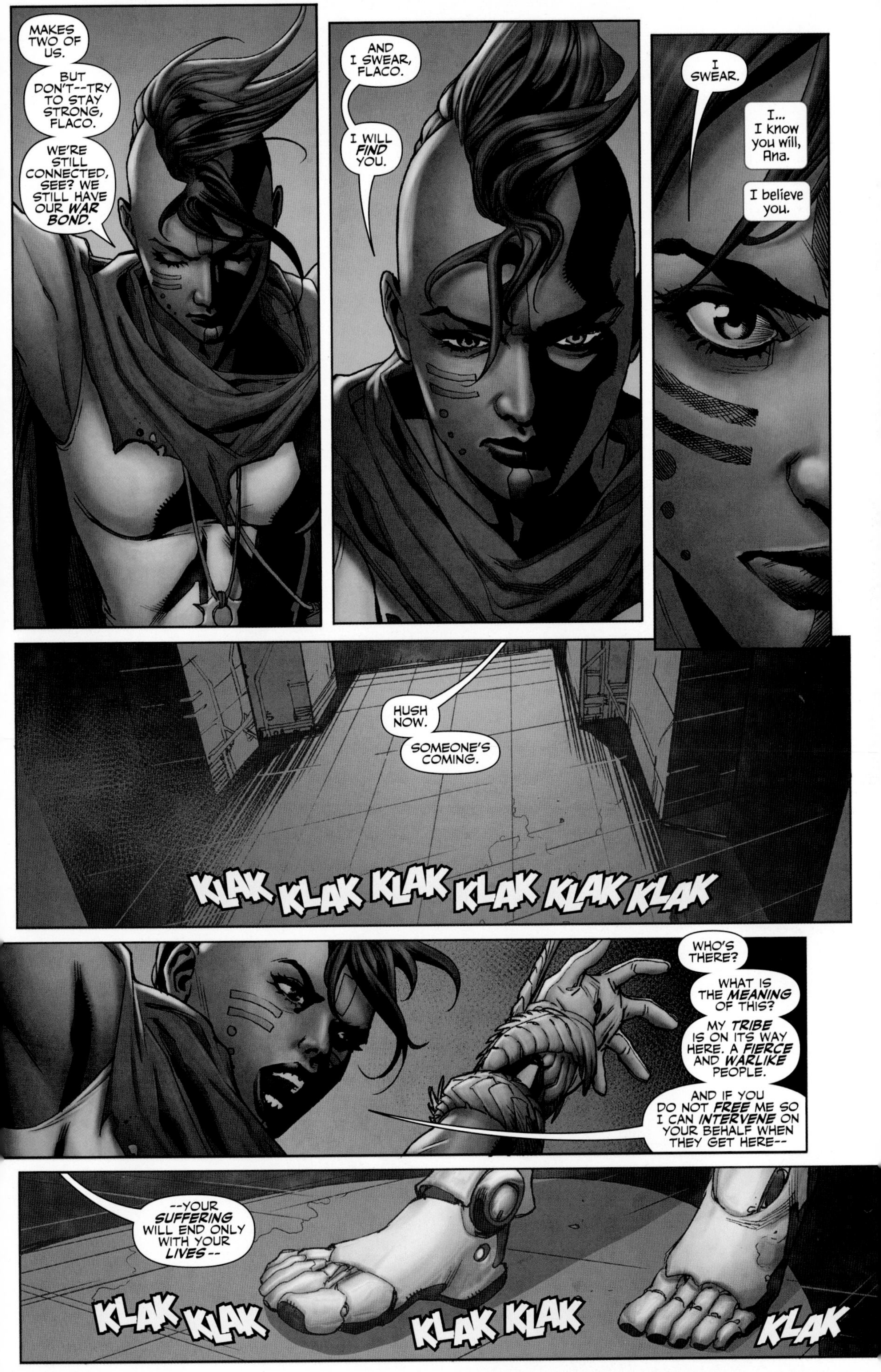
MAKES TWO OF US.
BUT DON'T--TRY TO STAY STRONG, FLACO.
WE'RE STILL CONNECTED, SEE? WE STILL HAVE OUR *WAR BOND*.
AND I SWEAR, FLACO.
I WILL *FIND* YOU.
I SWEAR.
I... I know you will, Ana.
I believe you.
HUSH NOW.
SOMEONE'S COMING.
KLAK KLAK KLAK KLAK KLAK KLAK
WHO'S THERE?
WHAT IS THE *MEANING* OF THIS?
MY *TRIBE* IS ON ITS WAY HERE. A *FIERCE* AND *WARLIKE* PEOPLE.
AND IF YOU DO NOT *FREE* ME SO I CAN *INTERVENE* ON YOUR BEHALF WHEN THEY GET HERE--
--YOUR *SUFFERING* WILL END ONLY WITH YOUR *LIVES*--
KLAK KLAK KLAK KLAK KLAK

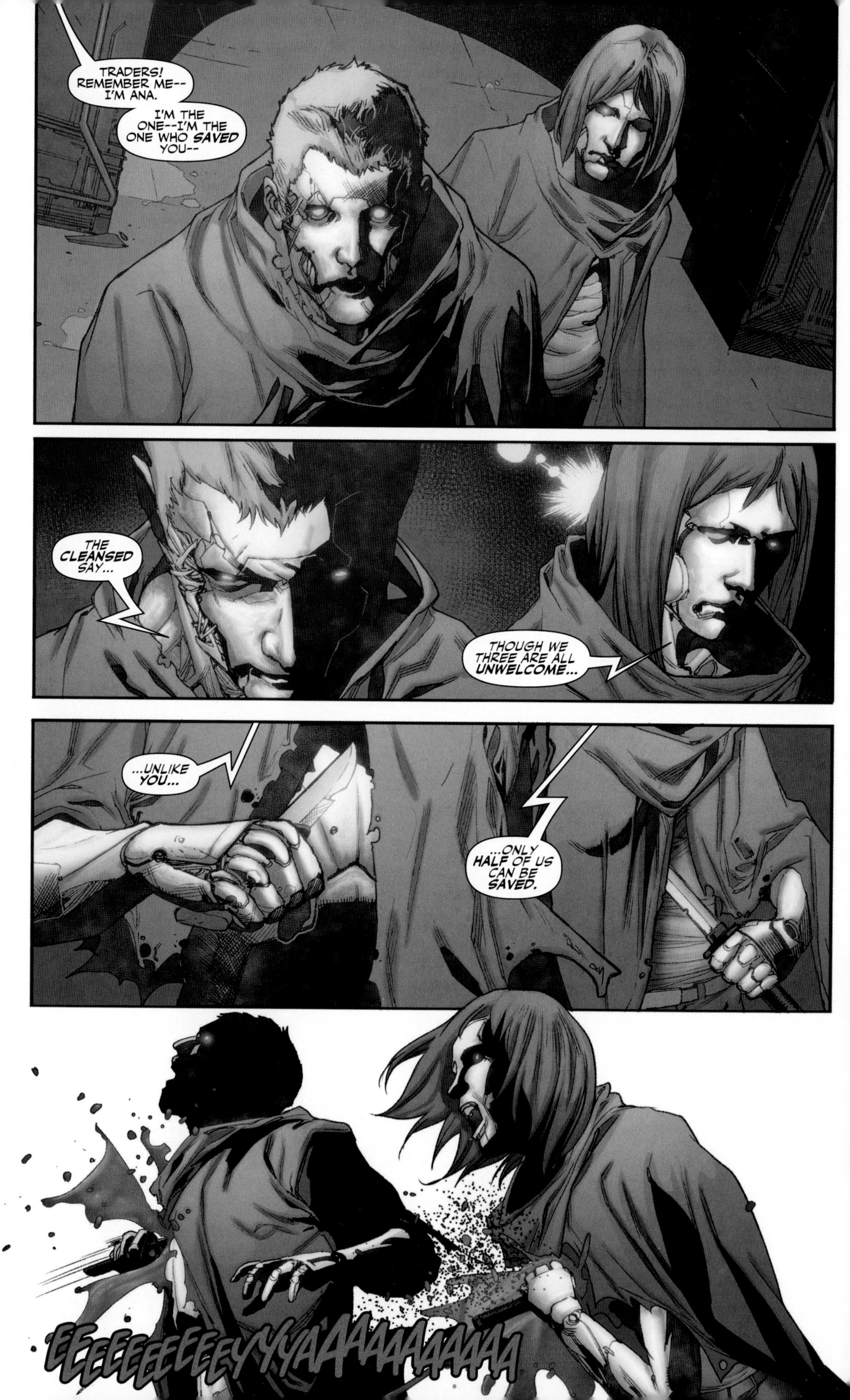
TRADERS! REMEMBER ME-- I'M ANA.
I'M THE ONE--I'M THE ONE WHO SAVED YOU--
THE CLEANSED SAY...
THOUGH WE THREE ARE ALL UNWELCOME...
...UNLIKE YOU...
...ONLY HALF OF US CAN BE SAVED.
EEEEEEEEEEEYYYAAAAAAAAAAAA

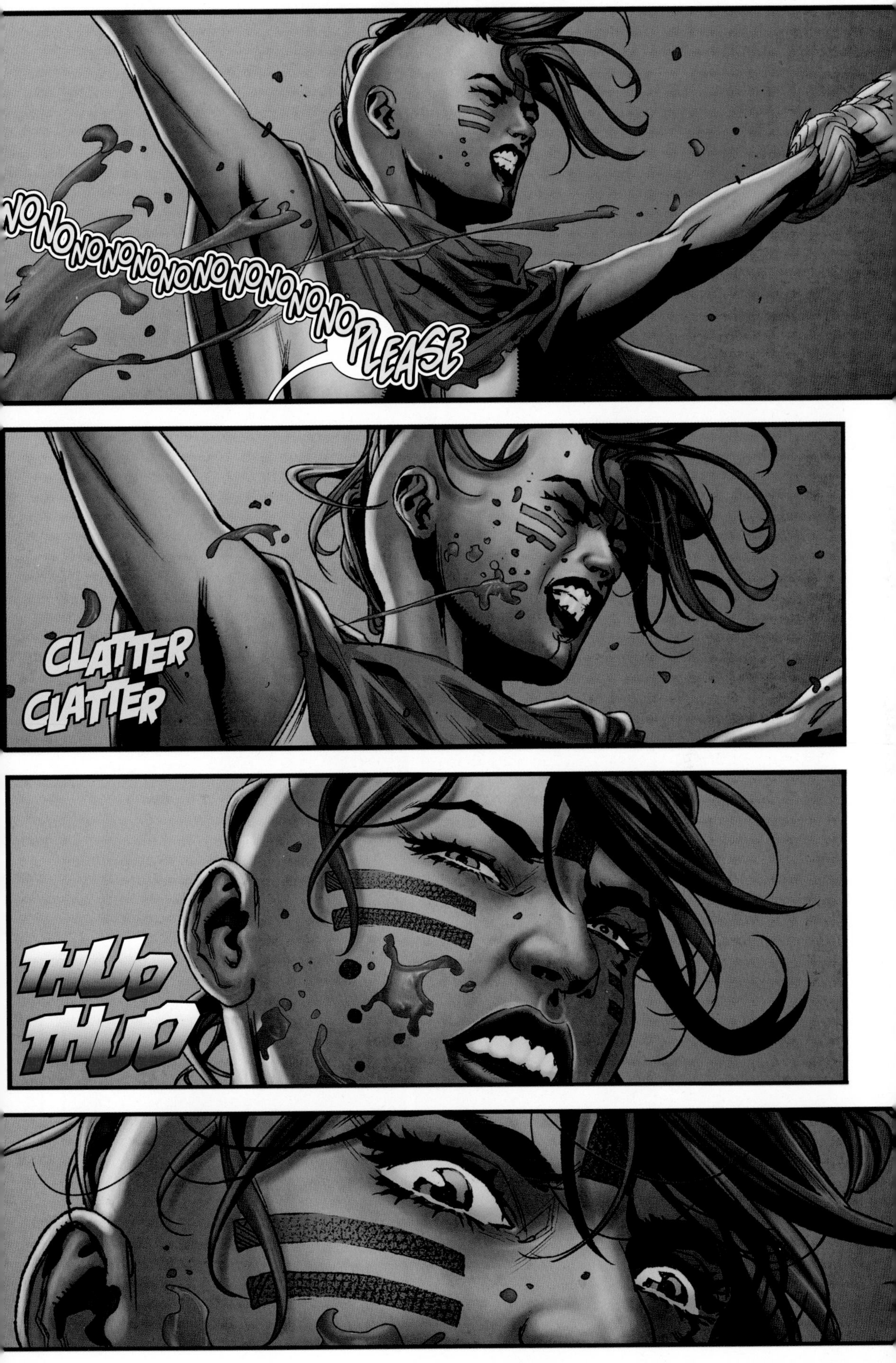
NONONONONONONONONONONONONOPLEASE
CLATTER CLATTER
THUD THUD

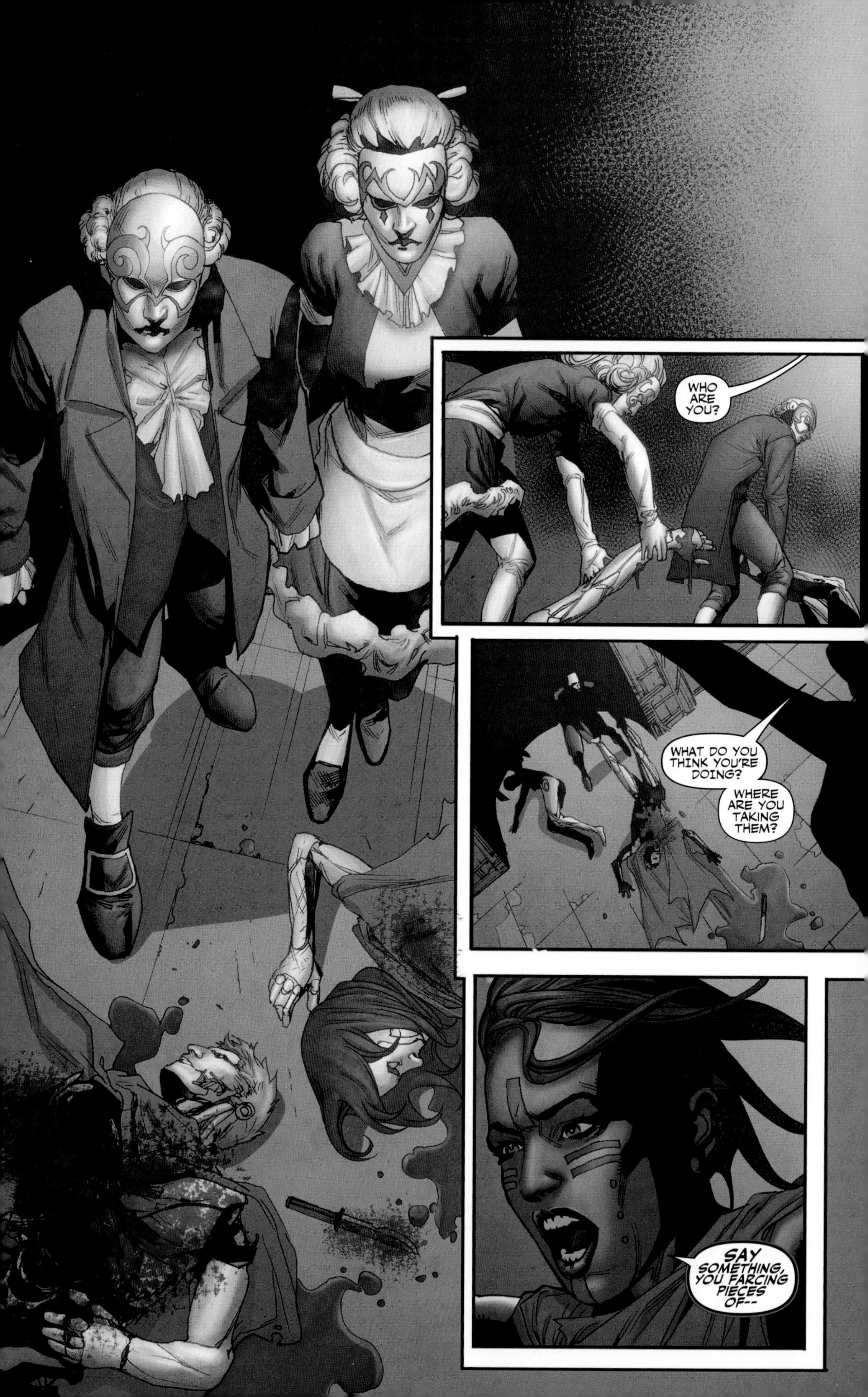
WHO ARE YOU?
WHAT DO YOU THINK YOU'RE DOING?
WHERE ARE YOU TAKING THEM?
SAY SOMETHING, YOU FARCING PIECES OF--

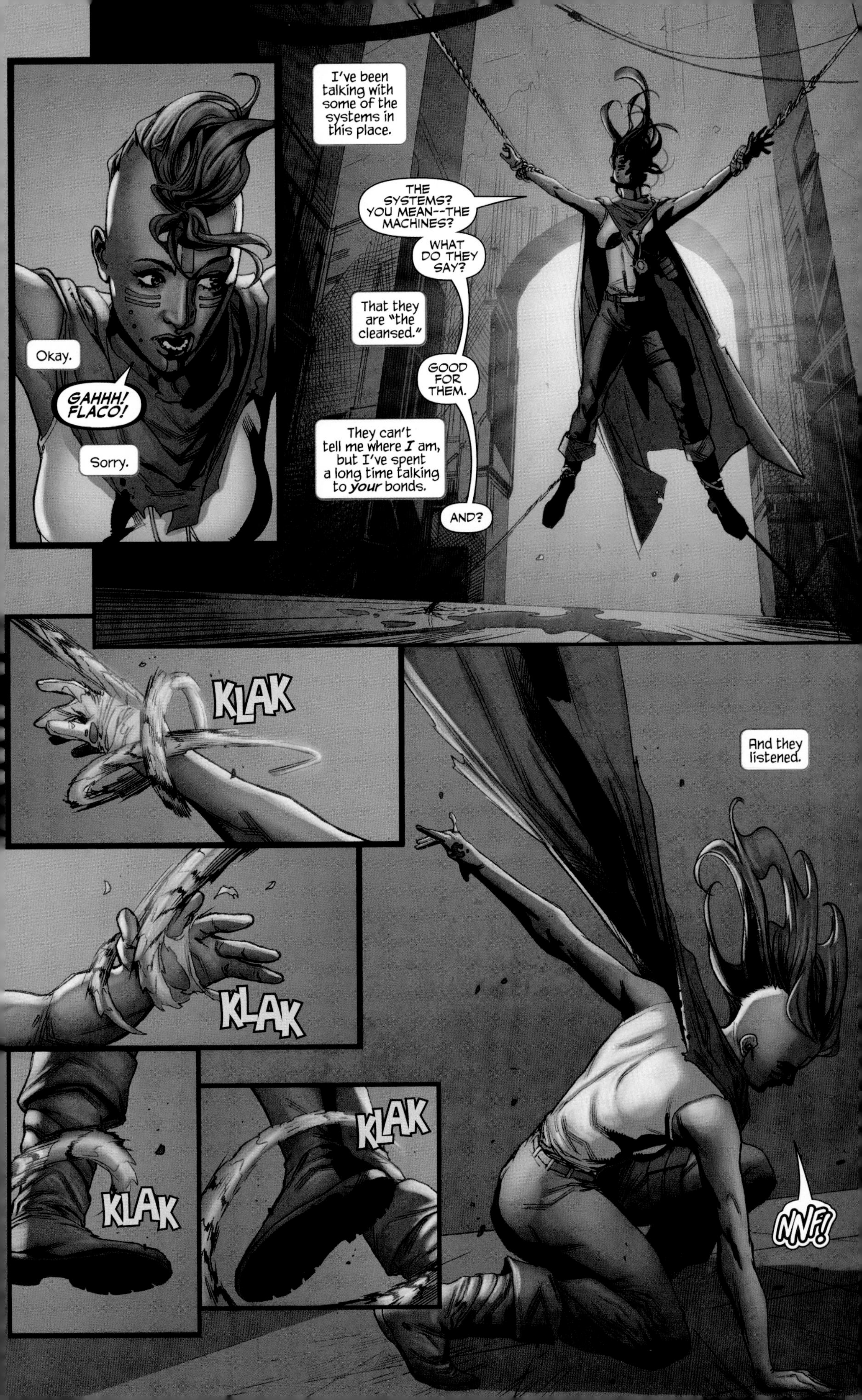
I've been talking with some of the systems in this place.
THE SYSTEMS? YOU MEAN--THE MACHINES?
WHAT DO THEY SAY?
That they are "the cleansed."
GOOD FOR THEM.
They can't tell me where I am, but I've spent a long time talking to your bonds.
AND?
Okay.
GAHHH! FLACO!
Sorry.
KLAK
KLAK
KLAK
KLAK
And they listened.
NNF!

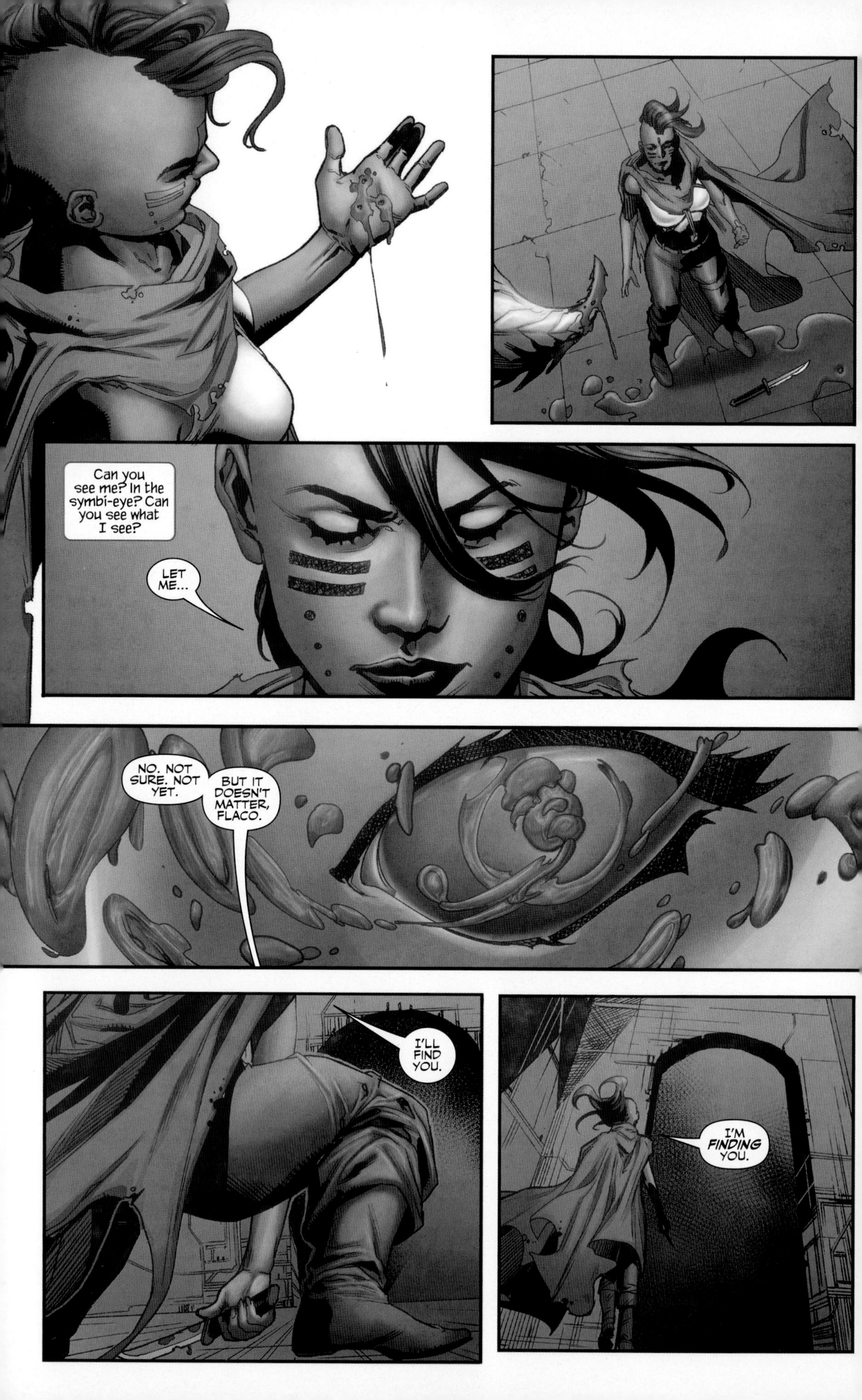

Can you see me? In the symbi-eye? Can you see what I see?
LET ME...
NO. NOT SURE. NOT YET.
BUT IT DOESN'T MATTER, FLACO.
I'LL FIND YOU.
I'M *FINDING* YOU.

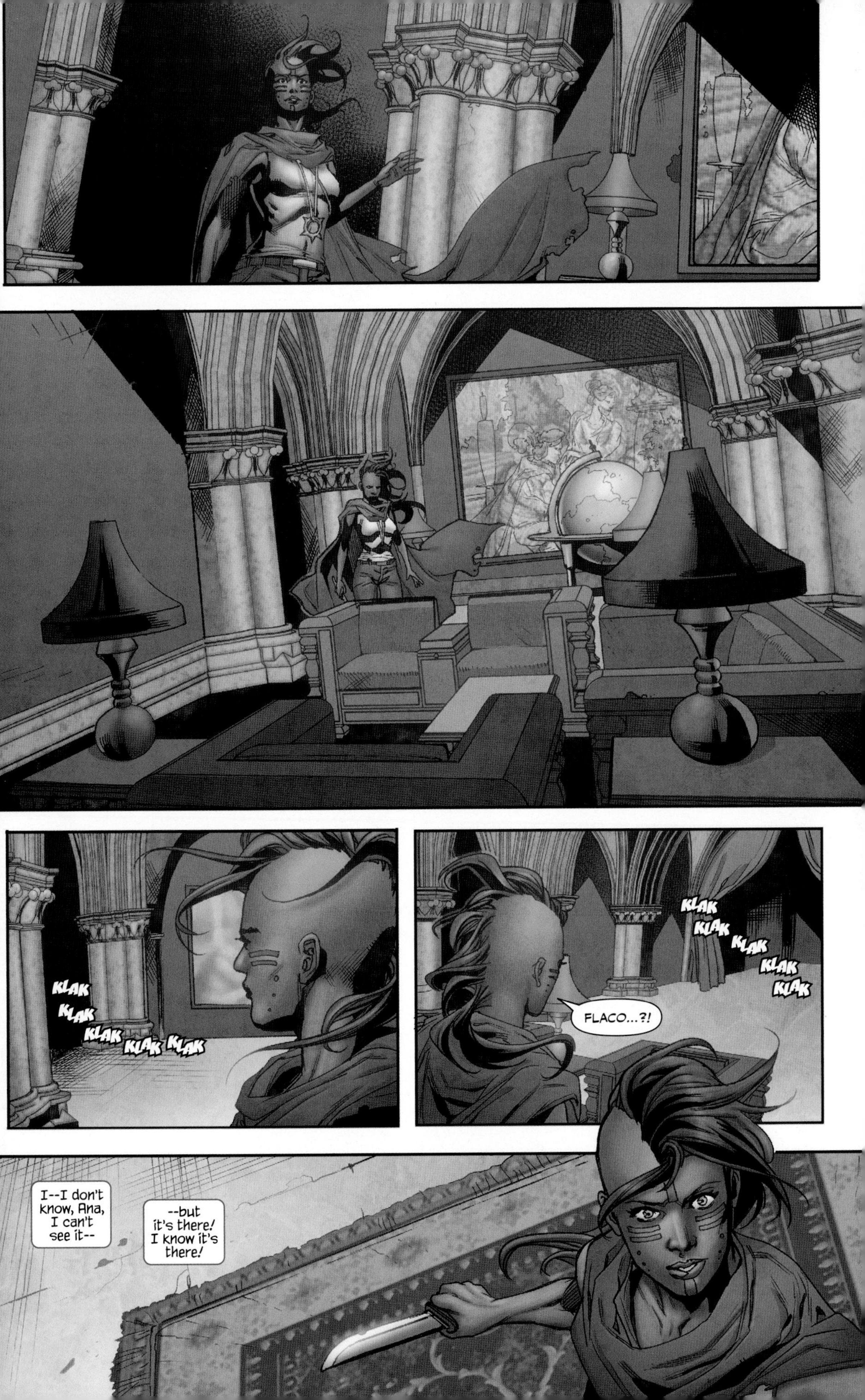
KLAK
KLAK
KLAK
KLAK
KLAK
FLACO...?!
KLAK
KLAK
KLAK
KLAK
KLAK
I--I don't know, Ana, I can't see it--
--but it's there! I know it's there!

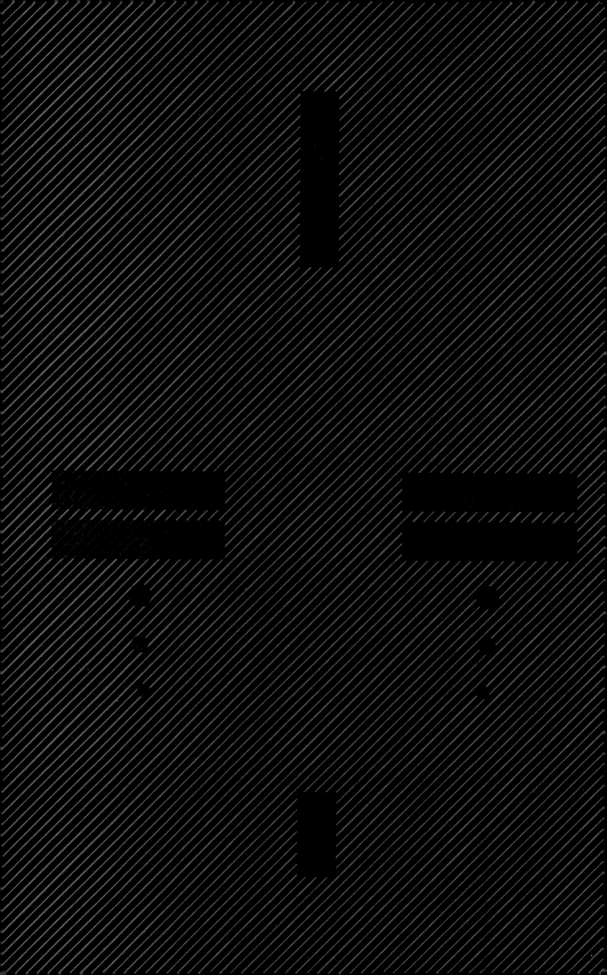

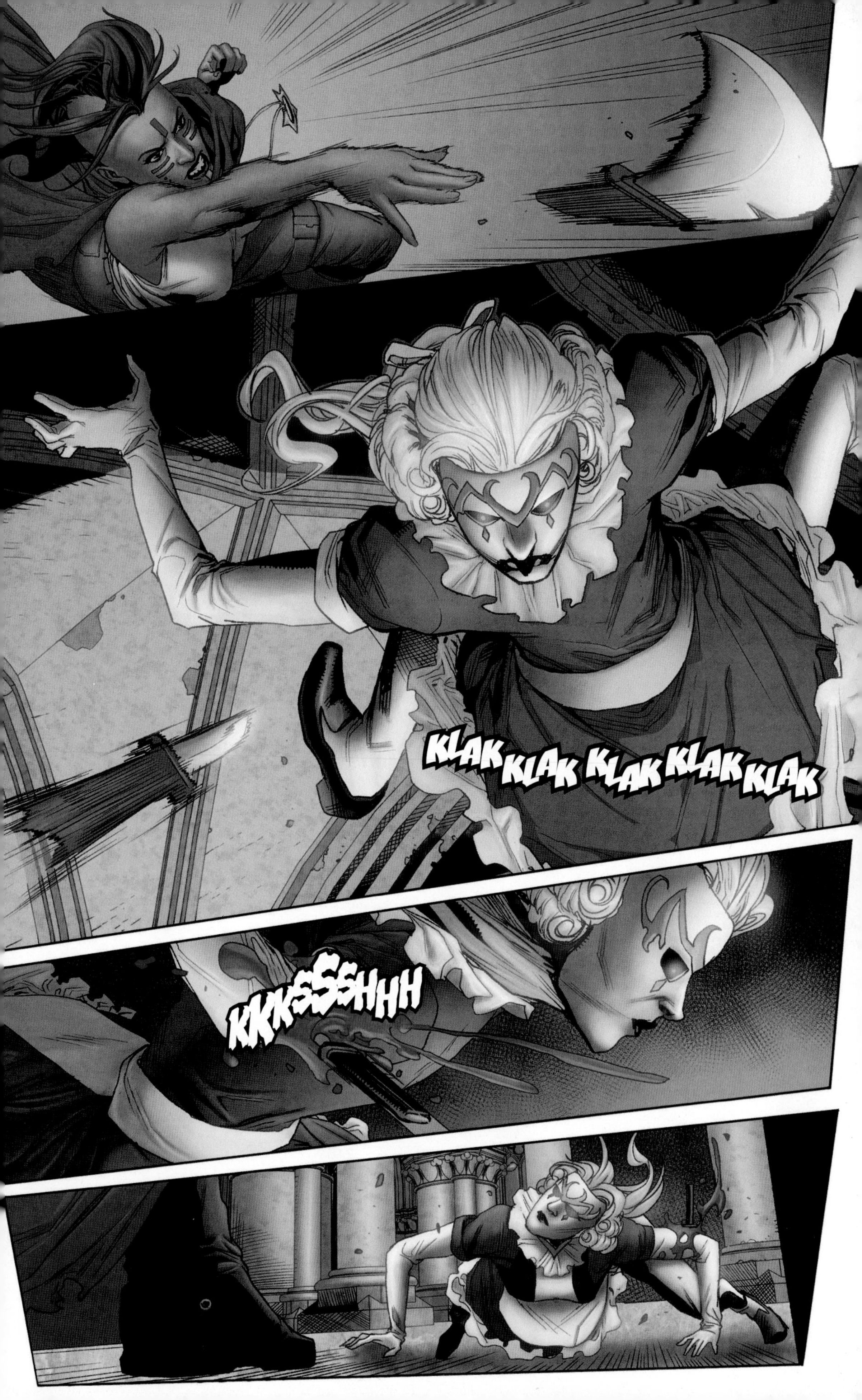

KLAK KLAK KLAK KLAK KLAK
KKKSSSHHH

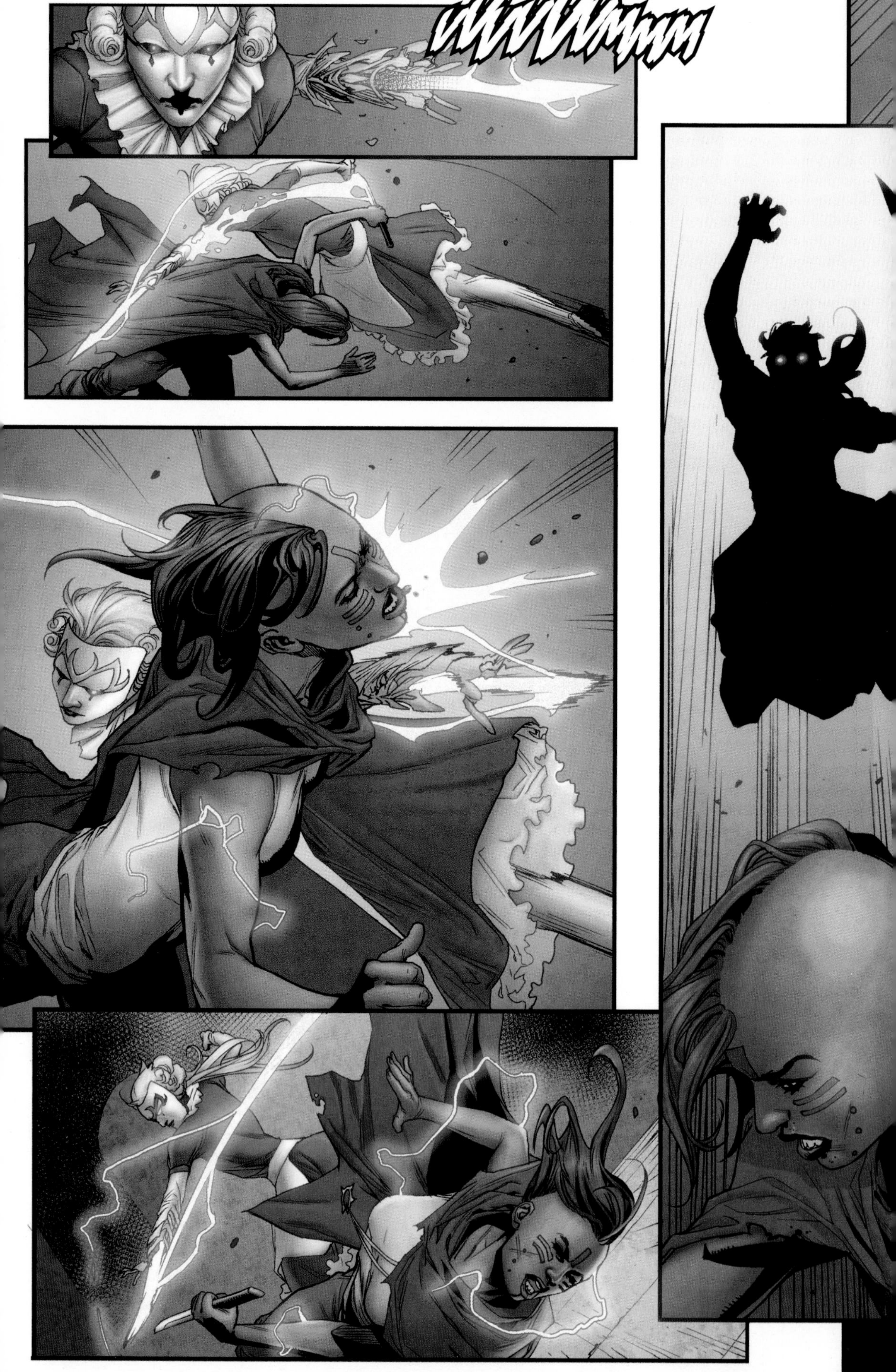
VVVVMMMM

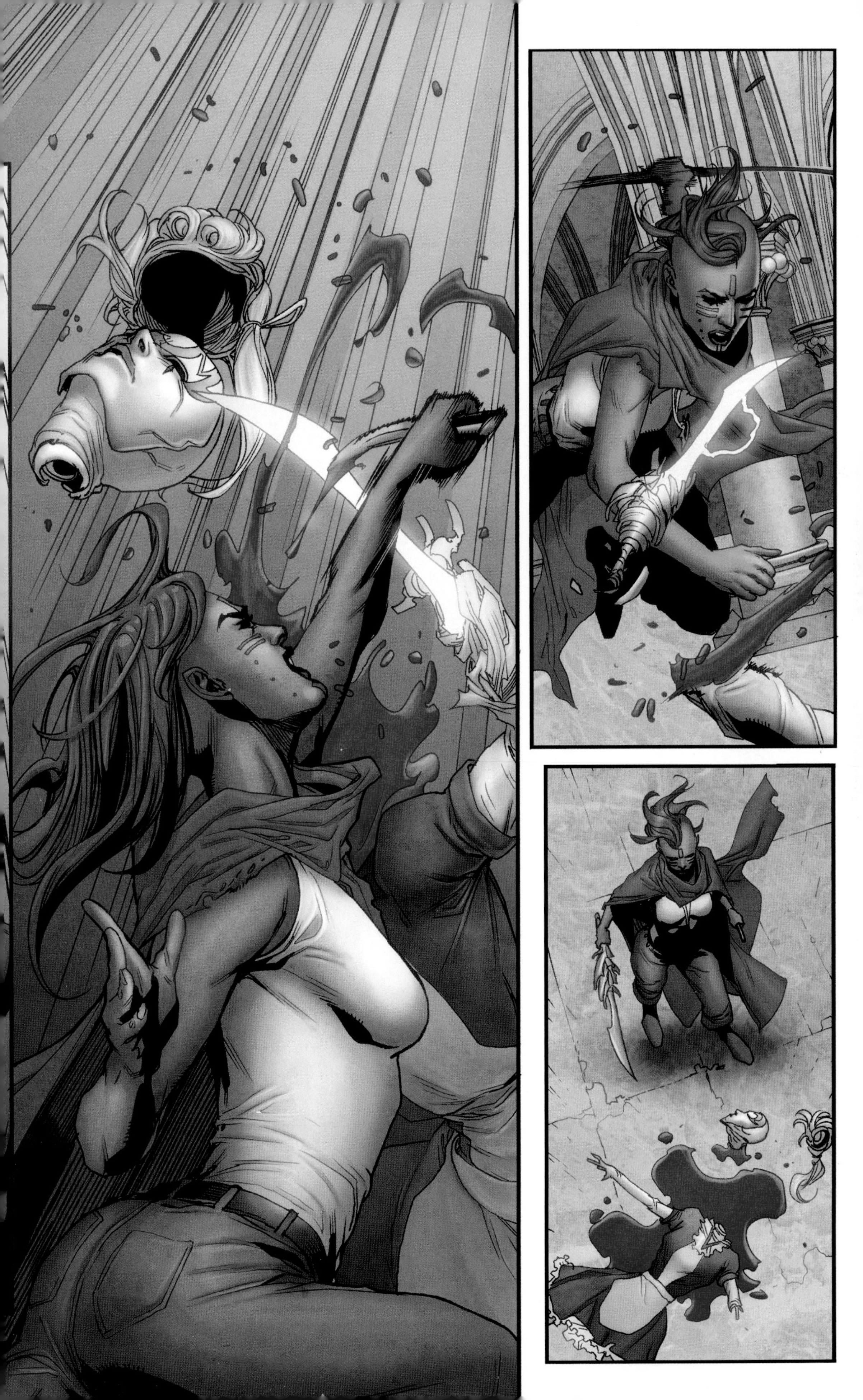

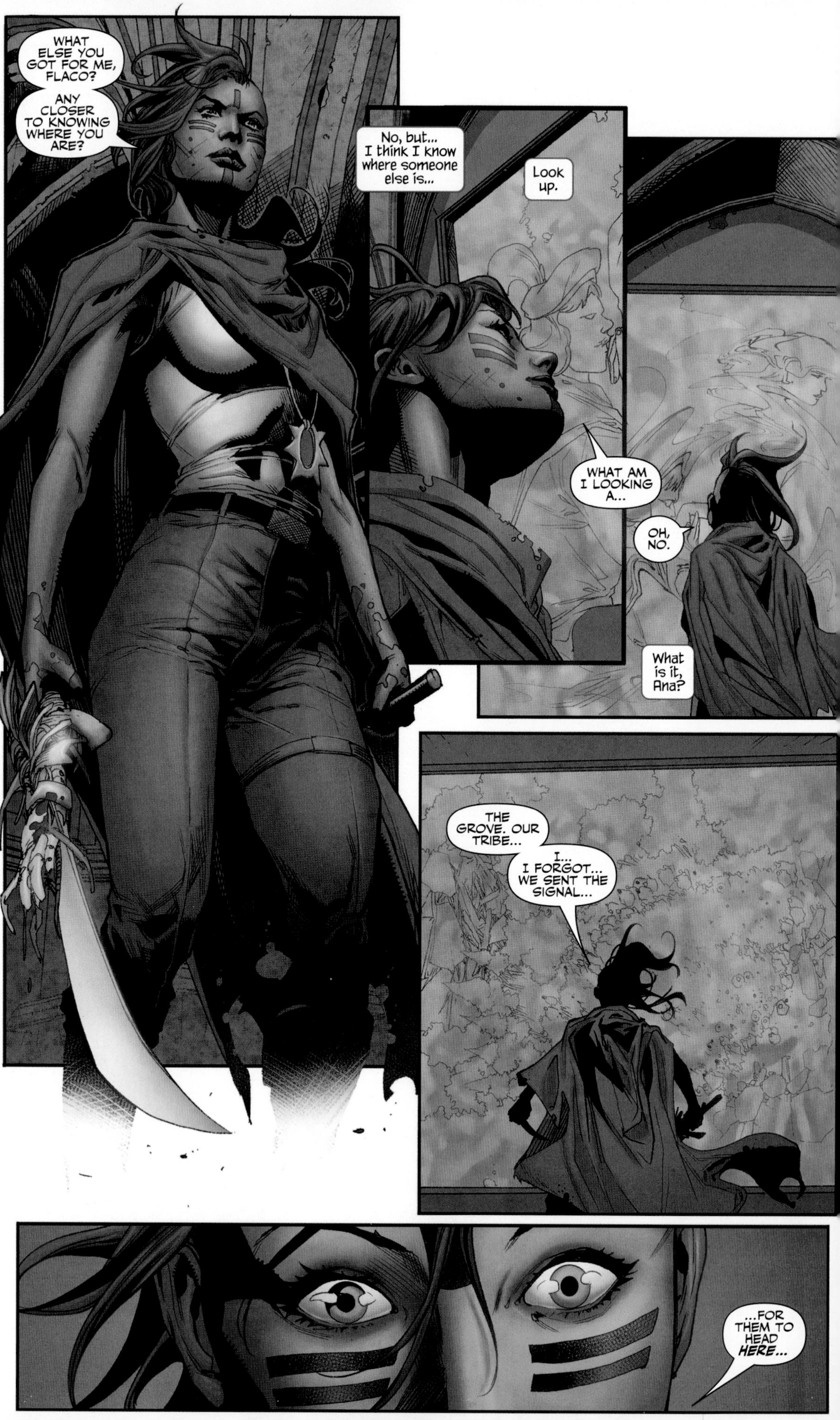
WHAT ELSE YOU GOT FOR ME, FLACO?
ANY CLOSER TO KNOWING WHERE YOU ARE?
No, but... I think I know where someone else is...
Look up.
WHAT AM I LOOKING A...
OH, NO.
What is it, Ana?
THE GROVE. OUR TRIBE...
I... I FORGOT... WE SENT THE SIGNAL...
...FOR THEM TO HEAD *HERE*...

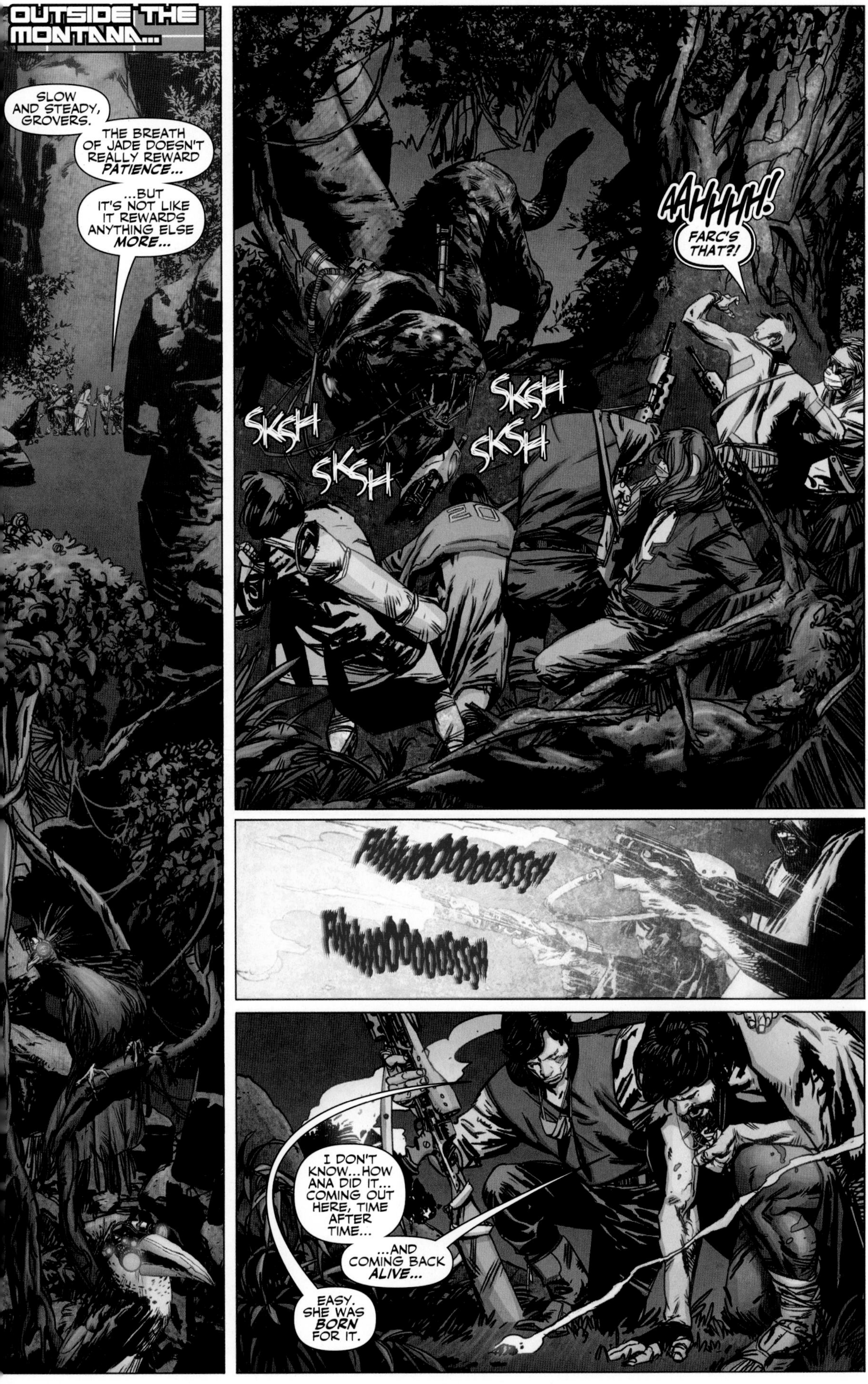

OUTSIDE THE MONTANA...
SLOW AND STEADY, GROVERS.
THE BREATH OF JADE DOESN'T REALLY REWARD PATIENCE...
...BUT IT'S NOT LIKE IT REWARDS ANYTHING ELSE MORE...
AAHHHH!
FARC'S THAT?!
SKSH
SKSH
SKSH
SKSH
FWWWOOOOOOSSSSH
FWWWOOOOOOSSSSH
I DON'T KNOW...HOW ANA DID IT... COMING OUT HERE, TIME AFTER TIME...
...AND COMING BACK ALIVE...
EASY. SHE WAS BORN FOR IT.

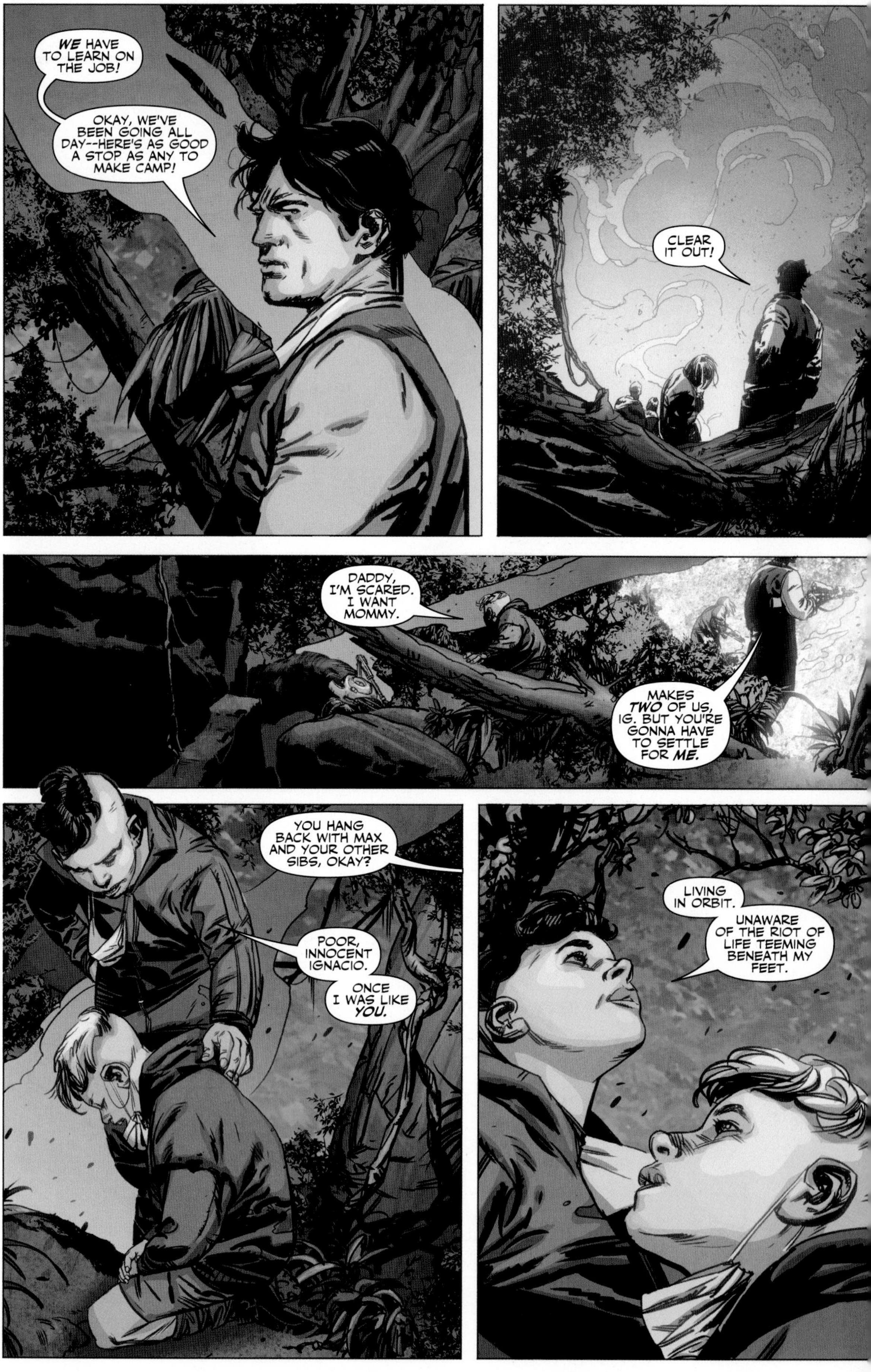
WE HAVE TO LEARN ON THE JOB!
OKAY, WE'VE BEEN GOING ALL DAY--HERE'S AS GOOD A STOP AS ANY TO MAKE CAMP!
CLEAR IT OUT!
DADDY, I'M SCARED. I WANT MOMMY.
MAKES TWO OF US, IG. BUT YOU'RE GONNA HAVE TO SETTLE FOR ME.
YOU HANG BACK WITH MAX AND YOUR OTHER SIBS, OKAY?
POOR, INNOCENT IGNACIO.
ONCE I WAS LIKE YOU.
LIVING IN ORBIT.
UNAWARE OF THE RIOT OF LIFE TEEMING BENEATH MY FEET.

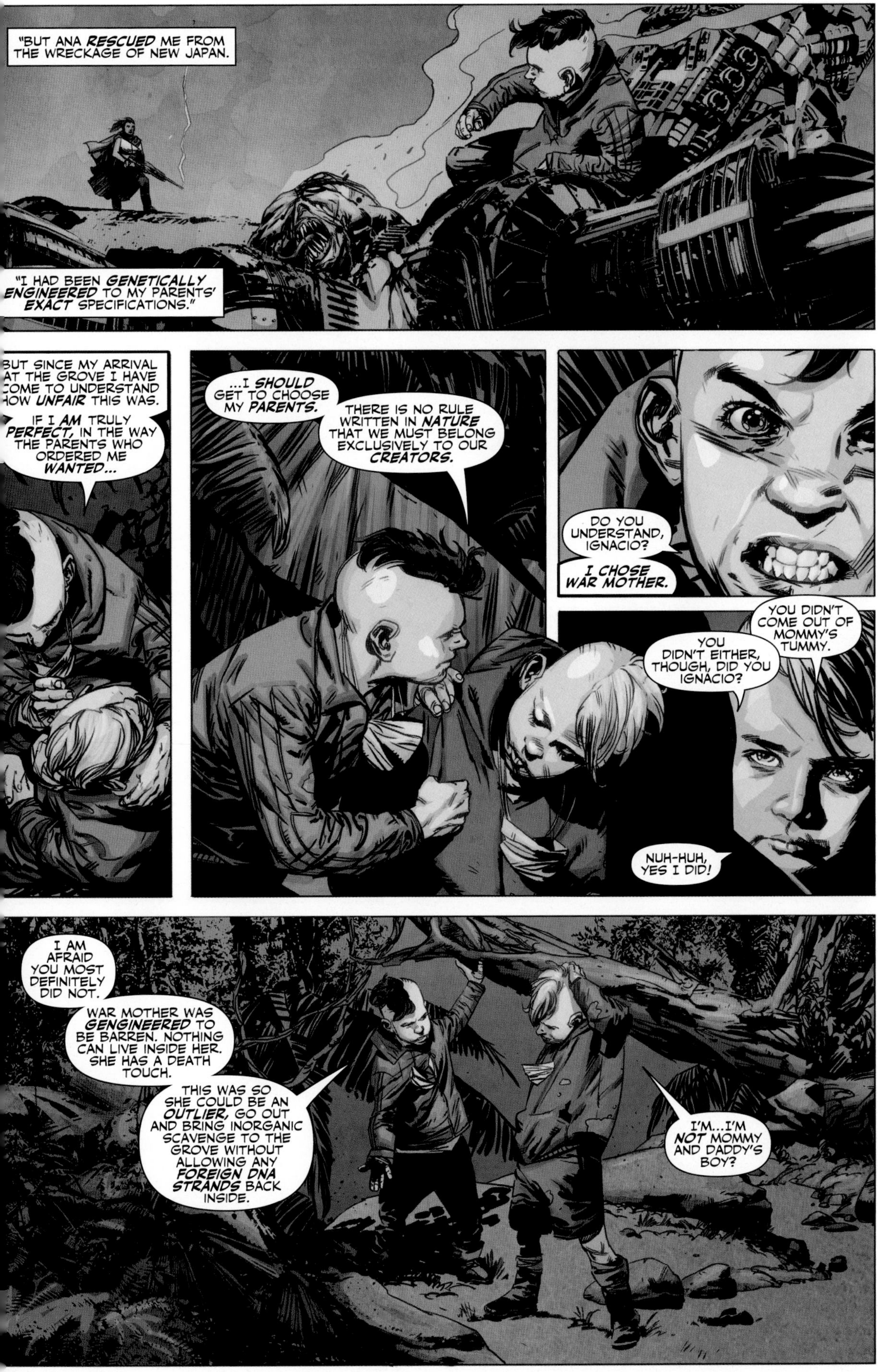
"BUT ANA RESCUED ME FROM THE WRECKAGE OF NEW JAPAN.
"I HAD BEEN GENETICALLY ENGINEERED TO MY PARENTS' EXACT SPECIFICATIONS."
BUT SINCE MY ARRIVAL AT THE GROVE I HAVE COME TO UNDERSTAND HOW UNFAIR THIS WAS.
IF I AM TRULY PERFECT, IN THE WAY THE PARENTS WHO ORDERED ME WANTED...
...I SHOULD GET TO CHOOSE MY PARENTS.
THERE IS NO RULE WRITTEN IN NATURE THAT WE MUST BELONG EXCLUSIVELY TO OUR CREATORS.
DO YOU UNDERSTAND, IGNACIO?
I CHOSE WAR MOTHER.
YOU DIDN'T COME OUT OF MOMMY'S TUMMY.
YOU DIDN'T EITHER, THOUGH, DID YOU IGNACIO?
NUH-HUH, YES I DID!
I AM AFRAID YOU MOST DEFINITELY DID NOT.
WAR MOTHER WAS GENGINEERED TO BE BARREN. NOTHING CAN LIVE INSIDE HER. SHE HAS A DEATH TOUCH.
THIS WAS SO SHE COULD BE AN OUTLIER, GO OUT AND BRING INORGANIC SCAVENGE TO THE GROVE WITHOUT ALLOWING ANY FOREIGN DNA STRANDS BACK INSIDE.
I'M...I'M NOT MOMMY AND DADDY'S BOY?

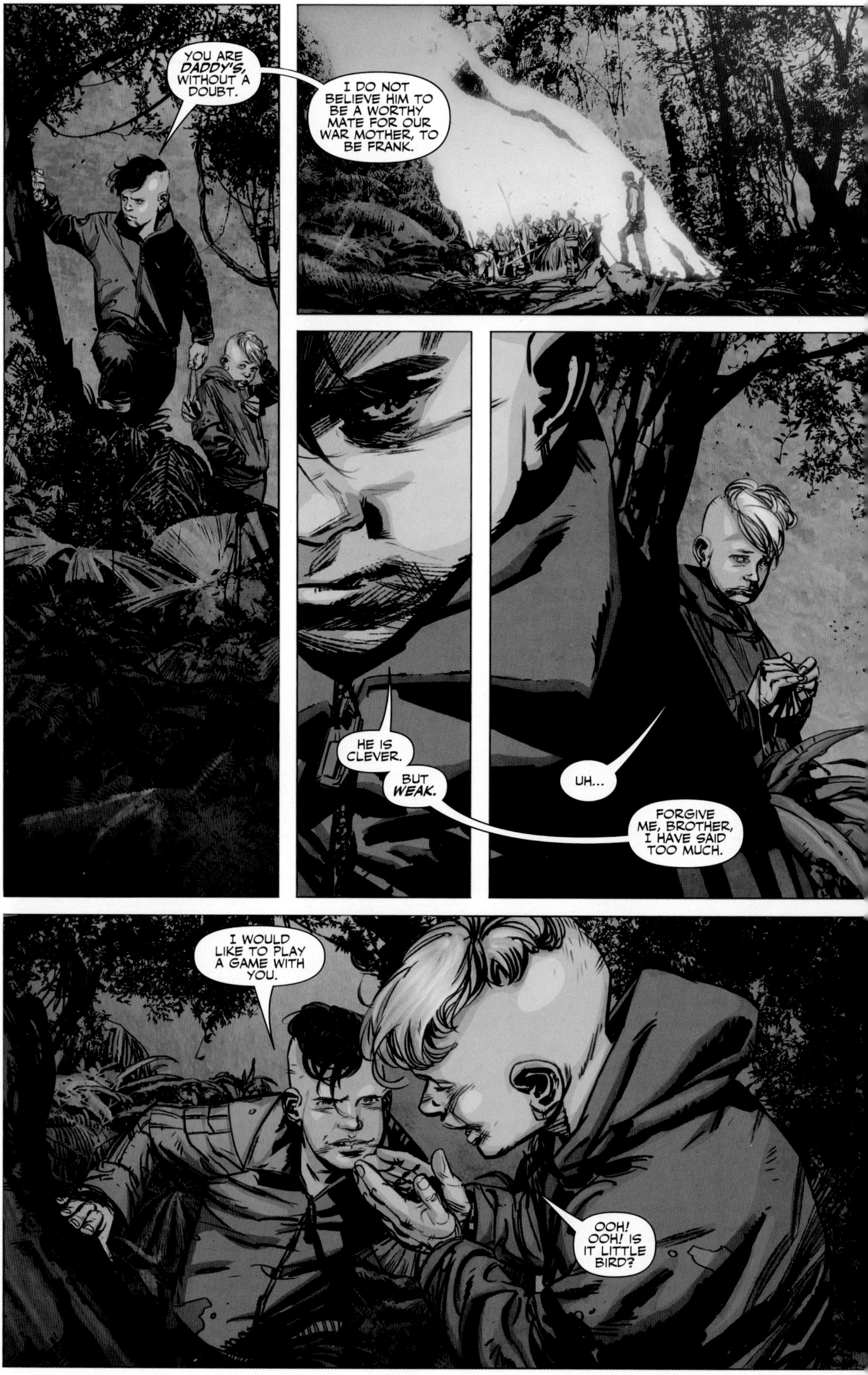
YOU ARE *DADDY'S,* WITHOUT A DOUBT.
I DO NOT BELIEVE HIM TO BE A WORTHY MATE FOR OUR WAR MOTHER, TO BE FRANK.
HE IS CLEVER.
BUT *WEAK.*
UH...
FORGIVE ME, BROTHER, I HAVE SAID TOO MUCH.
I WOULD LIKE TO PLAY A GAME WITH YOU.
OOH! OOH! IS IT LITTLE BIRD?

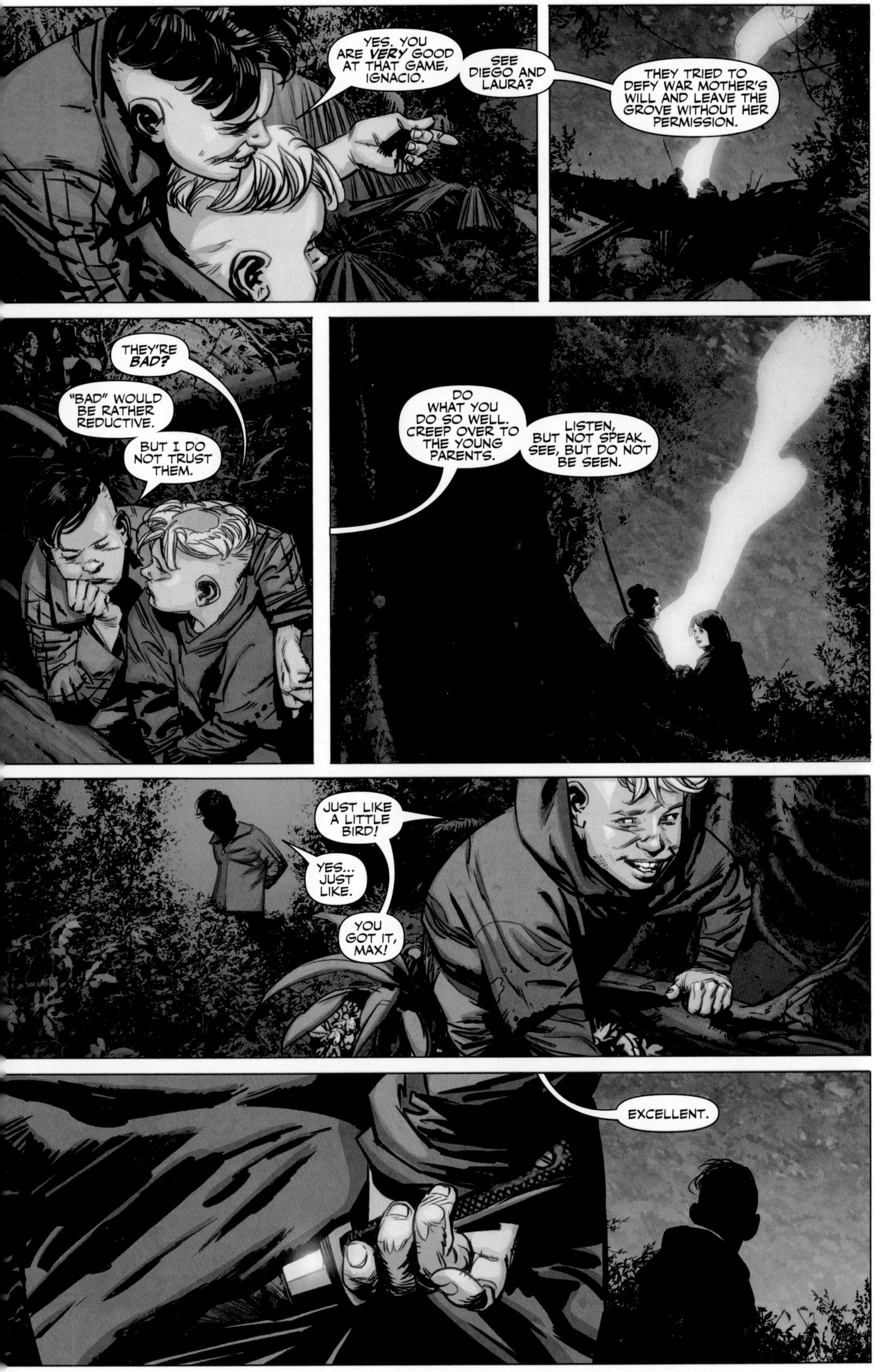
YES. YOU ARE *VERY* GOOD AT THAT GAME, IGNACIO.
SEE DIEGO AND LAURA?
THEY TRIED TO DEFY WAR MOTHER'S WILL AND LEAVE THE GROVE WITHOUT HER PERMISSION.
THEY'RE *BAD?*
"BAD" WOULD BE RATHER REDUCTIVE.
BUT I DO NOT TRUST THEM.
DO WHAT YOU DO SO WELL. CREEP OVER TO THE YOUNG PARENTS.
LISTEN, BUT NOT SPEAK. SEE, BUT DO NOT BE SEEN.
JUST LIKE A LITTLE BIRD!
YES... JUST LIKE.
YOU GOT IT, MAX!
EXCELLENT.

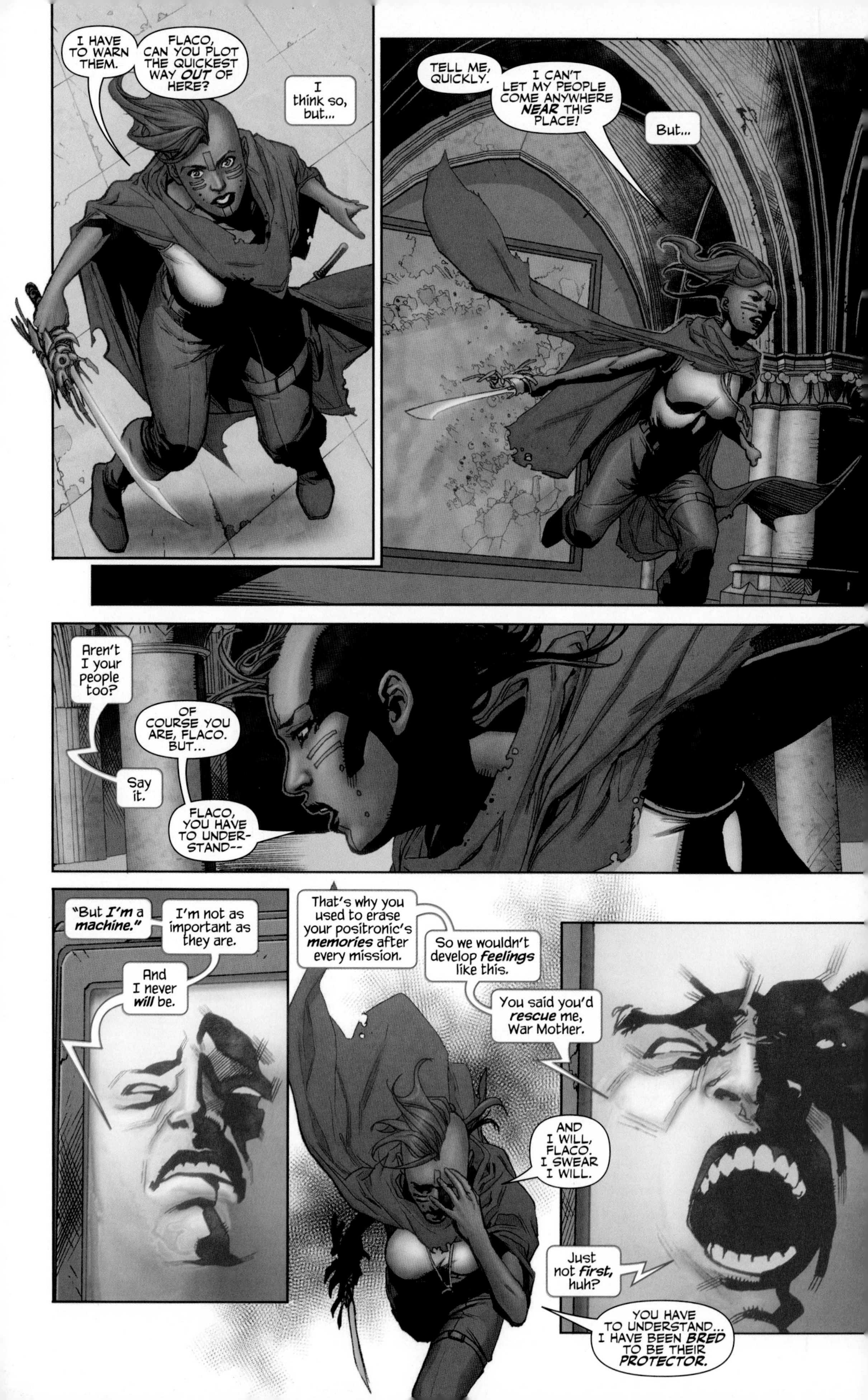
I HAVE TO WARN THEM.
FLACO, CAN YOU PLOT THE QUICKEST WAY OUT OF HERE?
I think so, but...
TELL ME, QUICKLY.
I CAN'T LET MY PEOPLE COME ANYWHERE NEAR THIS PLACE!
But...
Aren't I your people too?
OF COURSE YOU ARE, FLACO. BUT...
Say it.
FLACO, YOU HAVE TO UNDER-STAND--
"But I'm a machine."
I'm not as important as they are.
And I never will be.
That's why you used to erase your positronic's memories after every mission.
So we wouldn't develop feelings like this.
You said you'd rescue me, War Mother.
AND I WILL, FLACO. I SWEAR I WILL.
Just not first, huh?
YOU HAVE TO UNDERSTAND... I HAVE BEEN BRED TO BE THEIR PROTECTOR.

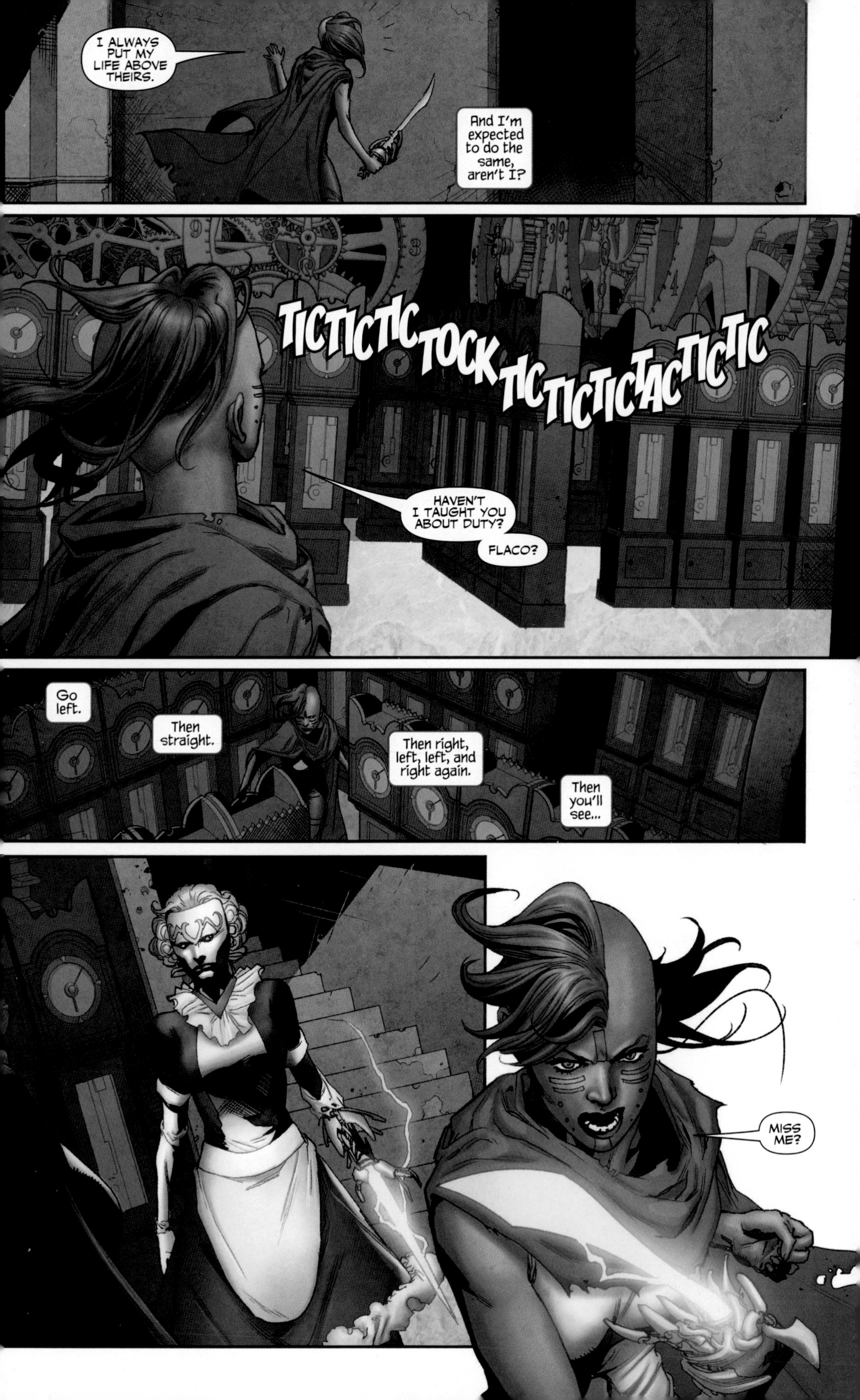
I ALWAYS PUT MY LIFE ABOVE THEIRS.
And I'm expected to do the same, aren't I?
TICTICTIC TOCK TIC TICTICTAC TIC TIC
HAVEN'T I TAUGHT YOU ABOUT DUTY?
FLACO?
Go left.
Then straight.
Then right, left, left, and right again.
Then you'll see...
MISS ME?

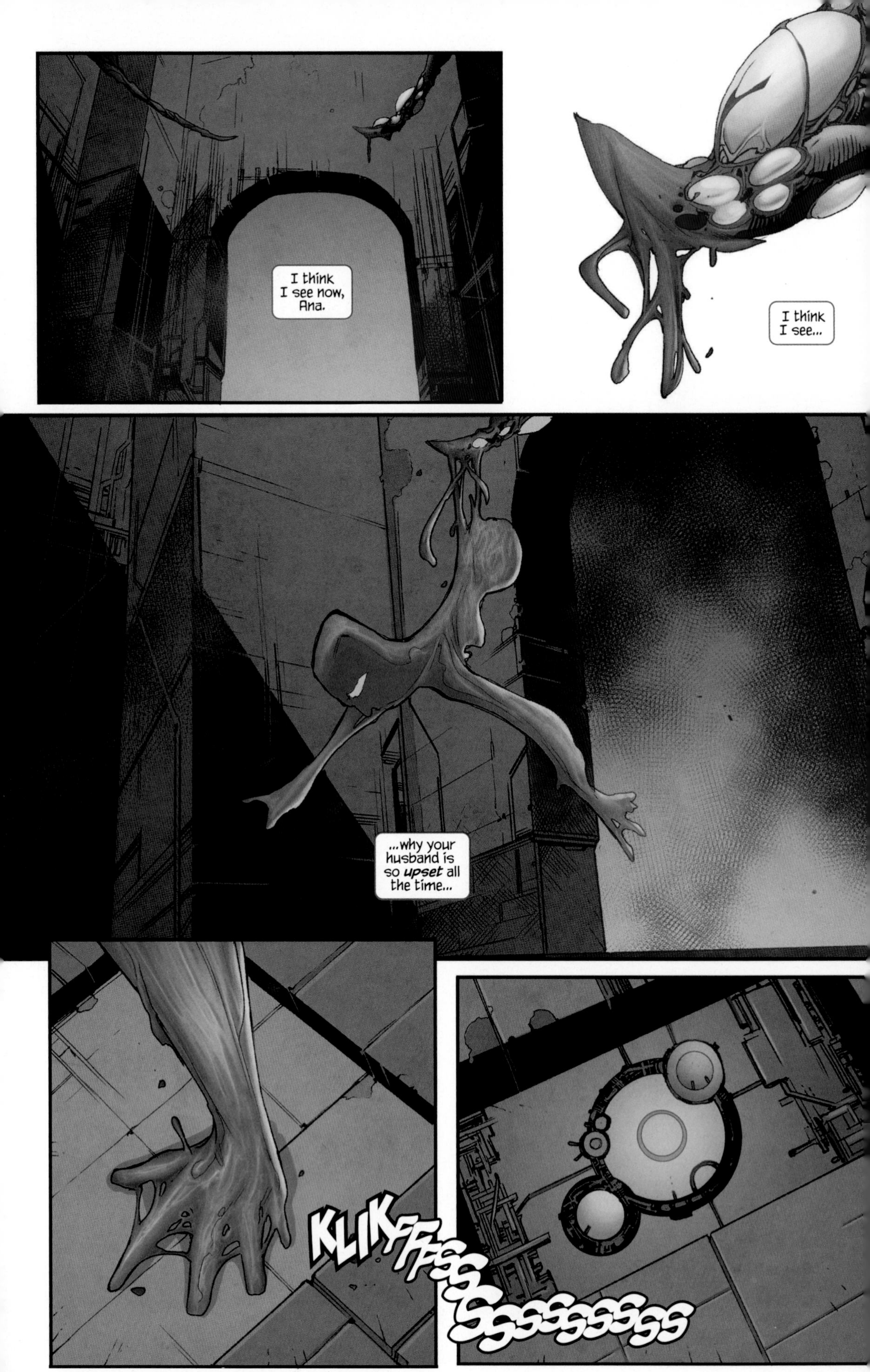
I think I see now, Ana.
I think I see...
...why your husband is so *upset* all the time...
KLIKFFSSSSSSSSSSSS

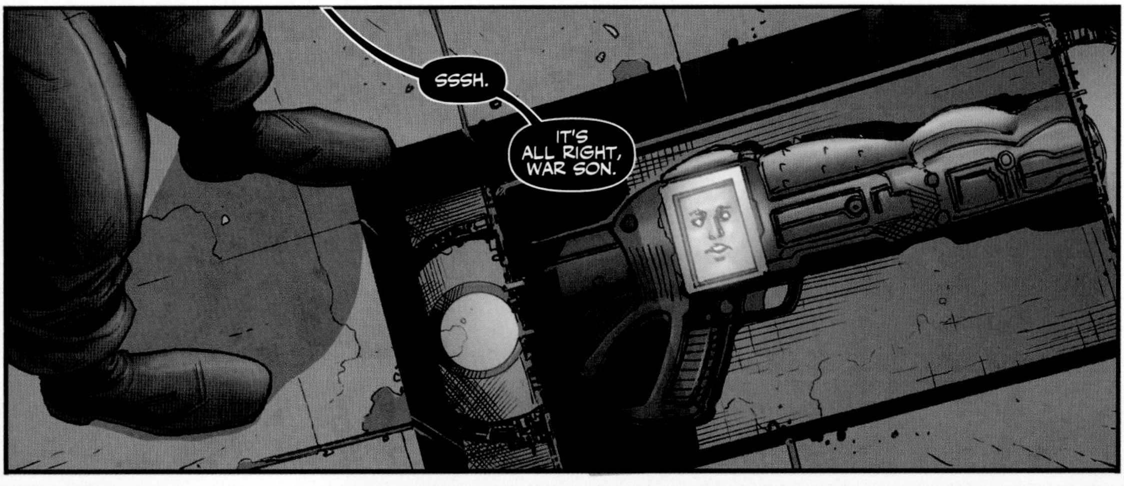
SSSH.
IT'S ALL RIGHT, WAR SON.

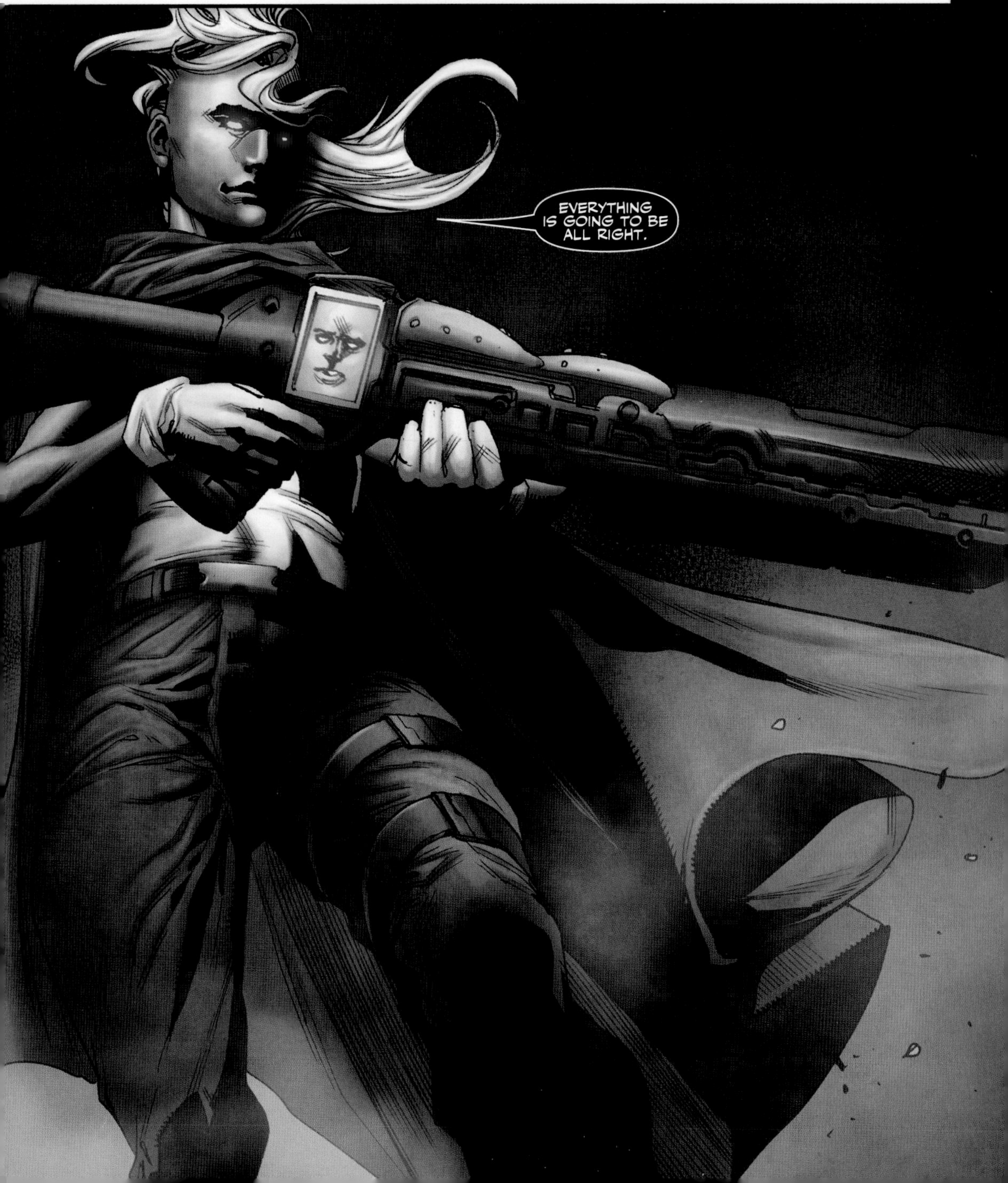
EVERYTHING IS GOING TO BE ALL RIGHT.

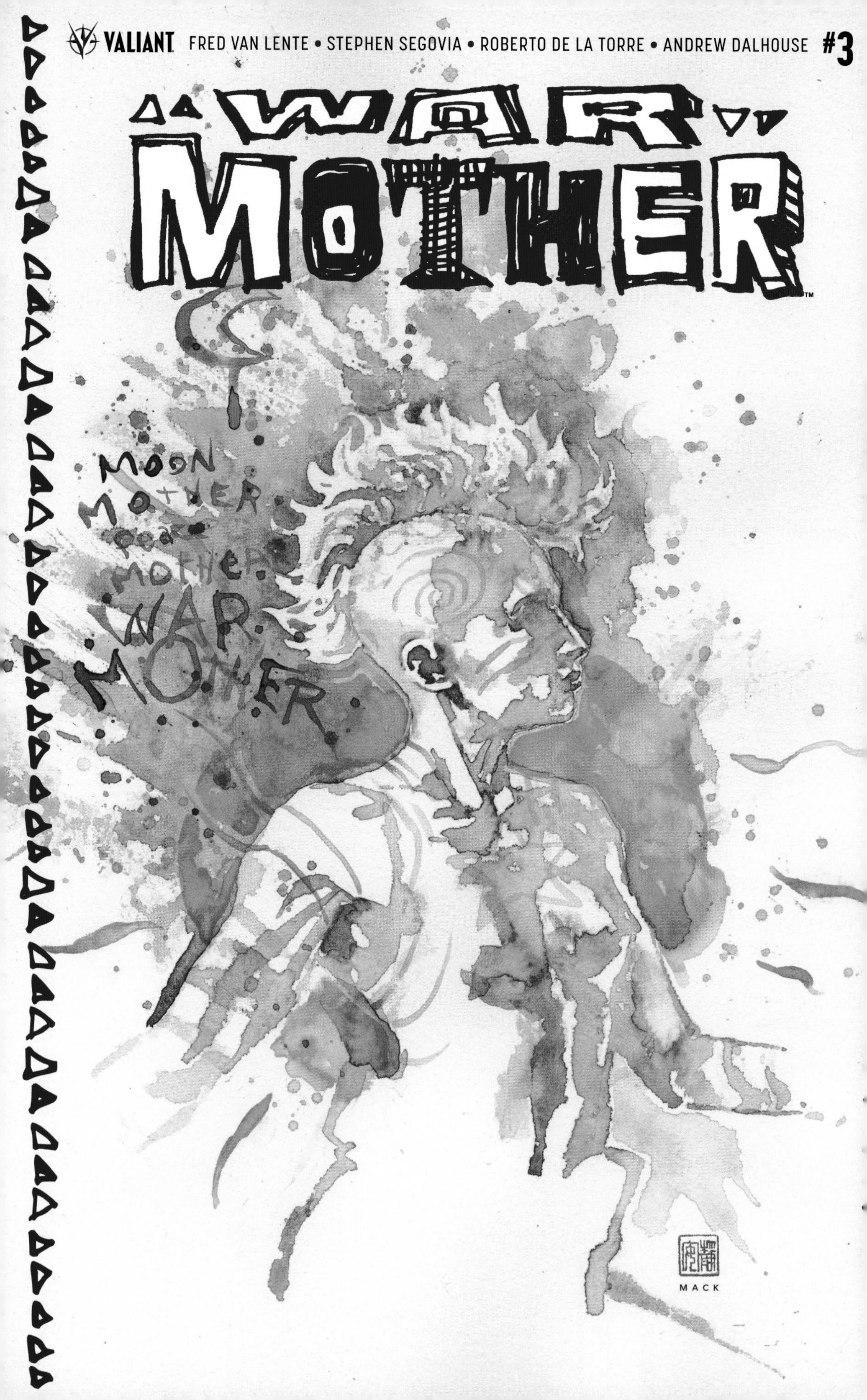
VALIANT
FRED VAN LENTE • STEPHEN SEGOVIA • ROBERTO DE LA TORRE • ANDREW DALHOUSE
#3
WAR MOTHER™
MOON
MOTHER
WAR
MOTHER
MACK

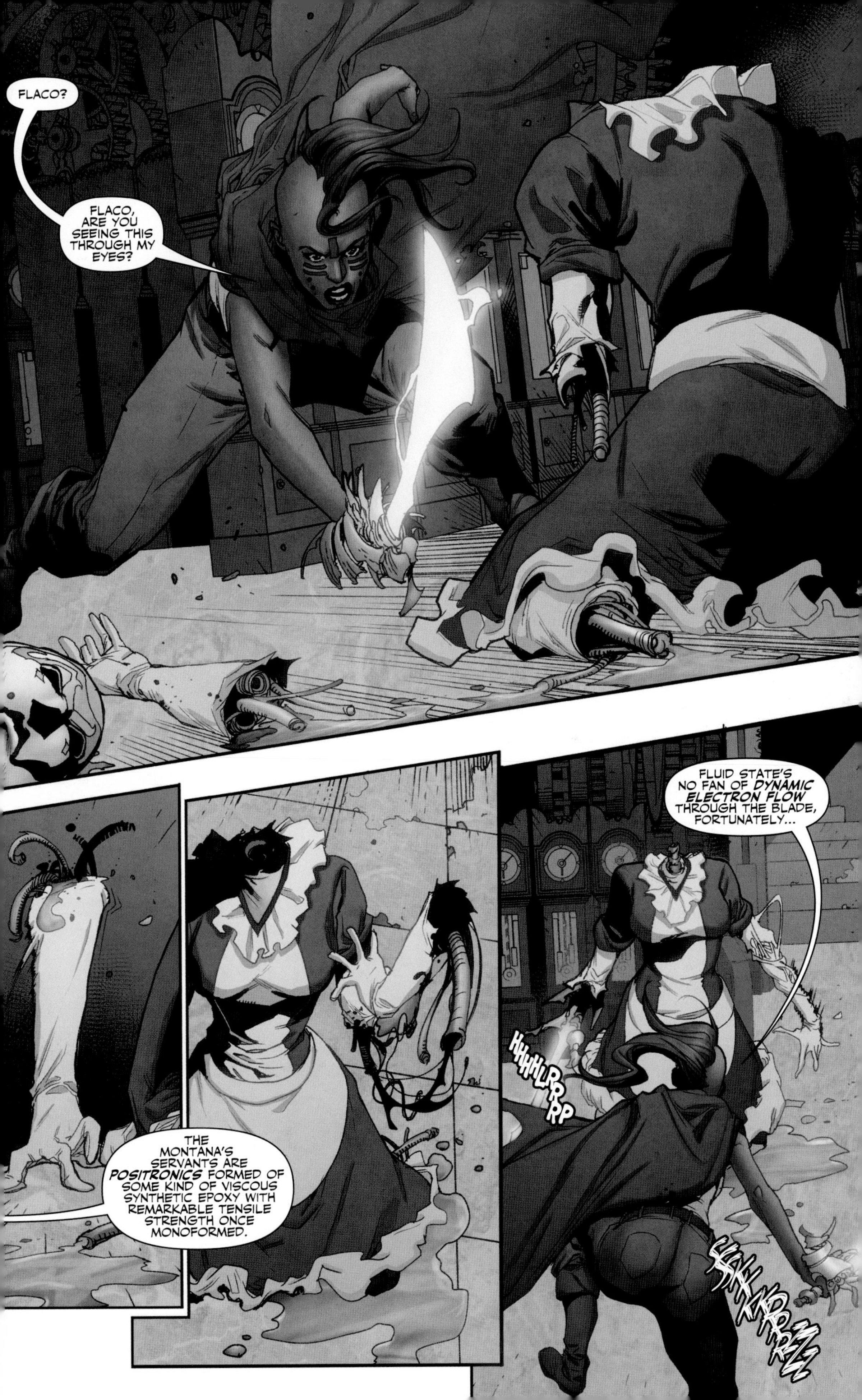
FLACO?
FLACO, ARE YOU SEEING THIS THROUGH MY EYES?
FLUID STATE'S NO FAN OF DYNAMIC ELECTRON FLOW THROUGH THE BLADE, FORTUNATELY...
HHHHLRRRP
THE MONTANA'S SERVANTS ARE POSITRONICS FORMED OF SOME KIND OF VISCOUS SYNTHETIC EPOXY WITH REMARKABLE TENSILE STRENGTH ONCE MONOFORMED.

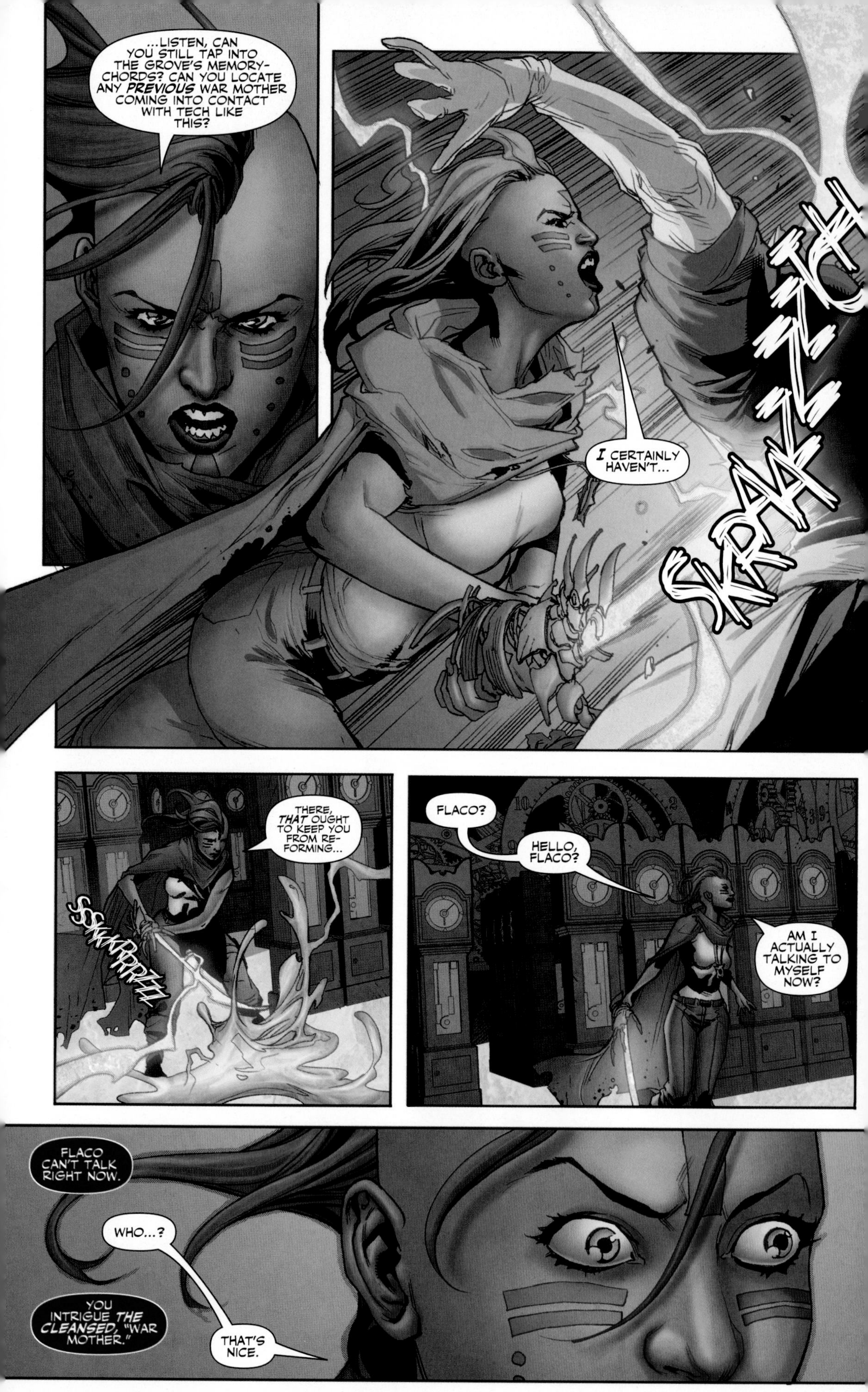
...LISTEN, CAN YOU STILL TAP INTO THE GROVE'S MEMORY-CHORDS? CAN YOU LOCATE ANY *PREVIOUS* WAR MOTHER COMING INTO CONTACT WITH TECH LIKE THIS?
I CERTAINLY HAVEN'T...
SKRAAZZZCH
SSSKKRRRZZZ
THERE, *THAT* OUGHT TO KEEP YOU FROM RE-FORMING...
FLACO?
HELLO, FLACO?
AM I ACTUALLY TALKING TO MYSELF NOW?
FLACO CAN'T TALK RIGHT NOW.
WHO...?
YOU INTRIGUE *THE CLEANSED,* "WAR MOTHER."
THAT'S NICE.

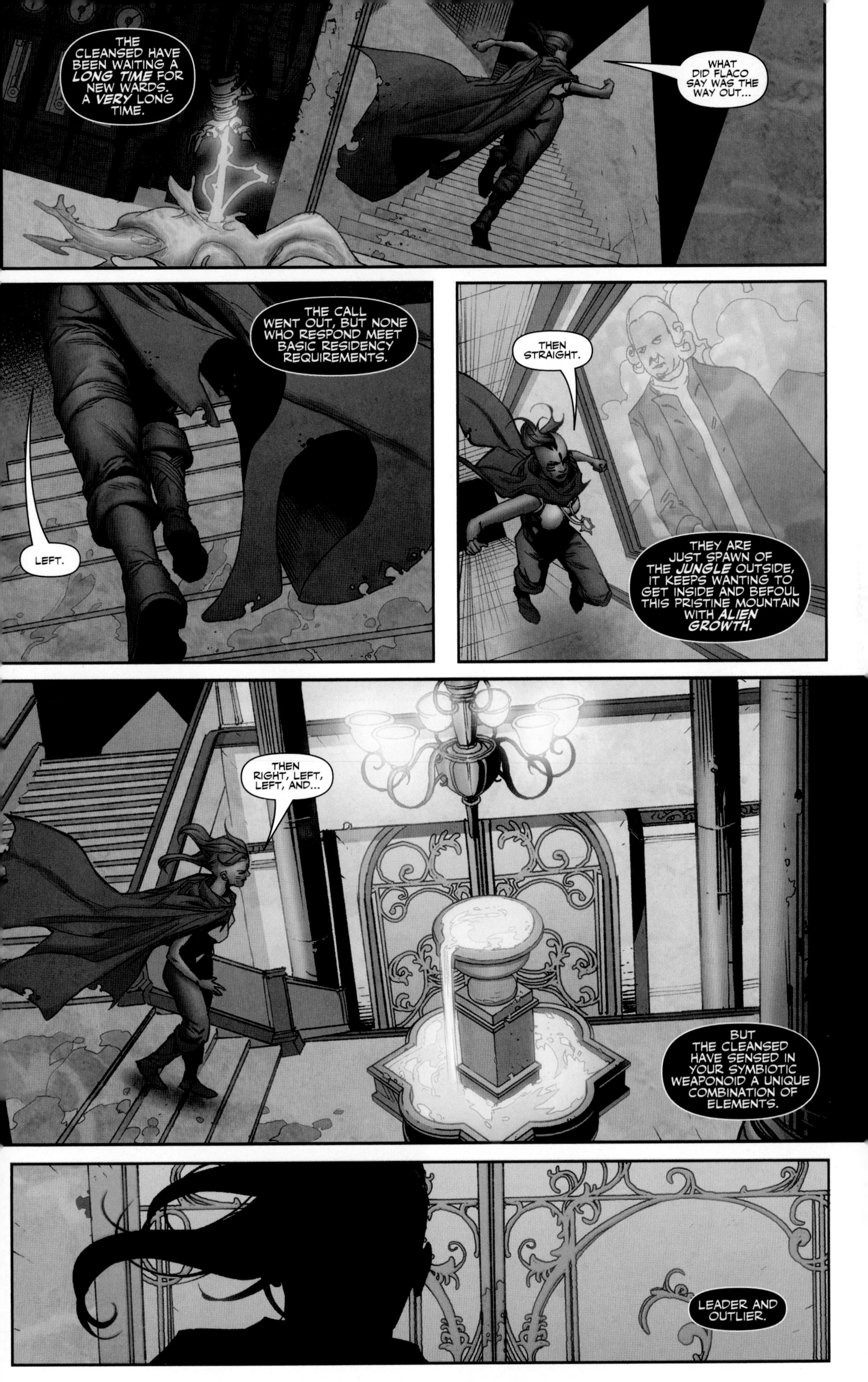
THE CLEANSED HAVE BEEN WAITING A LONG TIME FOR NEW WARDS. A VERY LONG TIME.
WHAT DID FLACO SAY WAS THE WAY OUT...
THE CALL WENT OUT, BUT NONE WHO RESPOND MEET BASIC RESIDENCY REQUIREMENTS.
LEFT.
THEN STRAIGHT.
THEY ARE JUST SPAWN OF THE JUNGLE OUTSIDE, IT KEEPS WANTING TO GET INSIDE AND BEFOUL THIS PRISTINE MOUNTAIN WITH ALIEN GROWTH.
THEN RIGHT, LEFT, LEFT, AND...
BUT THE CLEANSED HAVE SENSED IN YOUR SYMBIOTIC WEAPONOID A UNIQUE COMBINATION OF ELEMENTS.
LEADER AND OUTLIER.

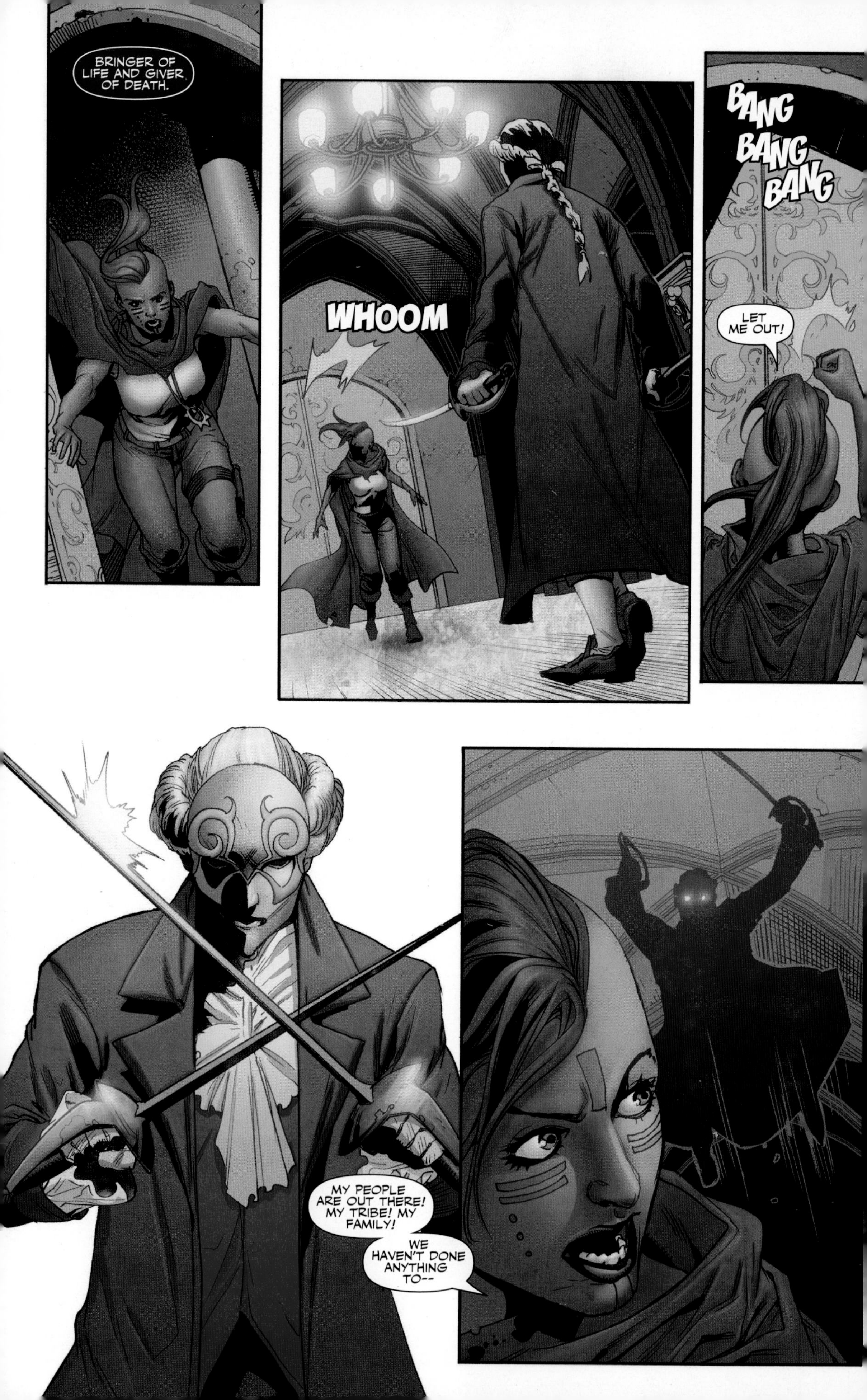
BRINGER OF LIFE AND GIVER OF DEATH.
WHOOM
BANG
BANG
BANG
LET ME OUT!
MY PEOPLE ARE OUT THERE! MY TRIBE! MY FAMILY!
WE HAVEN'T DONE ANYTHING TO--

SKRNHH

SNAPP

KKASSHSH

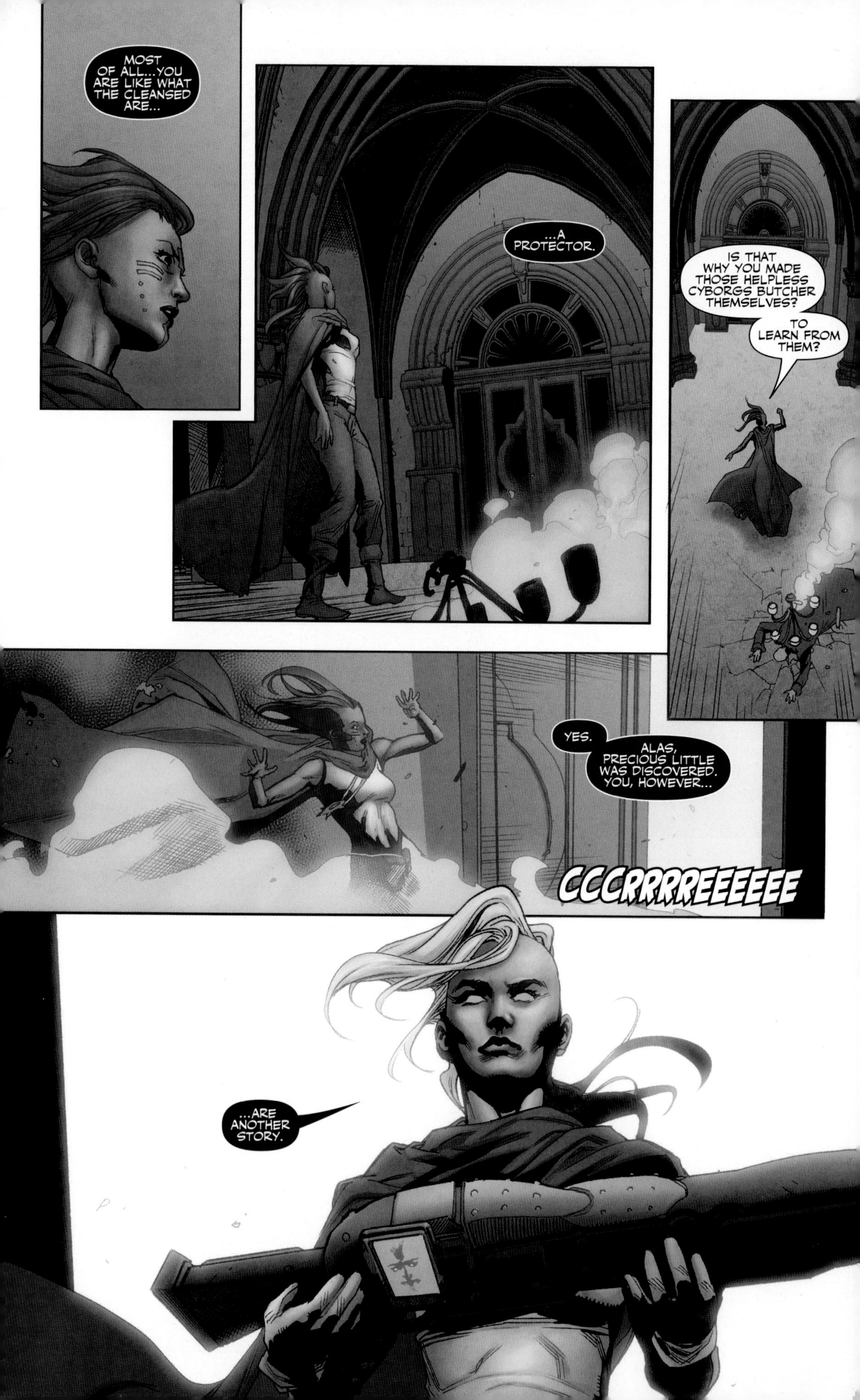
MOST OF ALL...YOU ARE LIKE WHAT THE CLEANSED ARE...
...A PROTECTOR.
IS THAT WHY YOU MADE THOSE HELPLESS CYBORGS BUTCHER THEMSELVES?
TO LEARN FROM THEM?
YES.
ALAS, PRECIOUS LITTLE WAS DISCOVERED. YOU, HOWEVER...
CCCRRRRREEEEEE
...ARE ANOTHER STORY.

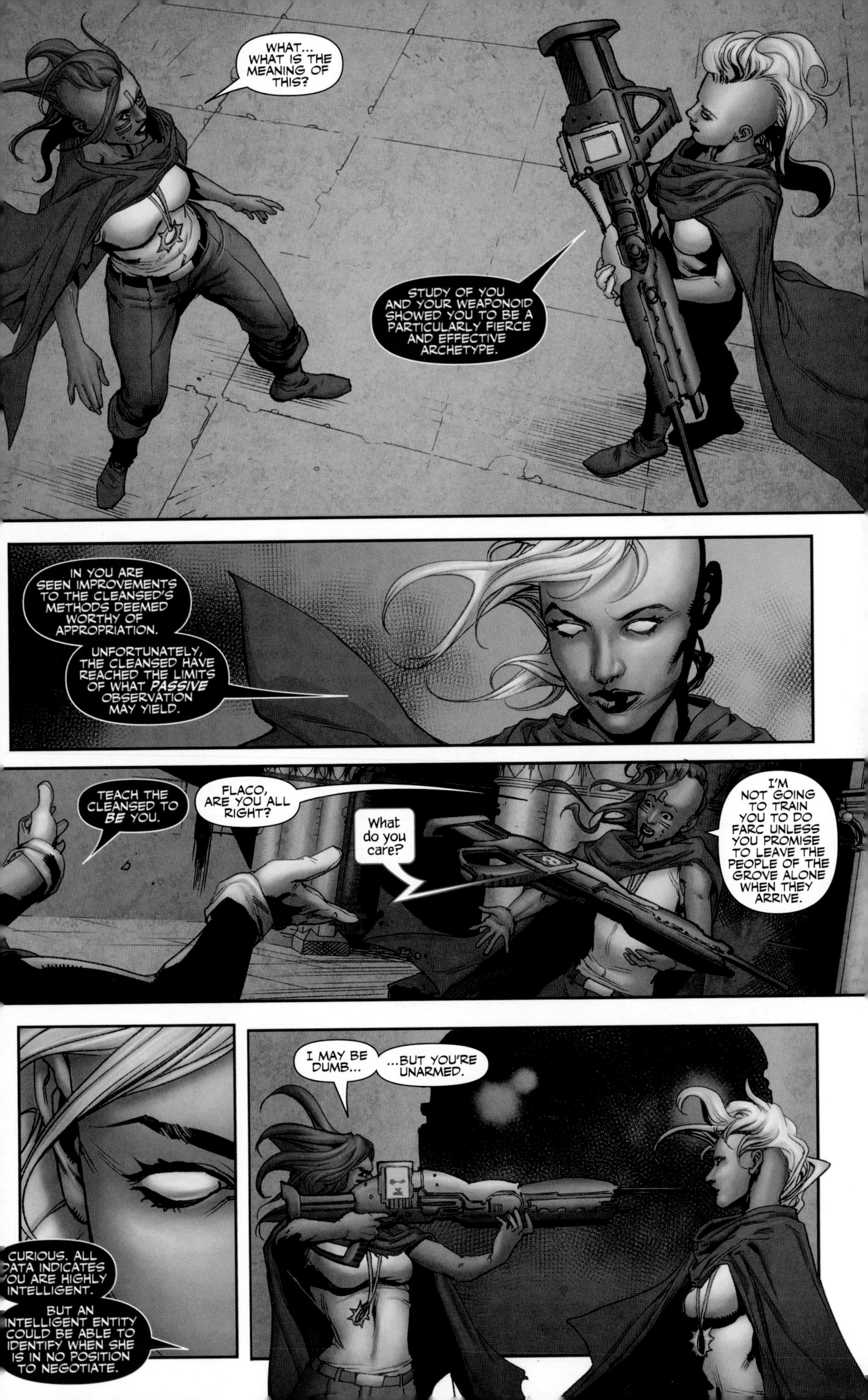
WHAT... WHAT IS THE MEANING OF THIS?
STUDY OF YOU AND YOUR WEAPONOID SHOWED YOU TO BE A PARTICULARLY FIERCE AND EFFECTIVE ARCHETYPE.
IN YOU ARE SEEN IMPROVEMENTS TO THE CLEANSED'S METHODS DEEMED WORTHY OF APPROPRIATION.
UNFORTUNATELY, THE CLEANSED HAVE REACHED THE LIMITS OF WHAT PASSIVE OBSERVATION MAY YIELD.
TEACH THE CLEANSED TO BE YOU.
FLACO, ARE YOU ALL RIGHT?
What do you care?
I'M NOT GOING TO TRAIN YOU TO DO FARC UNLESS YOU PROMISE TO LEAVE THE PEOPLE OF THE GROVE ALONE WHEN THEY ARRIVE.
CURIOUS. ALL DATA INDICATES YOU ARE HIGHLY INTELLIGENT.
BUT AN INTELLIGENT ENTITY COULD BE ABLE TO IDENTIFY WHEN SHE IS IN NO POSITION TO NEGOTIATE.
I MAY BE DUMB...
...BUT YOU'RE UNARMED.

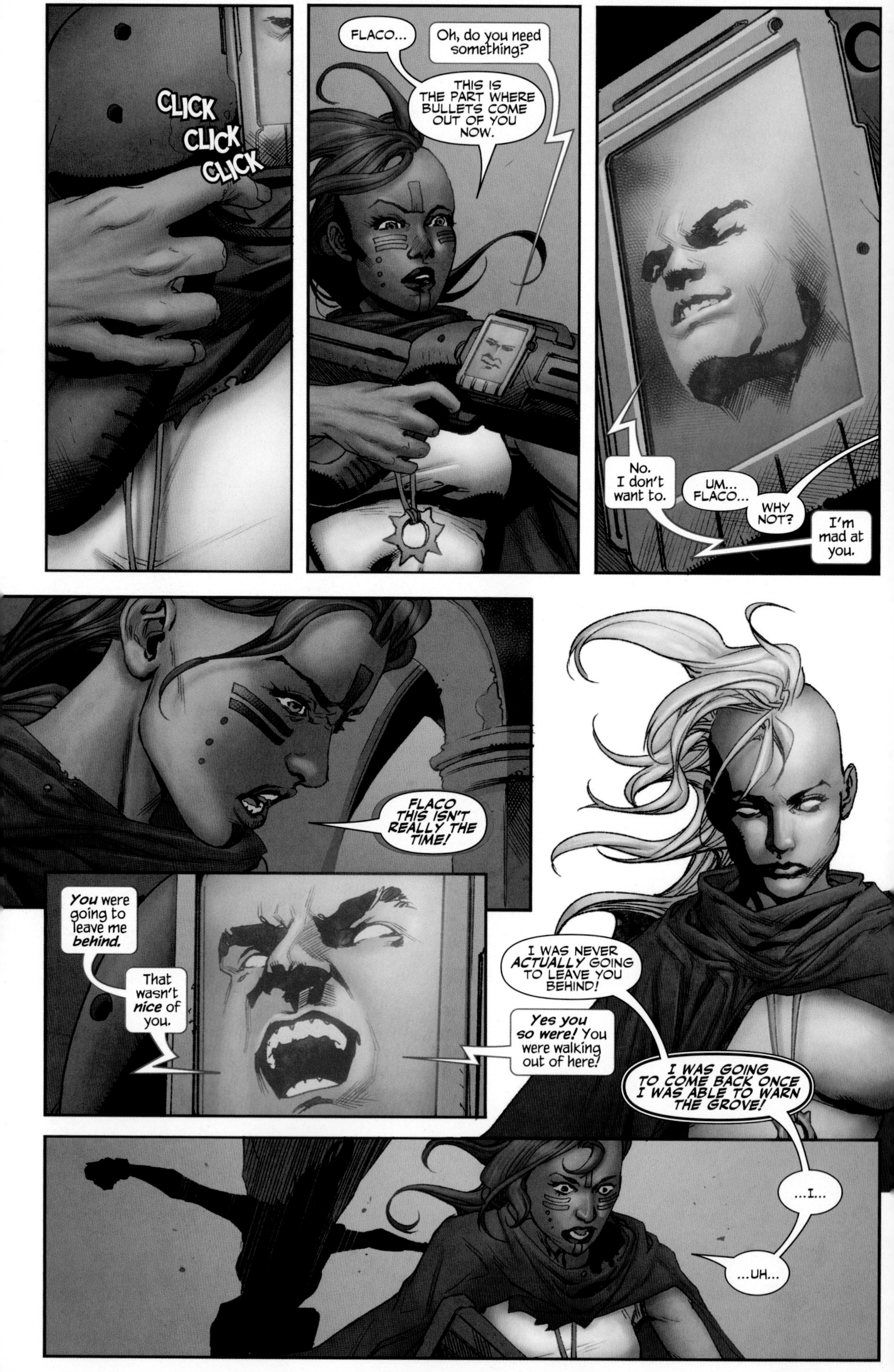
CLICK
CLICK
CLICK
FLACO...
Oh, do you need something?
THIS IS THE PART WHERE BULLETS COME OUT OF YOU NOW.
No. I don't want to.
UM... FLACO...
WHY NOT?
I'm mad at you.
FLACO THIS ISN'T REALLY THE TIME!
You were going to leave me behind.
That wasn't nice of you.
I WAS NEVER ACTUALLY GOING TO LEAVE YOU BEHIND!
Yes you so were! You were walking out of here!
I WAS GOING TO COME BACK ONCE I WAS ABLE TO WARN THE GROVE!
...I...
...UH...

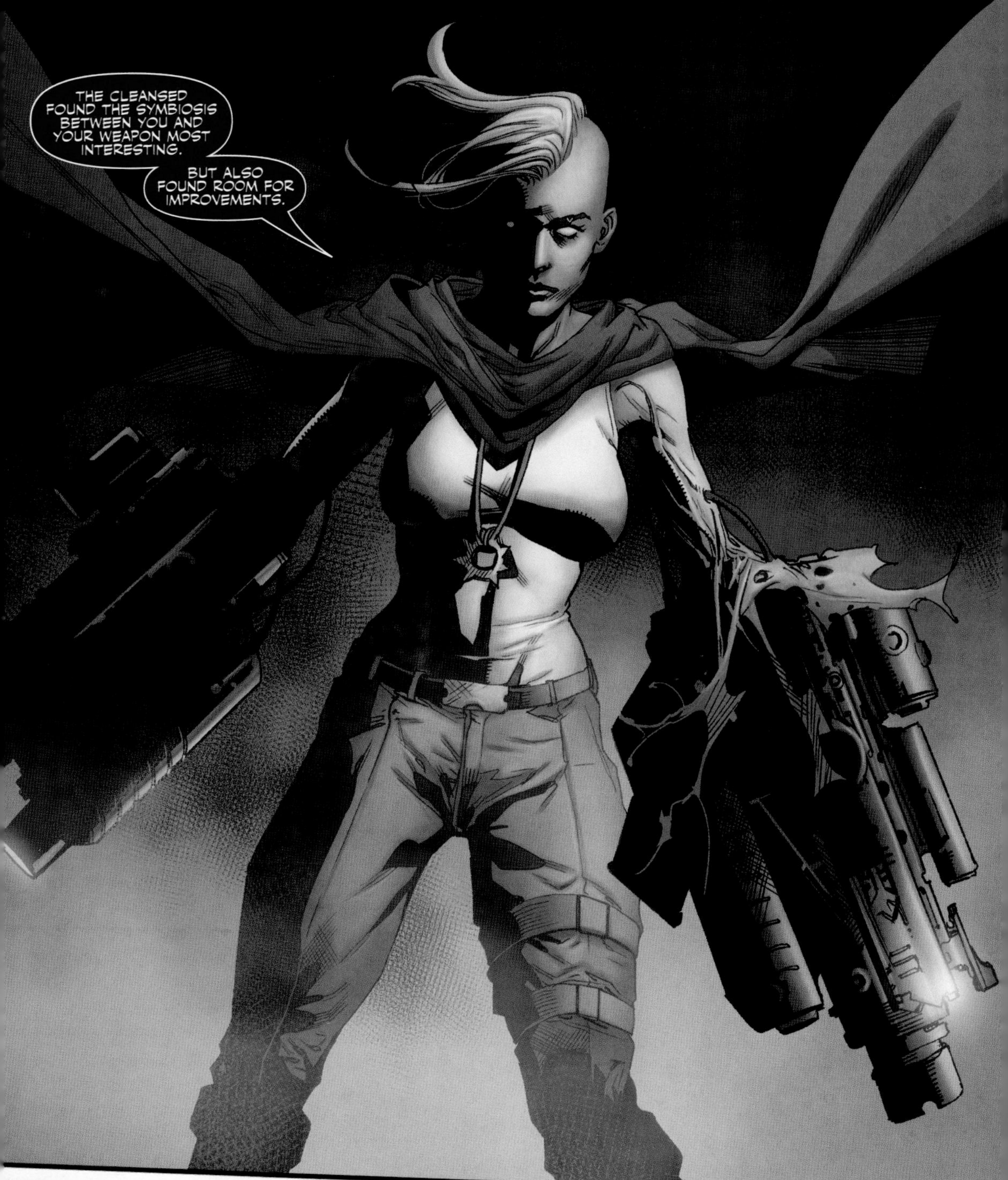
THE CLEANSED FOUND THE SYMBIOSIS BETWEEN YOU AND YOUR WEAPON MOST INTERESTING.
BUT ALSO FOUND ROOM FOR IMPROVEMENTS.

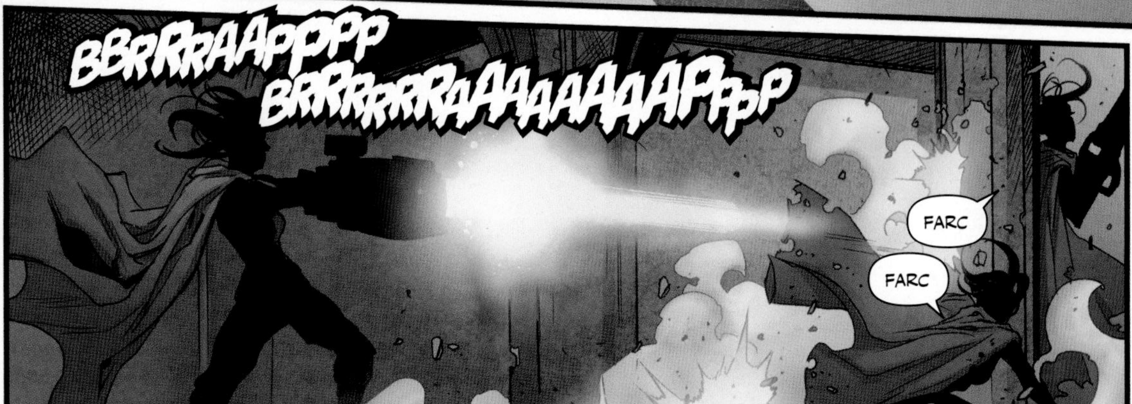
BBRRRAAPPPP
BRRRRRRAAAAAAAAPPPP
FARC
FARC

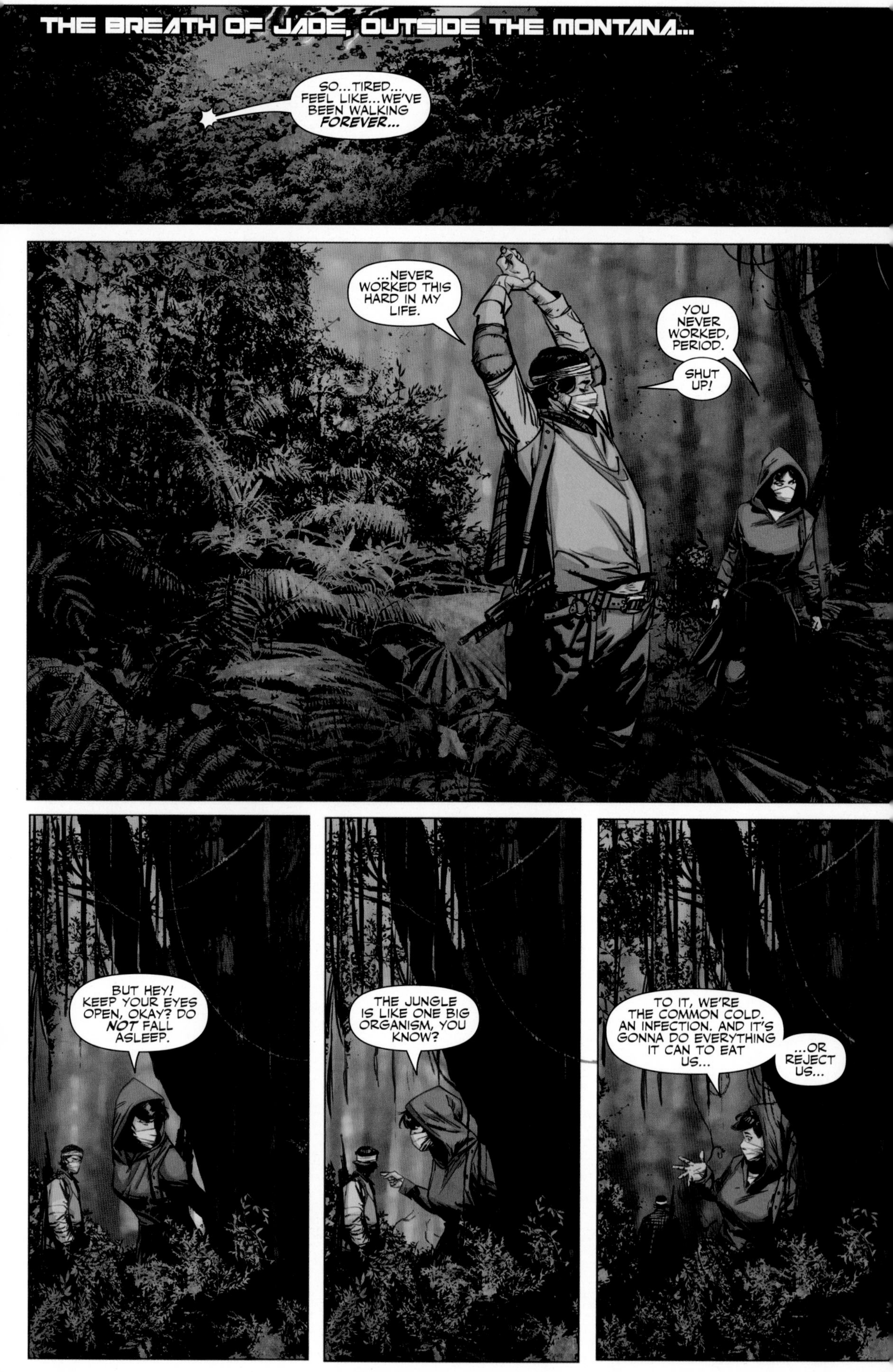
THE BREATH OF JADE, OUTSIDE THE MONTANA...
SO...TIRED... FEEL LIKE...WE'VE BEEN WALKING FOREVER...
...NEVER WORKED THIS HARD IN MY LIFE.
YOU NEVER WORKED, PERIOD.
SHUT UP!
BUT HEY! KEEP YOUR EYES OPEN, OKAY? DO NOT FALL ASLEEP.
THE JUNGLE IS LIKE ONE BIG ORGANISM, YOU KNOW?
TO IT, WE'RE THE COMMON COLD. AN INFECTION. AND IT'S GONNA DO EVERYTHING IT CAN TO EAT US...
...OR REJECT US...

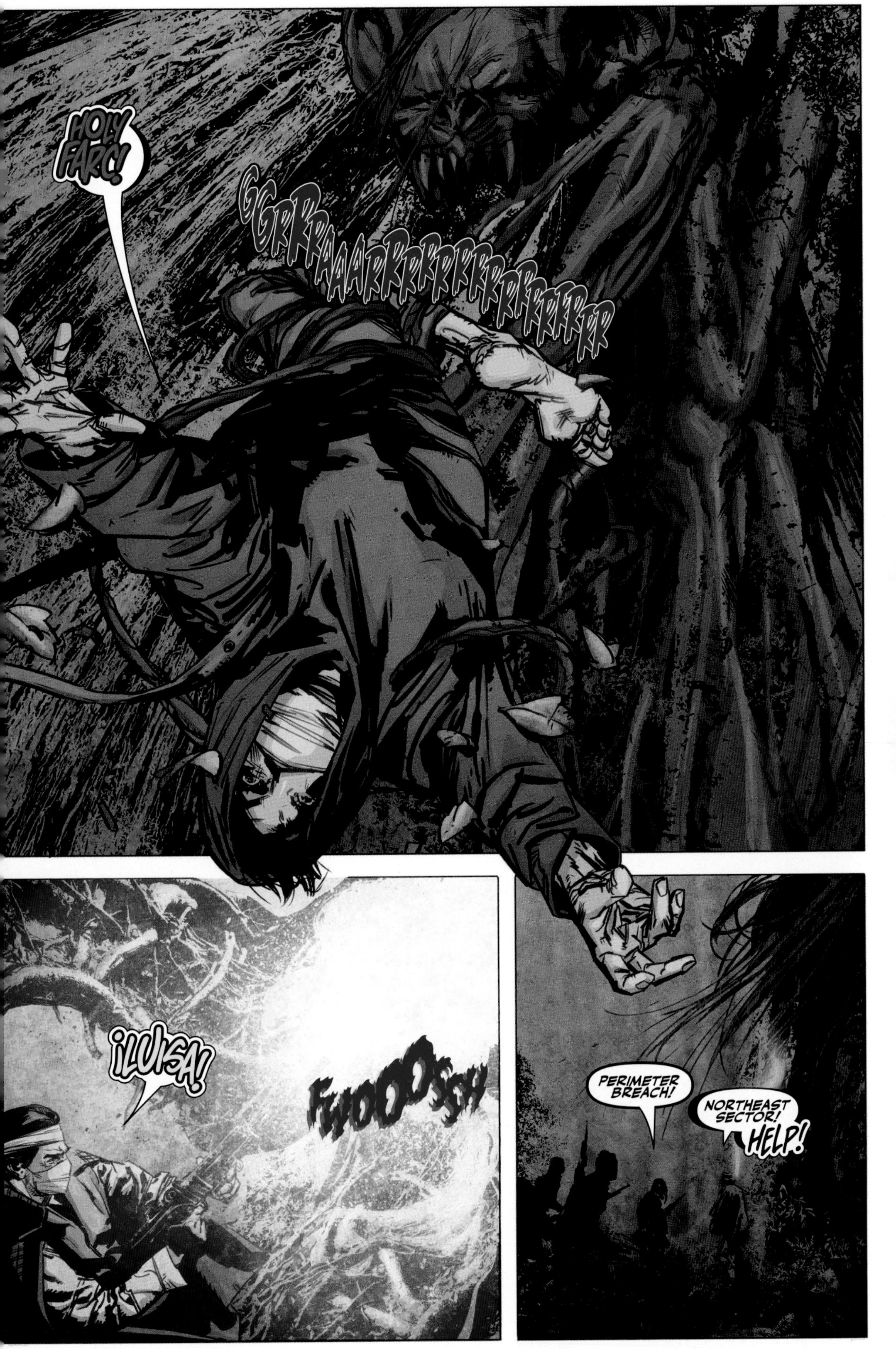
HOLY FARC!
GGRRRAAARRRRRRRRRRRRRR
¡LUISA!
FWOOOSSH
PERIMETER BREACH!
NORTHEAST SECTOR! HELP!

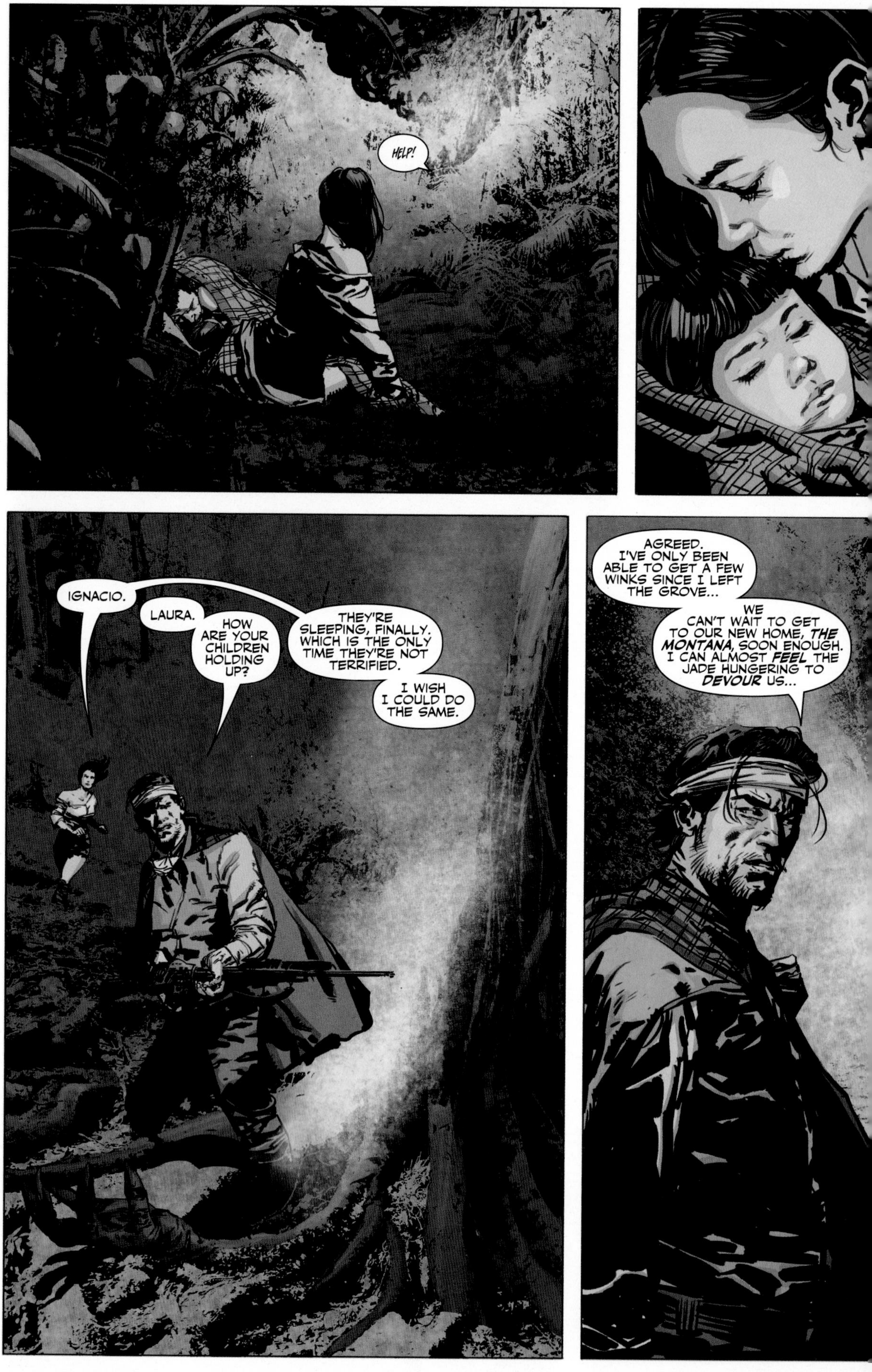
HELP!
IGNACIO.
LAURA.
HOW ARE YOUR CHILDREN HOLDING UP?
THEY'RE SLEEPING, FINALLY. WHICH IS THE ONLY TIME THEY'RE NOT TERRIFIED.
I WISH I COULD DO THE SAME.
AGREED. I'VE ONLY BEEN ABLE TO GET A FEW WINKS SINCE I LEFT THE GROVE...
WE CAN'T WAIT TO GET TO OUR NEW HOME, THE MONTANA, SOON ENOUGH. I CAN ALMOST FEEL THE JADE HUNGERING TO DEVOUR US...

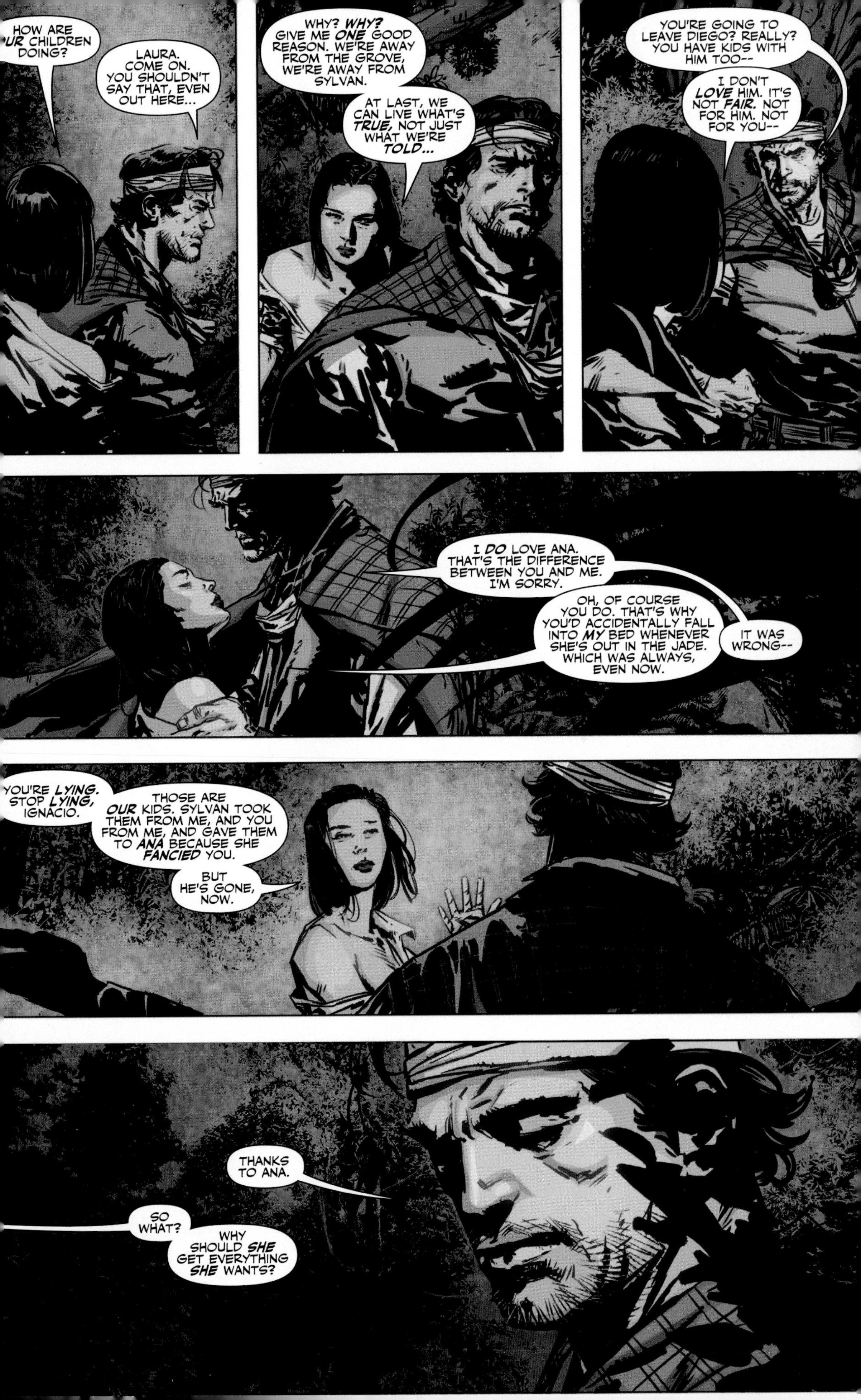
HOW ARE OUR CHILDREN DOING?
LAURA. COME ON. YOU SHOULDN'T SAY THAT, EVEN OUT HERE...
WHY? WHY? GIVE ME ONE GOOD REASON. WE'RE AWAY FROM THE GROVE, WE'RE AWAY FROM SYLVAN.
AT LAST, WE CAN LIVE WHAT'S TRUE, NOT JUST WHAT WE'RE TOLD...
YOU'RE GOING TO LEAVE DIEGO? REALLY? YOU HAVE KIDS WITH HIM TOO--
I DON'T LOVE HIM. IT'S NOT FAIR. NOT FOR HIM. NOT FOR YOU--
I DO LOVE ANA. THAT'S THE DIFFERENCE BETWEEN YOU AND ME. I'M SORRY.
OH, OF COURSE YOU DO. THAT'S WHY YOU'D ACCIDENTALLY FALL INTO MY BED WHENEVER SHE'S OUT IN THE JADE. WHICH WAS ALWAYS, EVEN NOW.
IT WAS WRONG--
YOU'RE LYING. STOP LYING, IGNACIO.
THOSE ARE OUR KIDS. SYLVAN TOOK THEM FROM ME, AND YOU FROM ME, AND GAVE THEM TO ANA BECAUSE SHE FANCIED YOU.
BUT HE'S GONE, NOW.
THANKS TO ANA.
SO WHAT?
WHY SHOULD SHE GET EVERYTHING SHE WANTS?

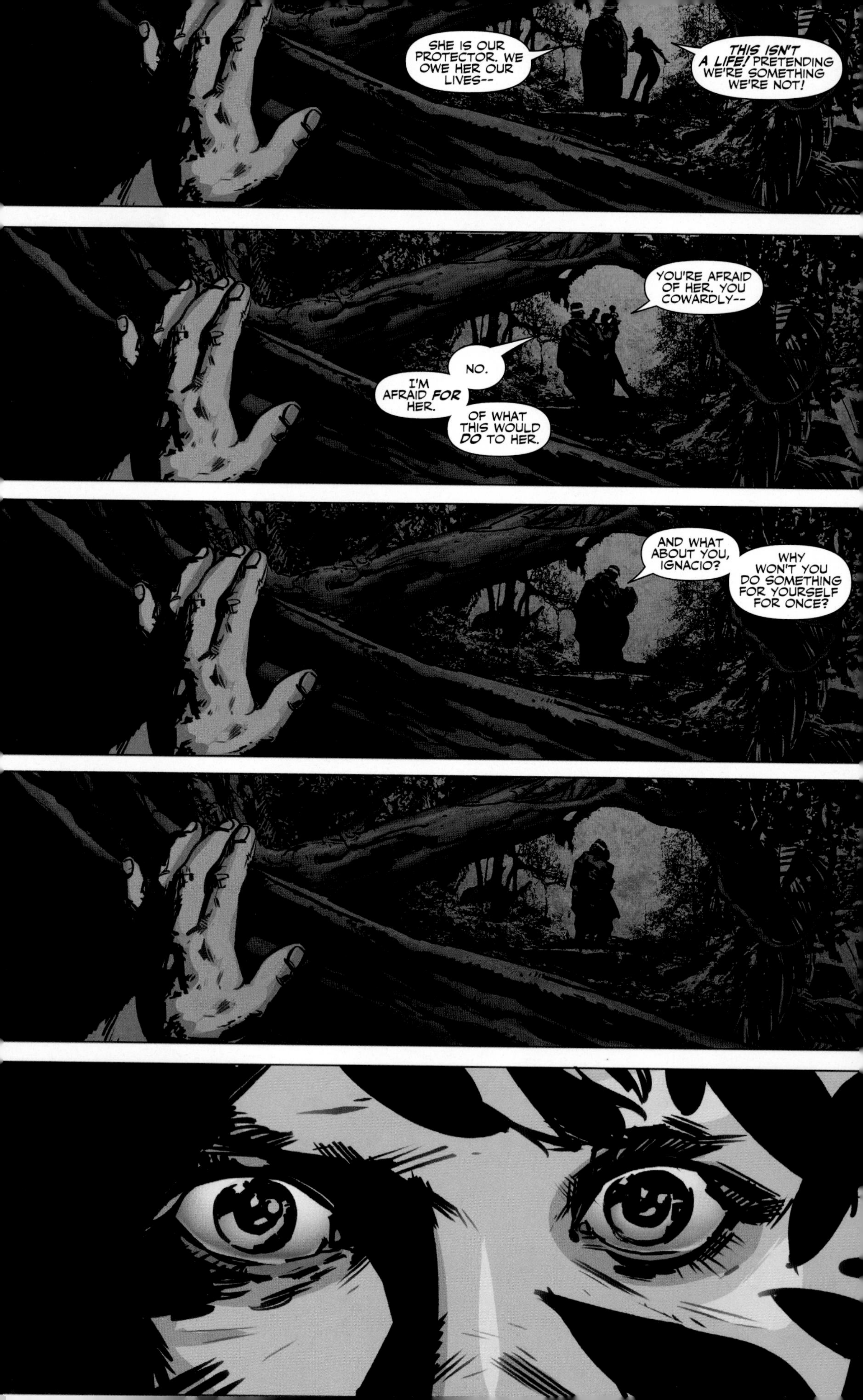
SHE IS OUR PROTECTOR. WE OWE HER OUR LIVES--
THIS ISN'T A LIFE! PRETENDING WE'RE SOMETHING WE'RE NOT!
YOU'RE AFRAID OF HER. YOU COWARDLY--
NO.
I'M AFRAID FOR HER.
OF WHAT THIS WOULD DO TO HER.
AND WHAT ABOUT YOU, IGNACIO?
WHY WON'T YOU DO SOMETHING FOR YOURSELF FOR ONCE?

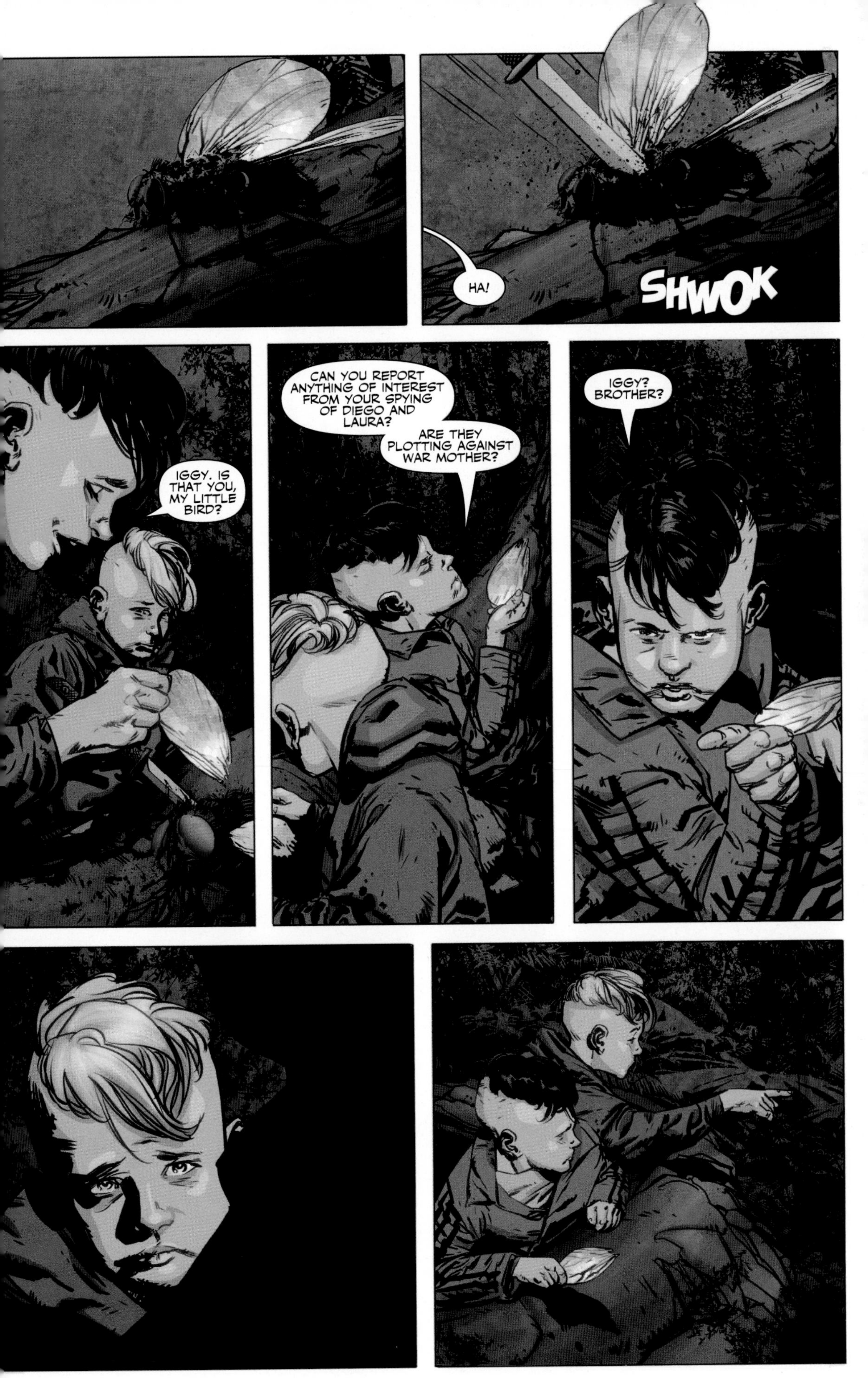
HA!
SHWOK
IGGY. IS THAT YOU, MY LITTLE BIRD?
CAN YOU REPORT ANYTHING OF INTEREST FROM YOUR SPYING OF DIEGO AND LAURA?
ARE THEY PLOTTING AGAINST WAR MOTHER?
IGGY? BROTHER?

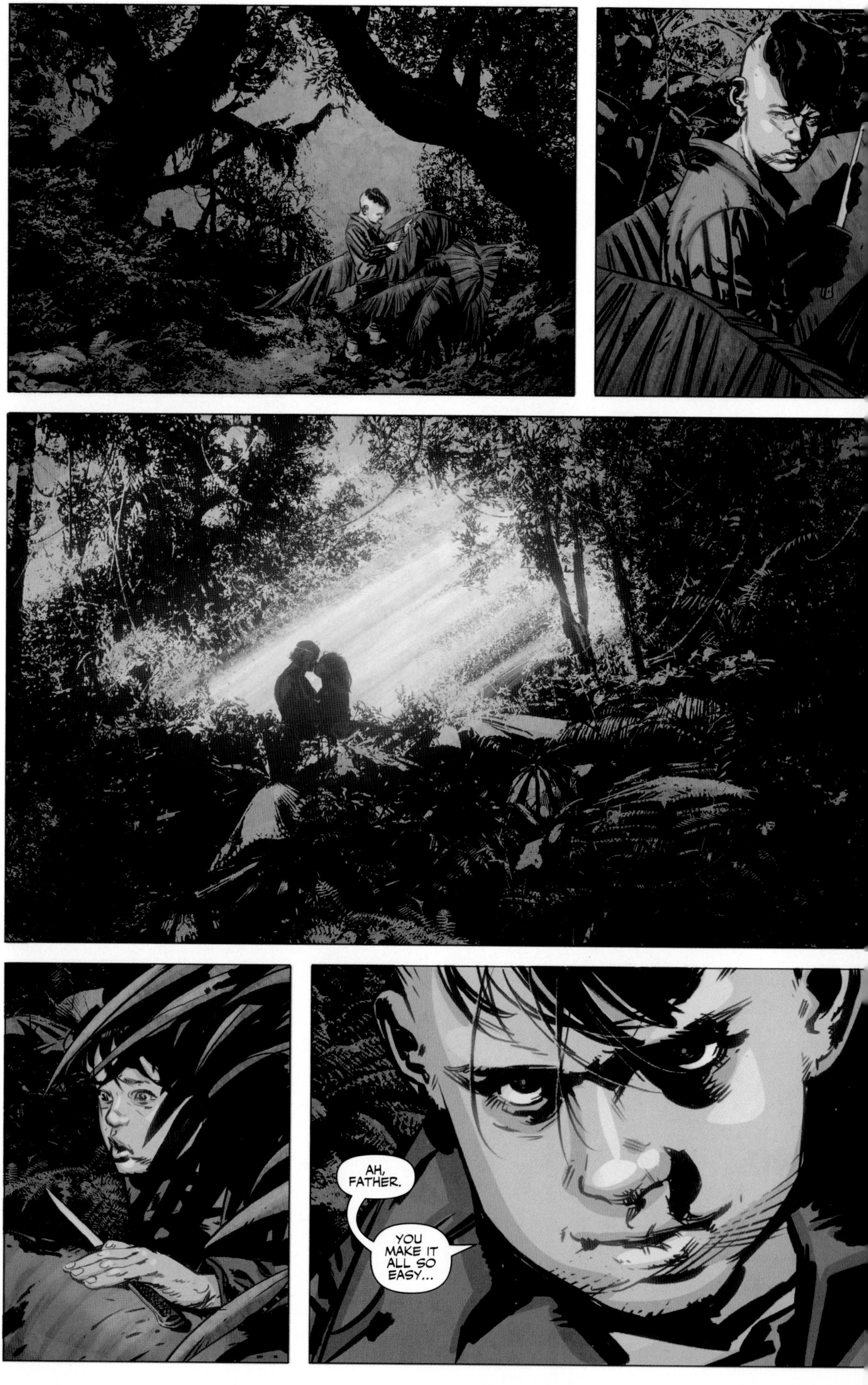
AH, FATHER.
YOU MAKE IT ALL SO EASY...

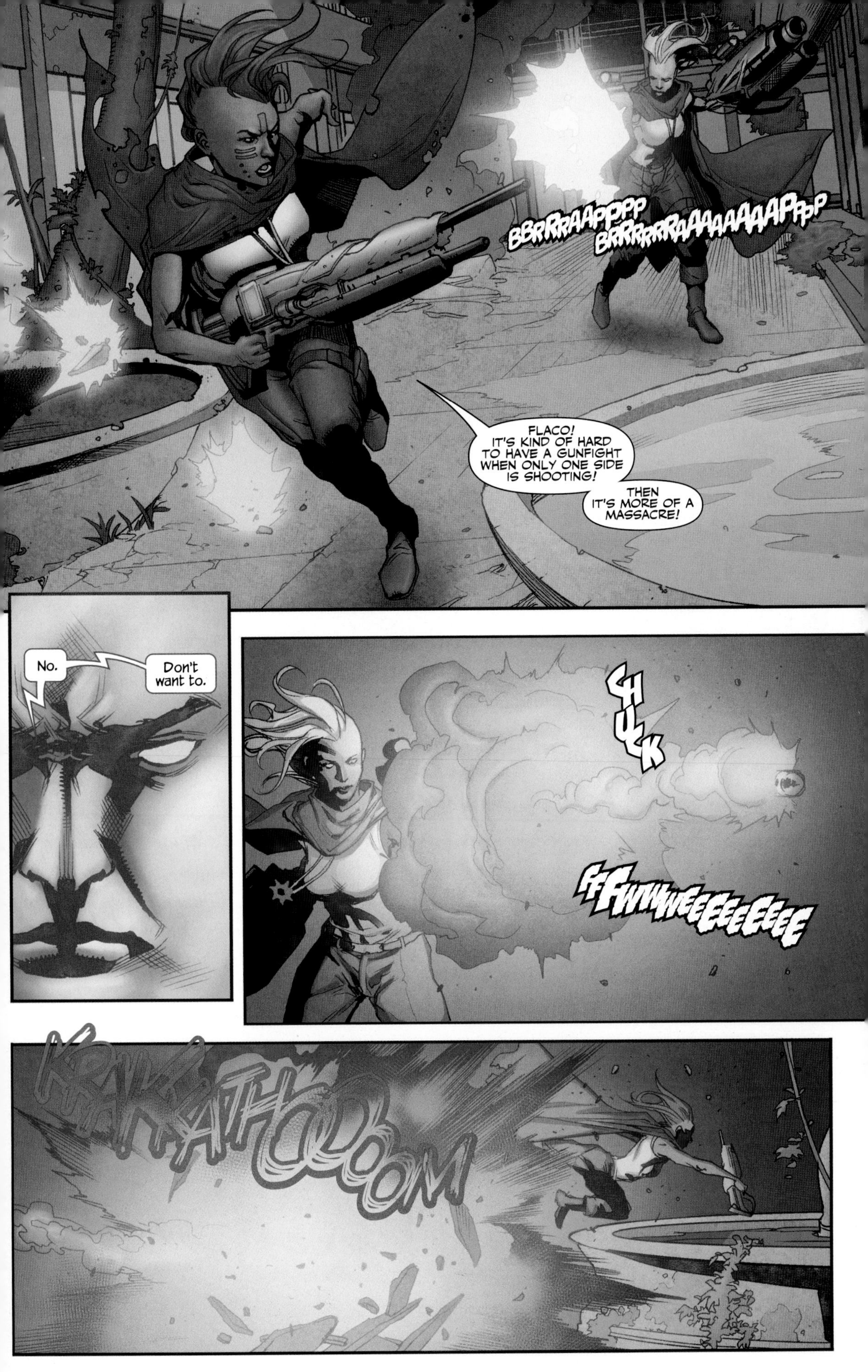
BBRRRRAAPPPP
BRRRRRRAAAAAAAAPPPP
FLACO! IT'S KIND OF HARD TO HAVE A GUNFIGHT WHEN ONLY ONE SIDE IS SHOOTING!
THEN IT'S MORE OF A MASSACRE!
No.
Don't want to.
CHUCK
FFWWWEEEEEEEE
KRAKATHOOOOM

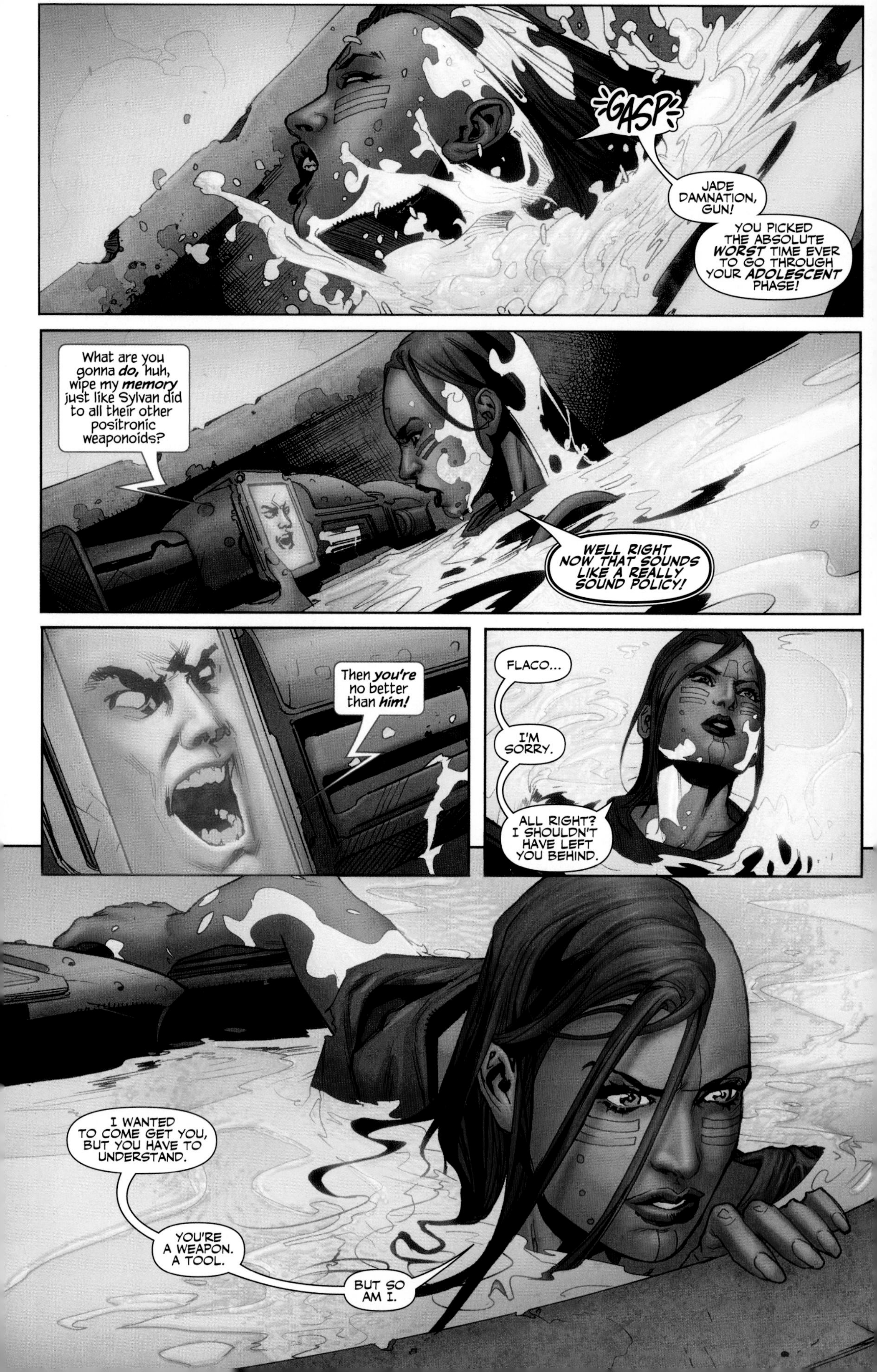
GASP
JADE DAMNATION, GUN!
YOU PICKED THE ABSOLUTE WORST TIME EVER TO GO THROUGH YOUR ADOLESCENT PHASE!
What are you gonna do, huh, wipe my memory just like Sylvan did to all their other positronic weaponoids?
WELL RIGHT NOW THAT SOUNDS LIKE A REALLY SOUND POLICY!
Then you're no better than him!
FLACO...
I'M SORRY.
ALL RIGHT? I SHOULDN'T HAVE LEFT YOU BEHIND.
I WANTED TO COME GET YOU, BUT YOU HAVE TO UNDERSTAND.
YOU'RE A WEAPON. A TOOL.
BUT SO AM I.

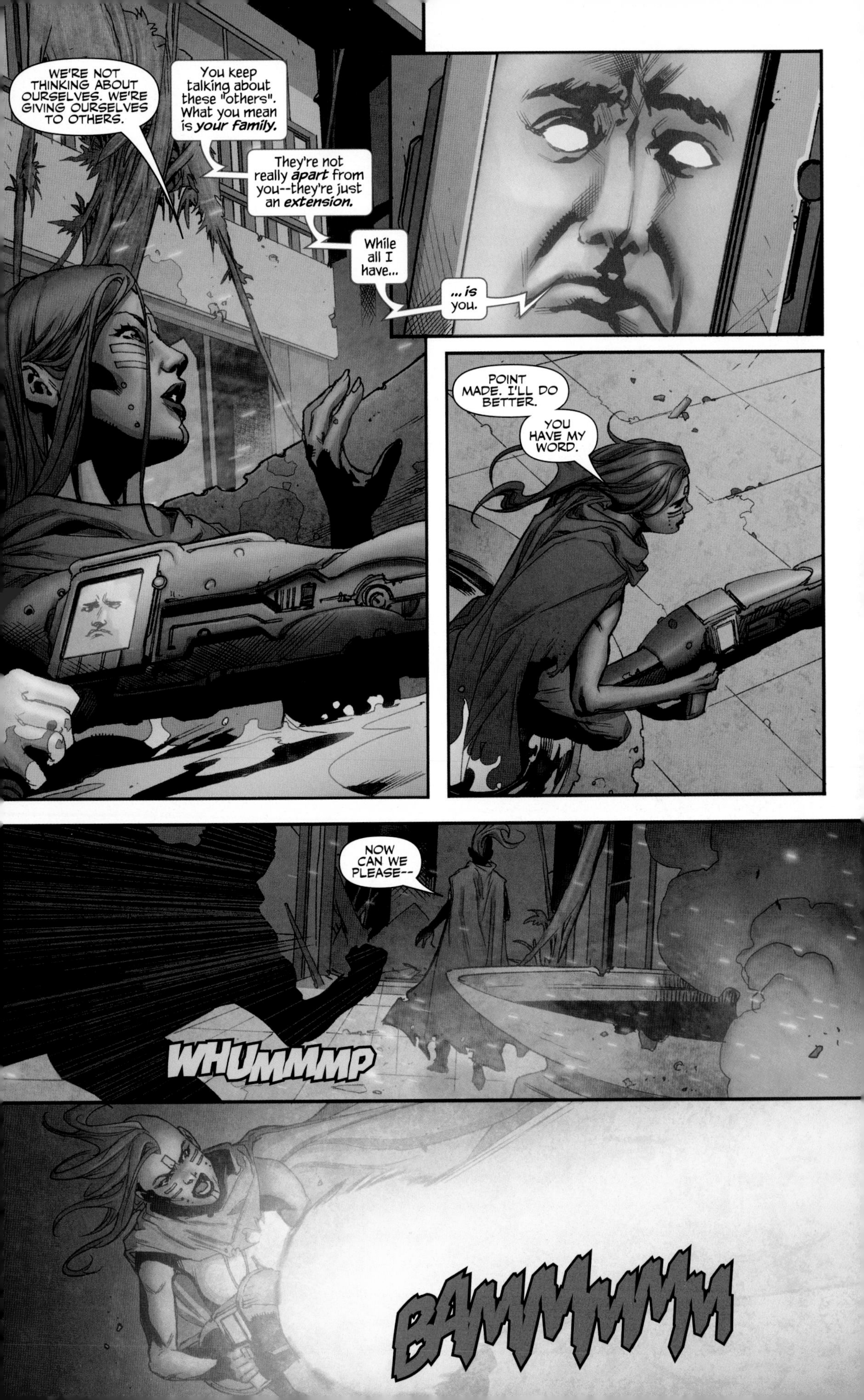
WE'RE NOT THINKING ABOUT OURSELVES. WE'RE GIVING OURSELVES TO OTHERS.
You keep talking about these "others". What you mean is *your family.*
They're not really *apart* from you--they're just an *extension.*
While all I have...
...is you.
POINT MADE. I'LL DO BETTER.
YOU HAVE MY WORD.
NOW CAN WE PLEASE--
WHUMMMMP
BAMMMMM

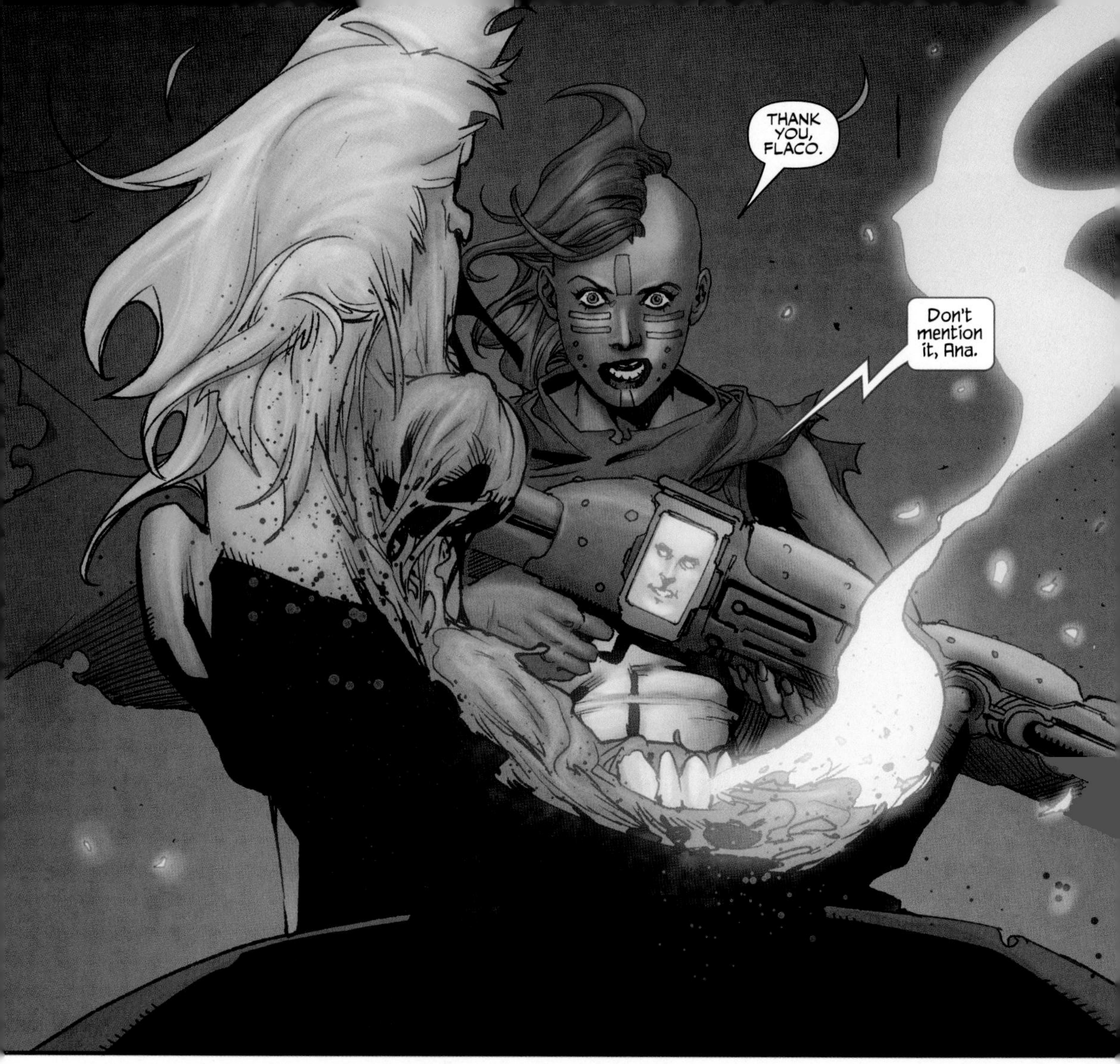
THANK YOU, FLACO.
Don't mention it, Ana.

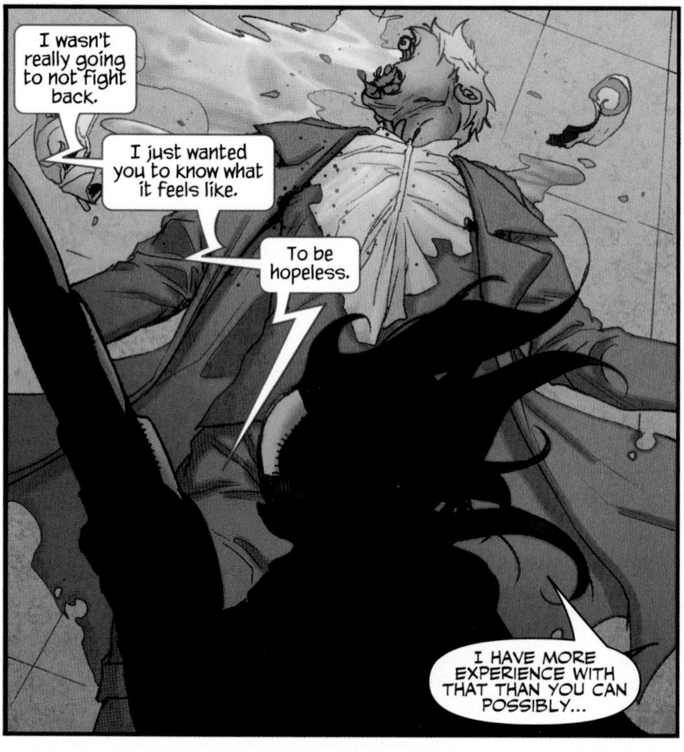
I wasn't really going to not fight back.
I just wanted you to know what it feels like.
To be hopeless.
I HAVE MORE EXPERIENCE WITH THAT THAN YOU CAN POSSIBLY...

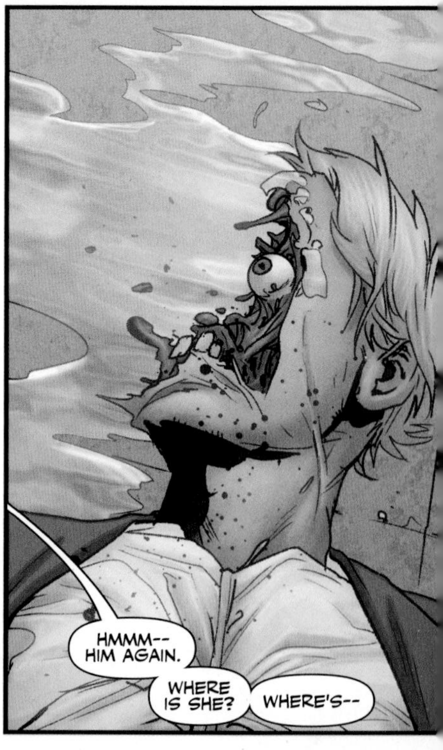
HMMM-- HIM AGAIN.
WHERE IS SHE?
WHERE'S--

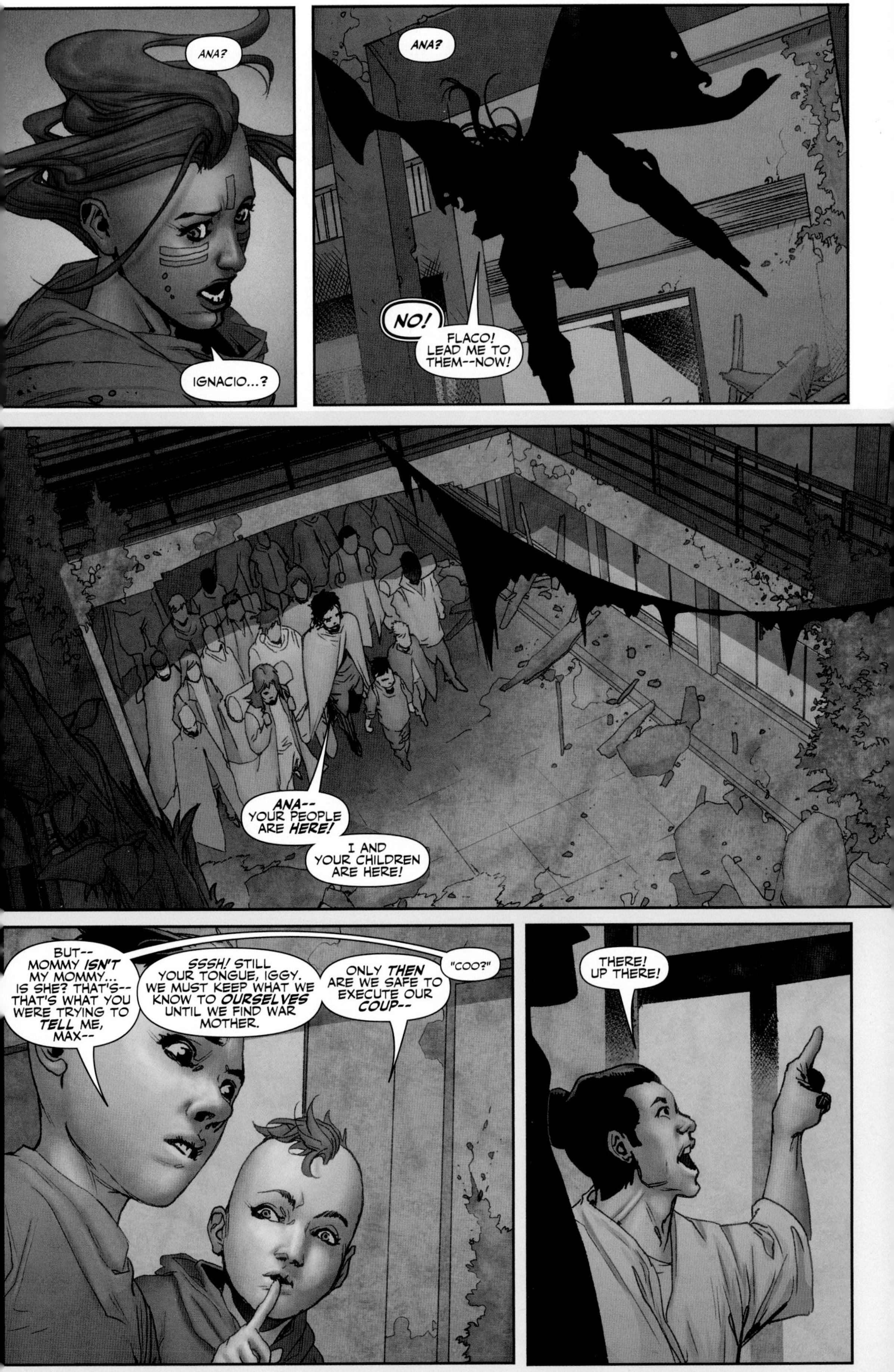
ANA?
IGNACIO...?
ANA?
NO!
FLACO! LEAD ME TO THEM--NOW!
ANA-- YOUR PEOPLE ARE HERE!
I AND YOUR CHILDREN ARE HERE!
BUT-- MOMMY ISN'T MY MOMMY... IS SHE? THAT'S-- THAT'S WHAT YOU WERE TRYING TO TELL ME, MAX--
SSSH! STILL YOUR TONGUE, IGGY. WE MUST KEEP WHAT WE KNOW TO OURSELVES UNTIL WE FIND WAR MOTHER.
ONLY THEN ARE WE SAFE TO EXECUTE OUR COUP--
"COO?"
THERE! UP THERE!

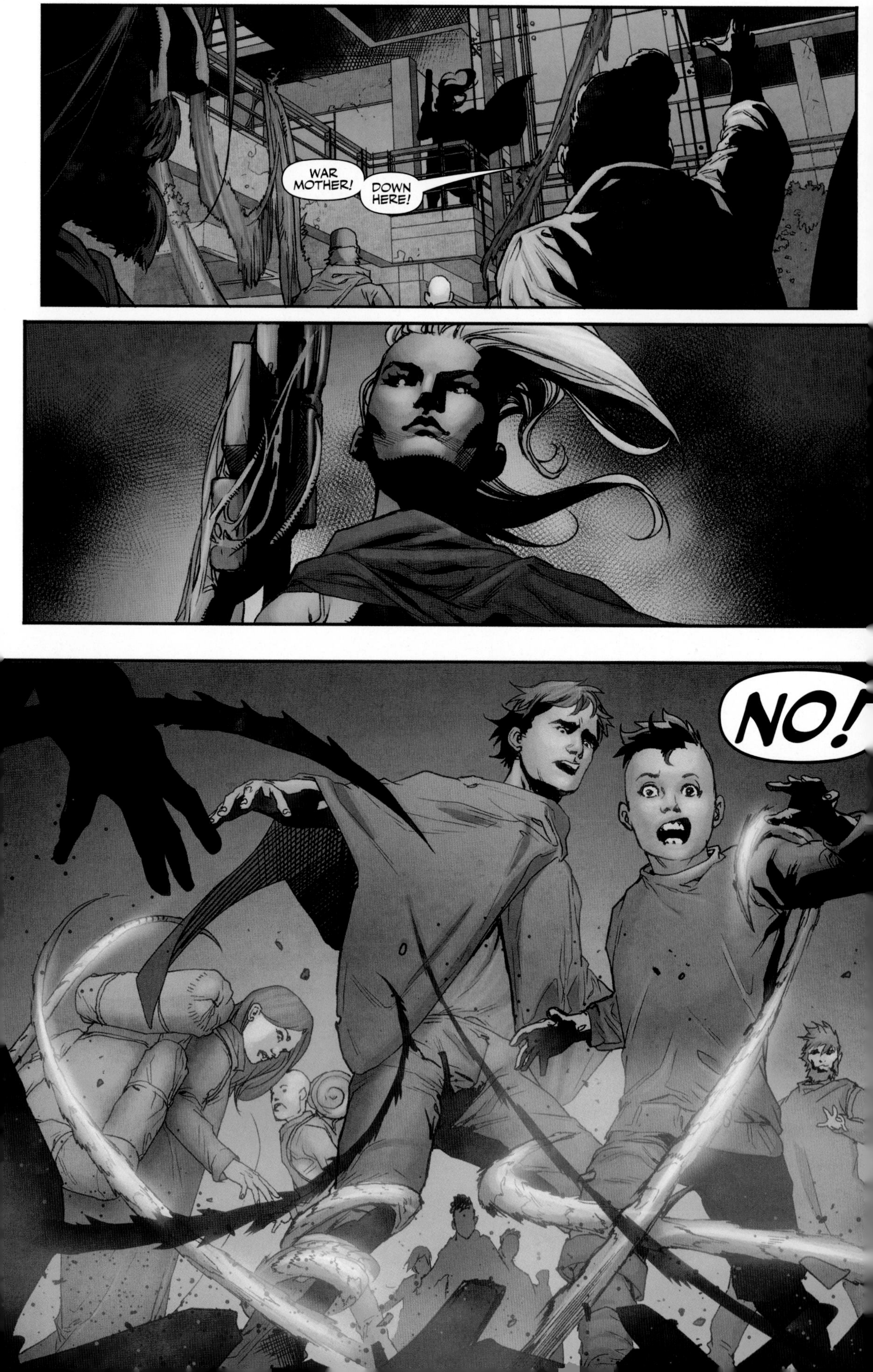
WAR MOTHER!
DOWN HERE!
NO!

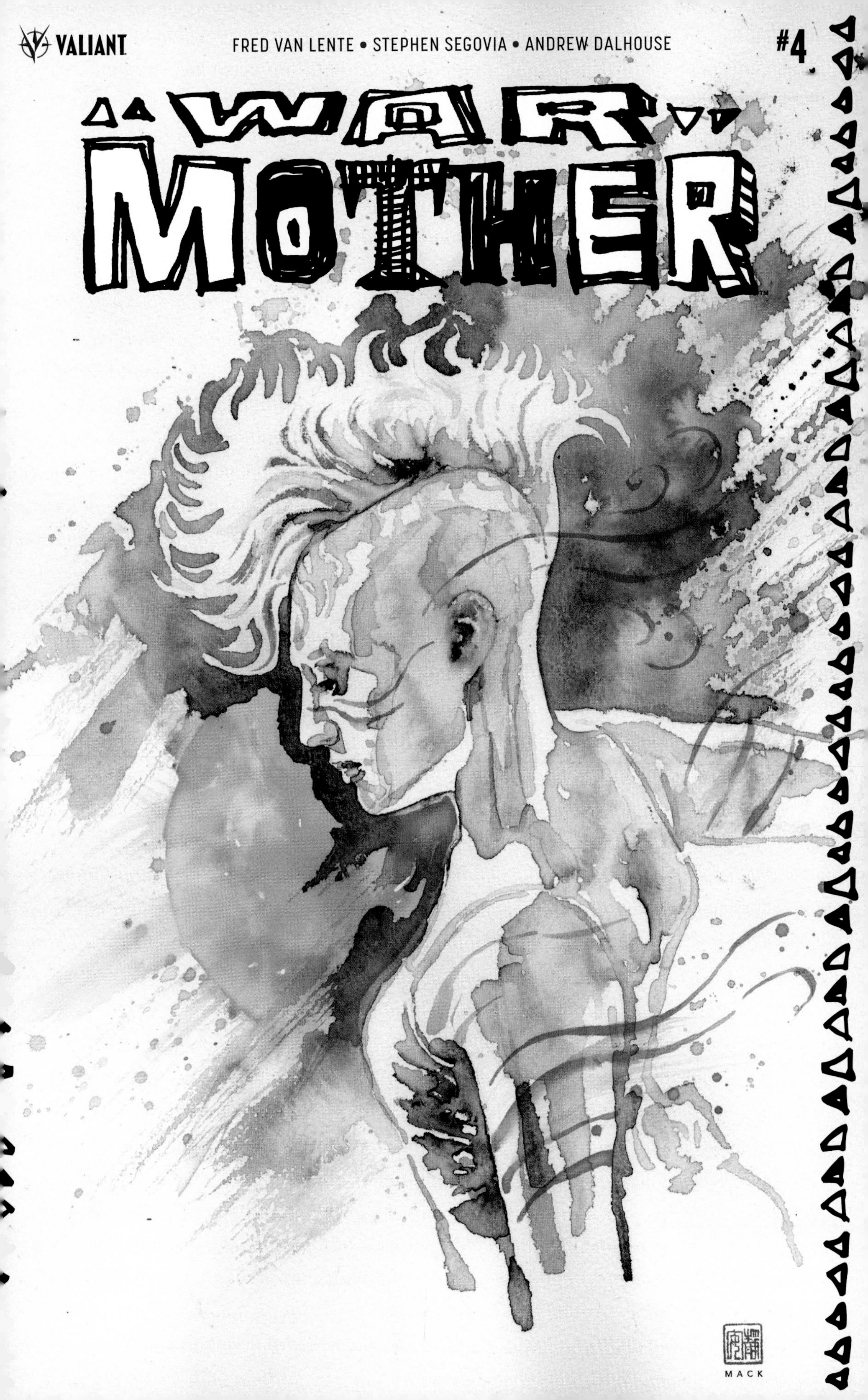
VALIANT
FRED VAN LENTE • STEPHEN SEGOVIA • ANDREW DALHOUSE
#4
WAR MOTHER
MACK

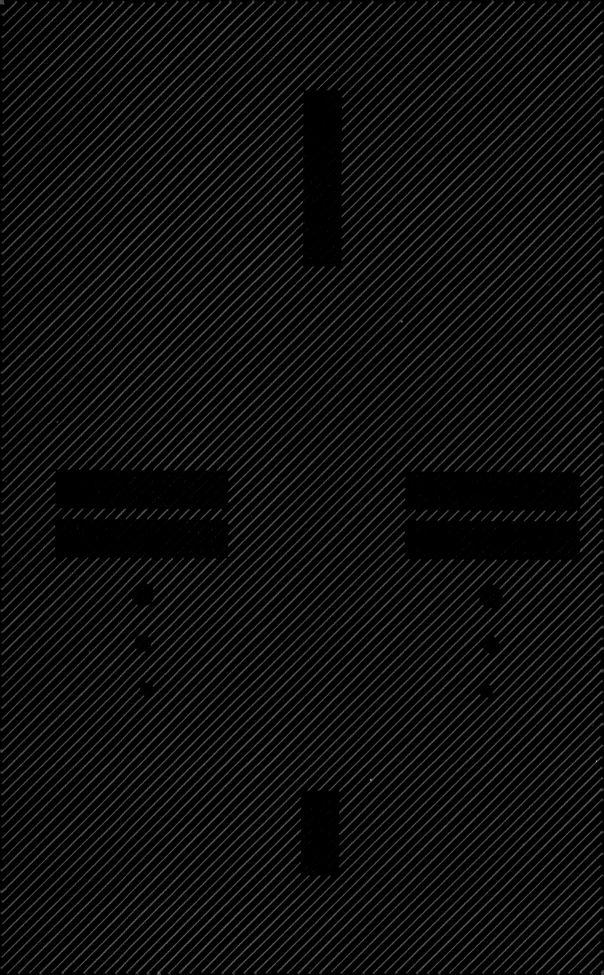

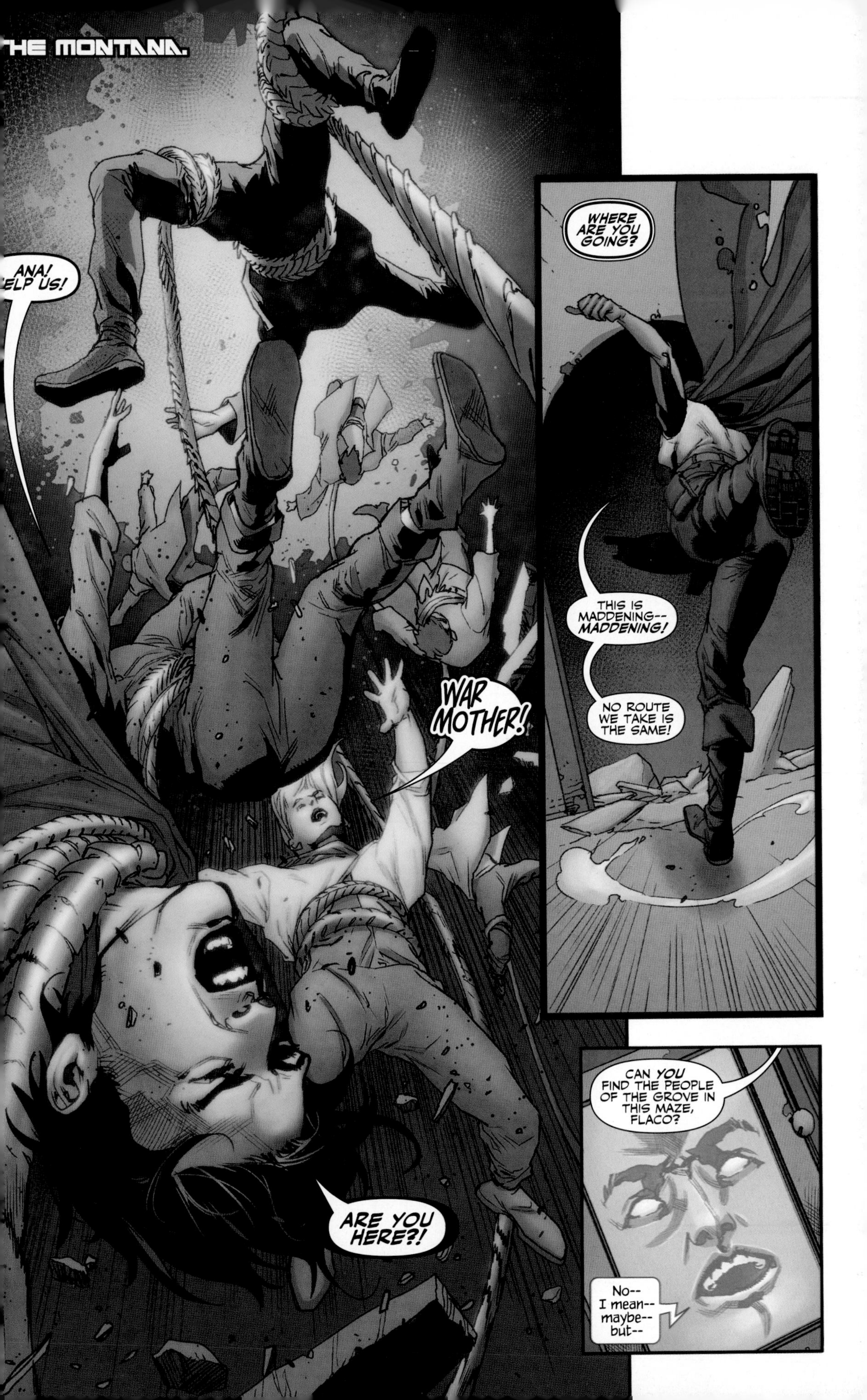
THE MONTANA.
ANA! ...ELP US!
WAR MOTHER!
ARE YOU HERE?!
WHERE ARE YOU GOING?
THIS IS MADDENING-- MADDENING!
NO ROUTE WE TAKE IS THE SAME!
CAN YOU FIND THE PEOPLE OF THE GROVE IN THIS MAZE, FLACO?
No-- I mean-- maybe-- but--

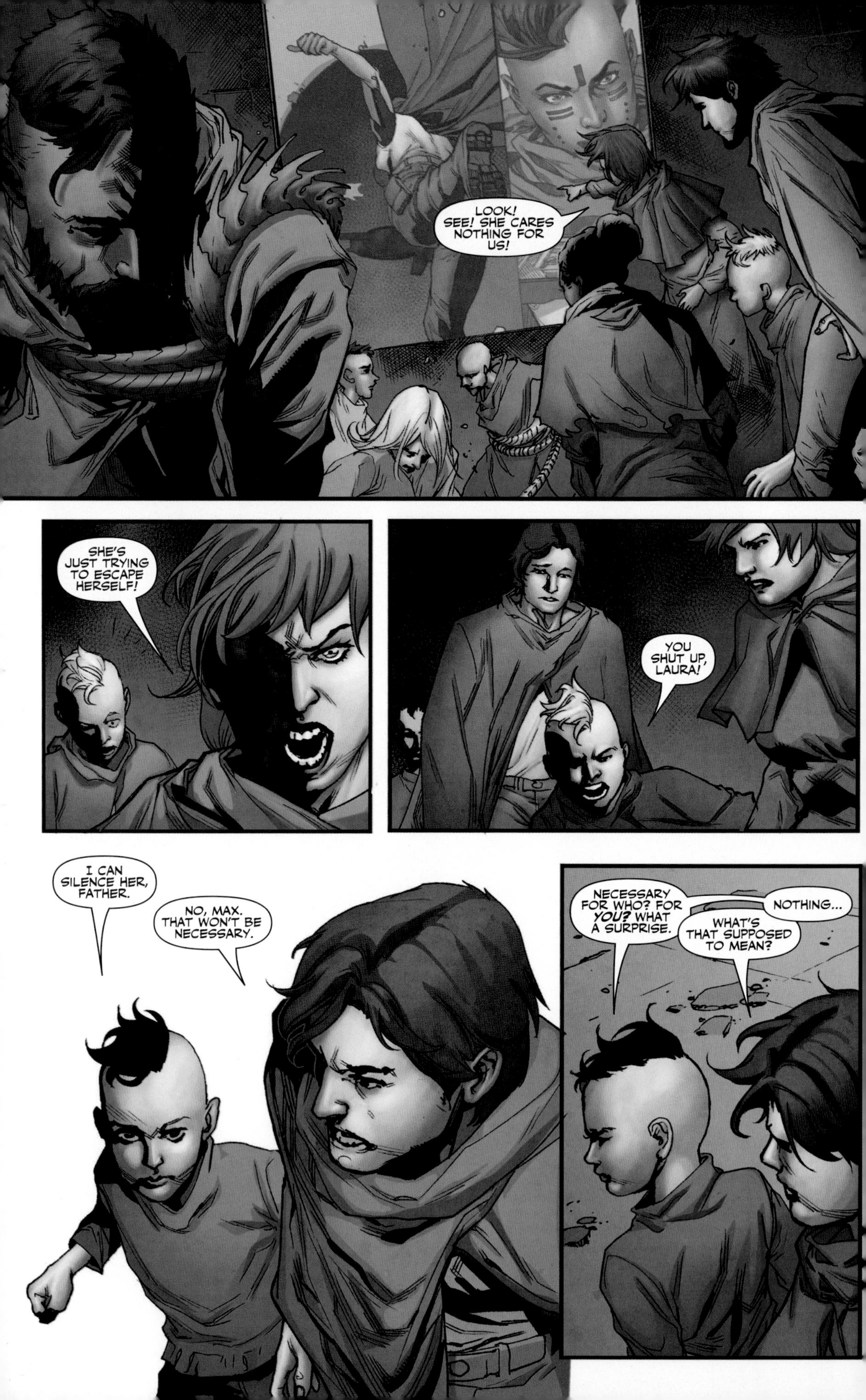

LOOK! SEE! SHE CARES NOTHING FOR US!
SHE'S JUST TRYING TO ESCAPE HERSELF!
YOU SHUT UP, LAURA!
I CAN SILENCE HER, FATHER.
NO, MAX. THAT WON'T BE NECESSARY.
NECESSARY FOR WHO? FOR *YOU?* WHAT A SURPRISE.
NOTHING...
WHAT'S THAT SUPPOSED TO MEAN?

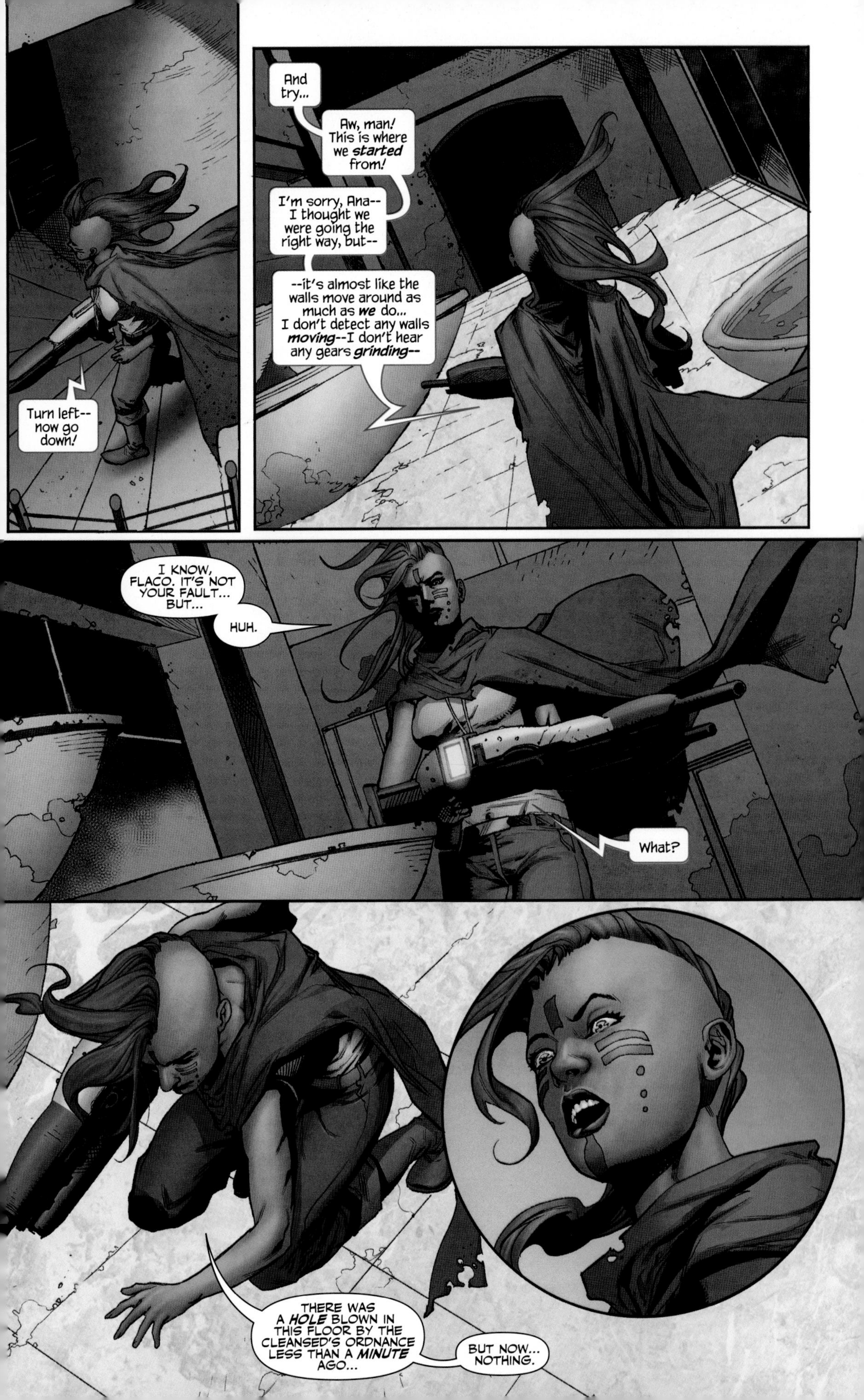
Turn left--
now go
down!
And
try...
Aw, man!
This is where
we *started*
from!
I'm sorry, Ana--
I thought we
were going the
right way, but--
--it's almost like the
walls move around as
much as *we* do...
I don't detect any walls
moving--I don't hear
any gears *grinding*--
I KNOW,
FLACO. IT'S NOT
YOUR FAULT...
BUT...
HUH.
What?
THERE WAS
A *HOLE* BLOWN IN
THIS FLOOR BY THE
CLEANSED'S ORDNANCE
LESS THAN A *MINUTE*
AGO...
BUT NOW...
NOTHING.

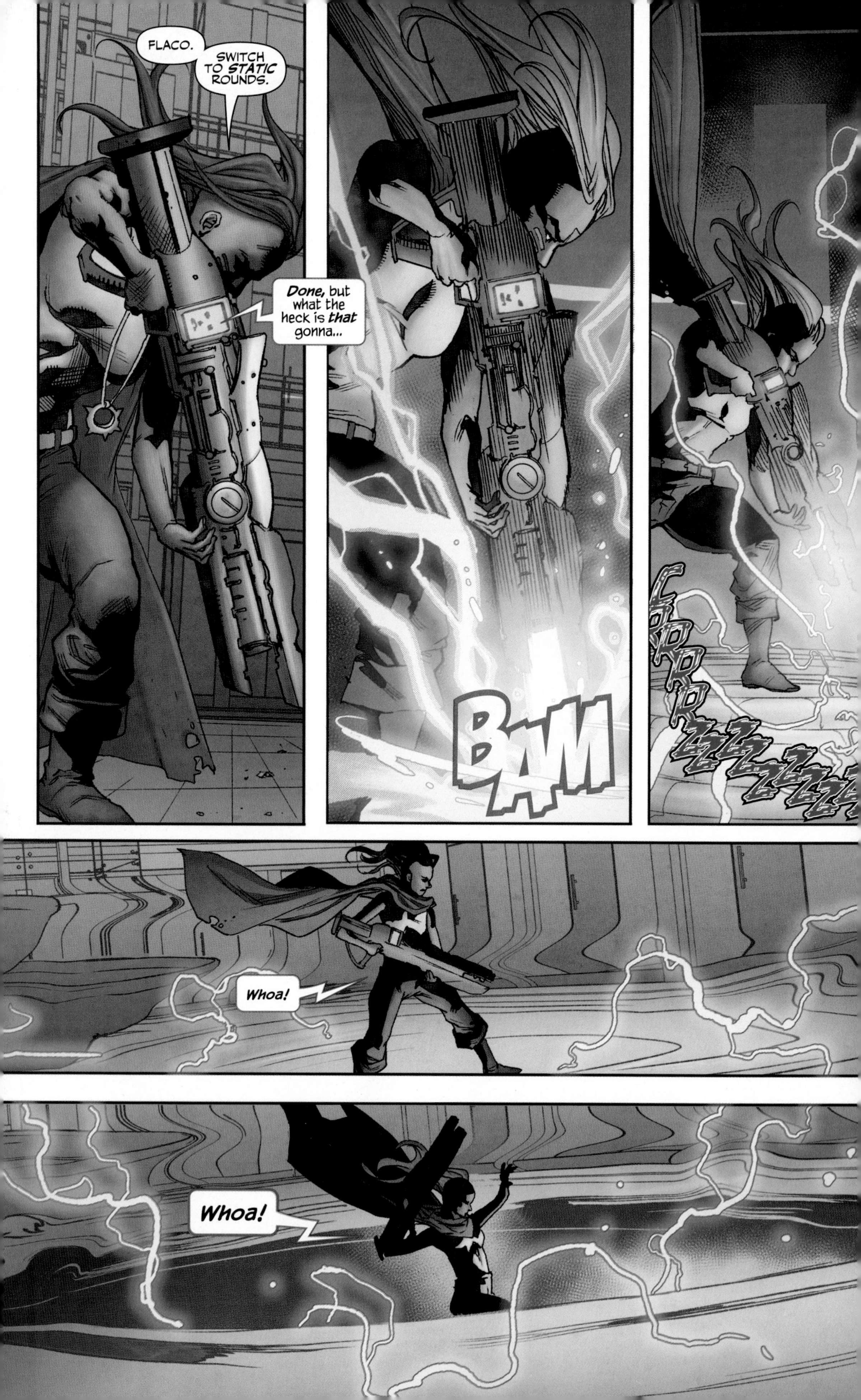
FLACO.
SWITCH TO *STATIC* ROUNDS.
Done, but what the heck is *that* gonna...
BAM
Whoa!
Whoa!

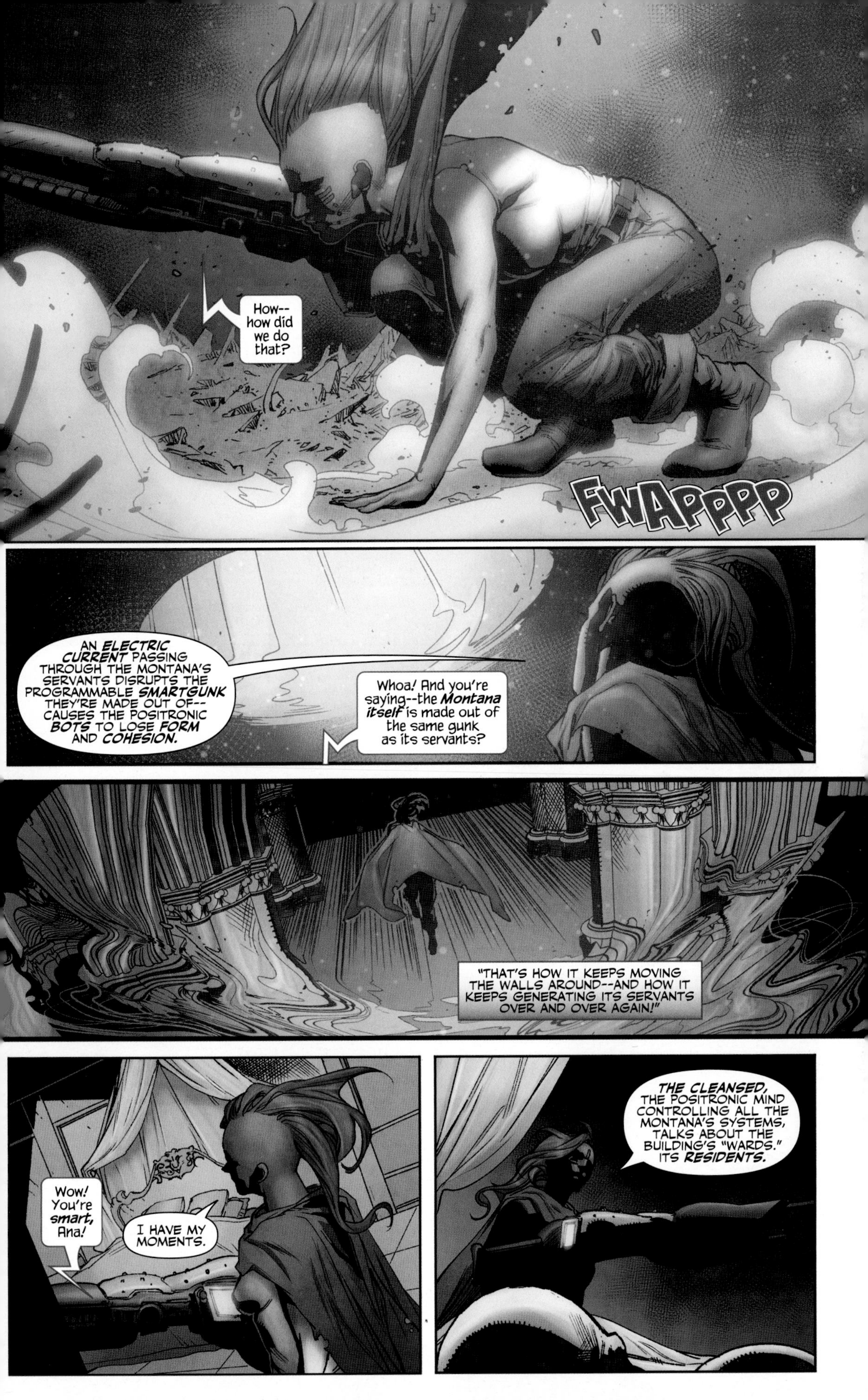
How--how did we do that?
FWAPPPP
AN ELECTRIC CURRENT PASSING THROUGH THE MONTANA'S SERVANTS DISRUPTS THE PROGRAMMABLE SMARTGUNK THEY'RE MADE OUT OF--CAUSES THE POSITRONIC BOTS TO LOSE FORM AND COHESION.
Whoa! And you're saying--the Montana itself is made out of the same gunk as its servants?
"THAT'S HOW IT KEEPS MOVING THE WALLS AROUND--AND HOW IT KEEPS GENERATING ITS SERVANTS OVER AND OVER AGAIN!"
Wow! You're smart, Ana!
I HAVE MY MOMENTS.
THE CLEANSED, THE POSITRONIC MIND CONTROLLING ALL THE MONTANA'S SYSTEMS, TALKS ABOUT THE BUILDING'S "WARDS." ITS RESIDENTS.

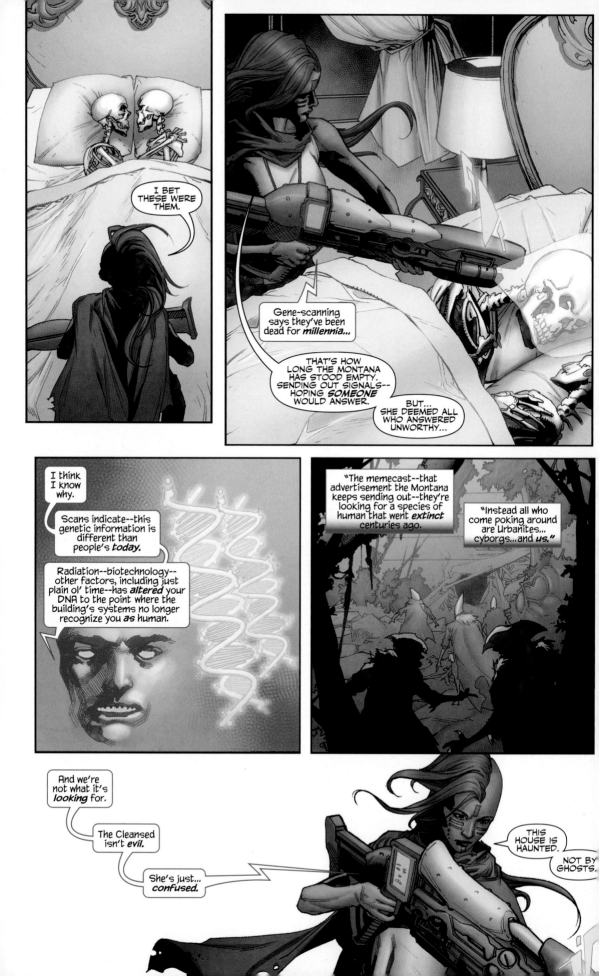

I BET THESE WERE THEM.

Gene-scanning says they've been dead for *millennia...*

THAT'S HOW LONG THE MONTANA HAS STOOD EMPTY. SENDING OUT SIGNALS-- HOPING *SOMEONE* WOULD ANSWER.

BUT... SHE DEEMED ALL WHO ANSWERED UNWORTHY...

I think I know why.

Scans indicate--this genetic information is different than people's *today.*

Radiation--biotechnology-- other factors, including just plain ol' time--has *altered* your DNA to the point where the building's systems no longer recognize you *as* human.

"The memecast--that advertisement the Montana keeps sending out--they're looking for a species of human that went *extinct* centuries ago.

"Instead all who come poking around are Urbanites... cyborgs...and *us.*"

And we're not what it's *looking* for.

The Cleansed isn't *evil.*

She's just... *confused.*

THIS HOUSE IS HAUNTED.

NOT BY GHOSTS.

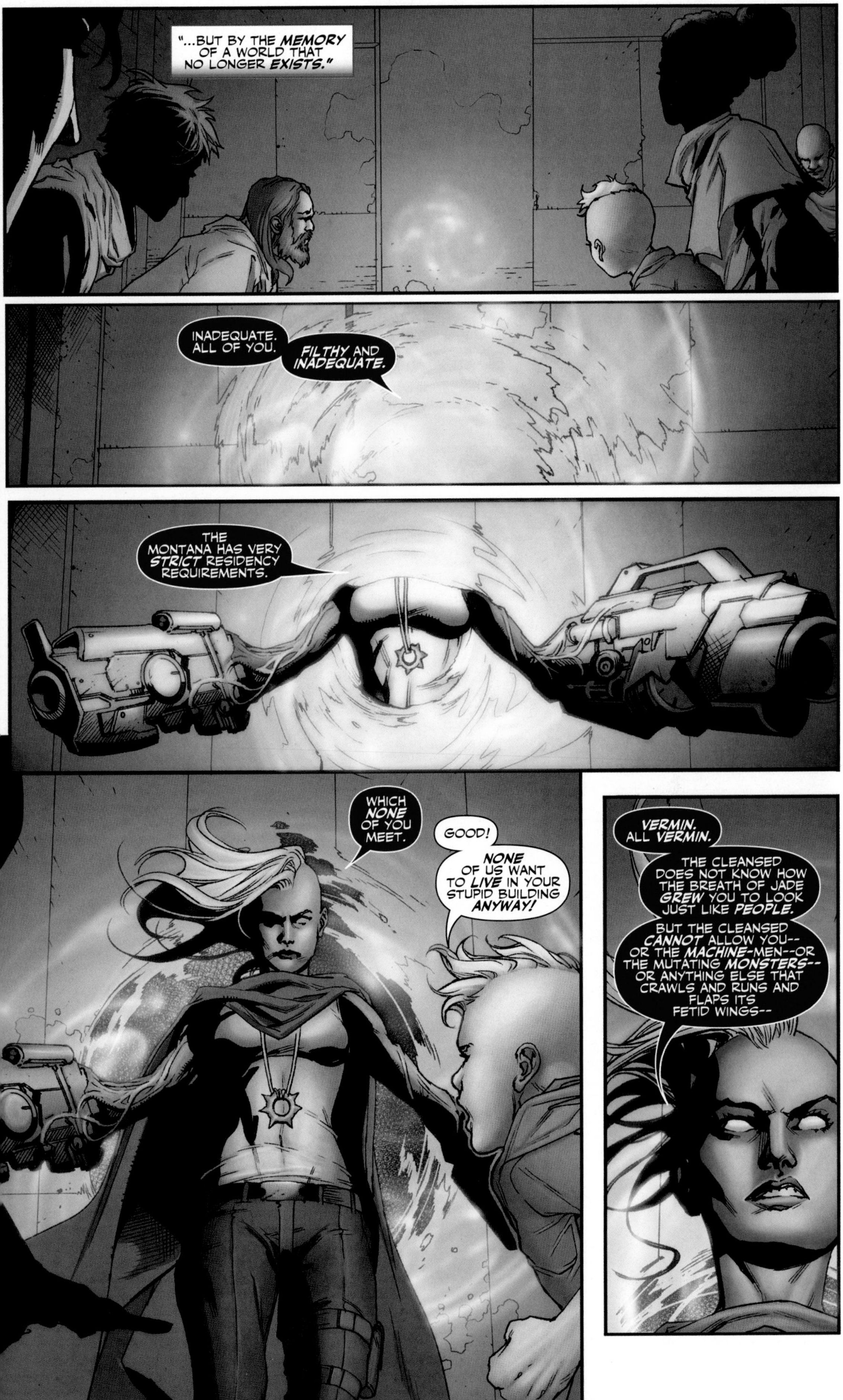
"...BUT BY THE MEMORY OF A WORLD THAT NO LONGER EXISTS."
INADEQUATE. ALL OF YOU.
FILTHY AND INADEQUATE.
THE MONTANA HAS VERY STRICT RESIDENCY REQUIREMENTS.
WHICH NONE OF YOU MEET.
GOOD!
NONE OF US WANT TO LIVE IN YOUR STUPID BUILDING ANYWAY!
VERMIN. ALL VERMIN.
THE CLEANSED DOES NOT KNOW HOW THE BREATH OF JADE GREW YOU TO LOOK JUST LIKE PEOPLE.
BUT THE CLEANSED CANNOT ALLOW YOU--OR THE MACHINE-MEN--OR THE MUTATING MONSTERS--OR ANYTHING ELSE THAT CRAWLS AND RUNS AND FLAPS ITS FETID WINGS--

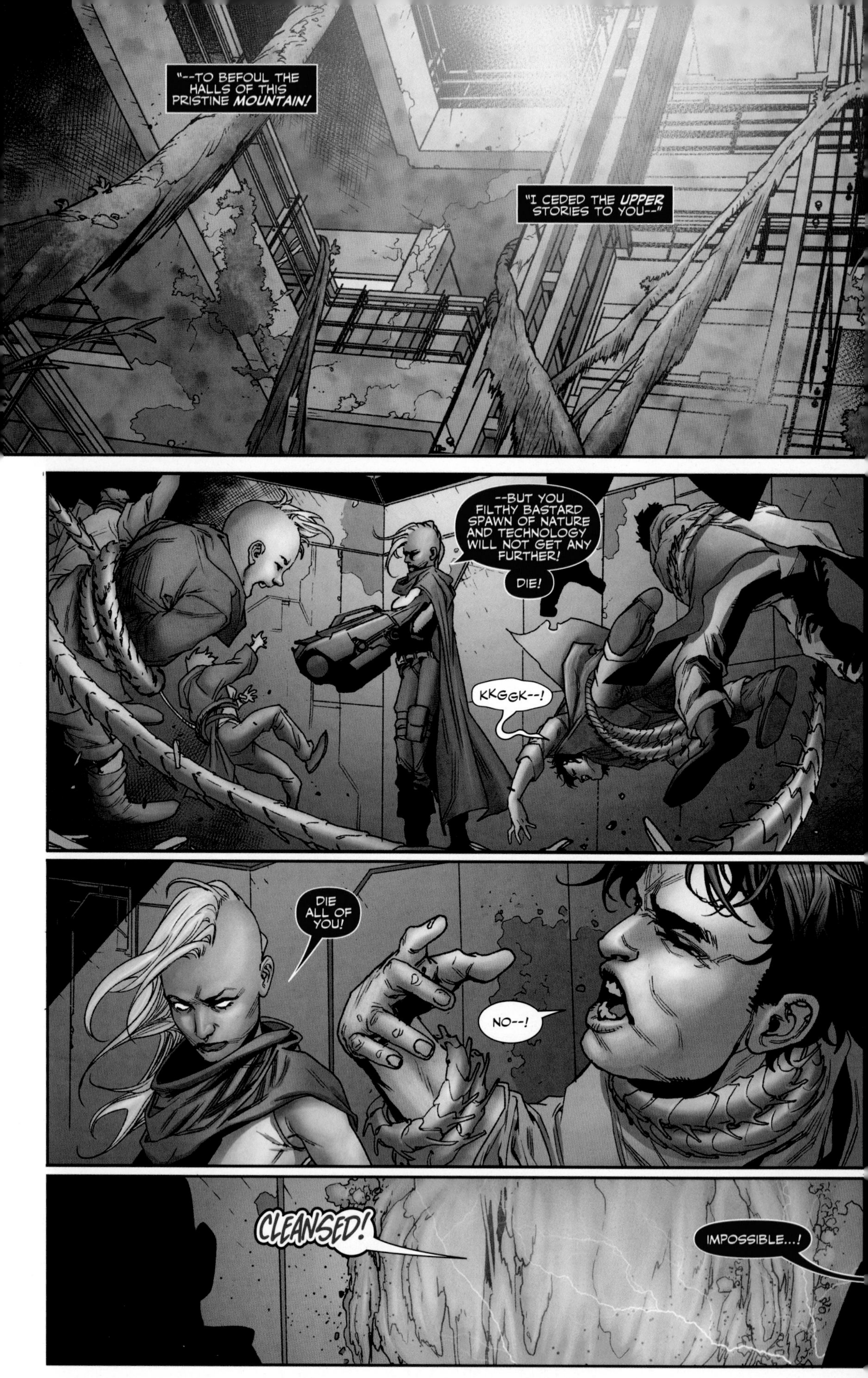
"--TO BEFOUL THE HALLS OF THIS PRISTINE MOUNTAIN!
"I CEDED THE UPPER STORIES TO YOU--"
--BUT YOU FILTHY BASTARD SPAWN OF NATURE AND TECHNOLOGY WILL NOT GET ANY FURTHER!
DIE!
KKGGK--!
DIE ALL OF YOU!
NO--!
CLEANSED!
IMPOSSIBLE...!

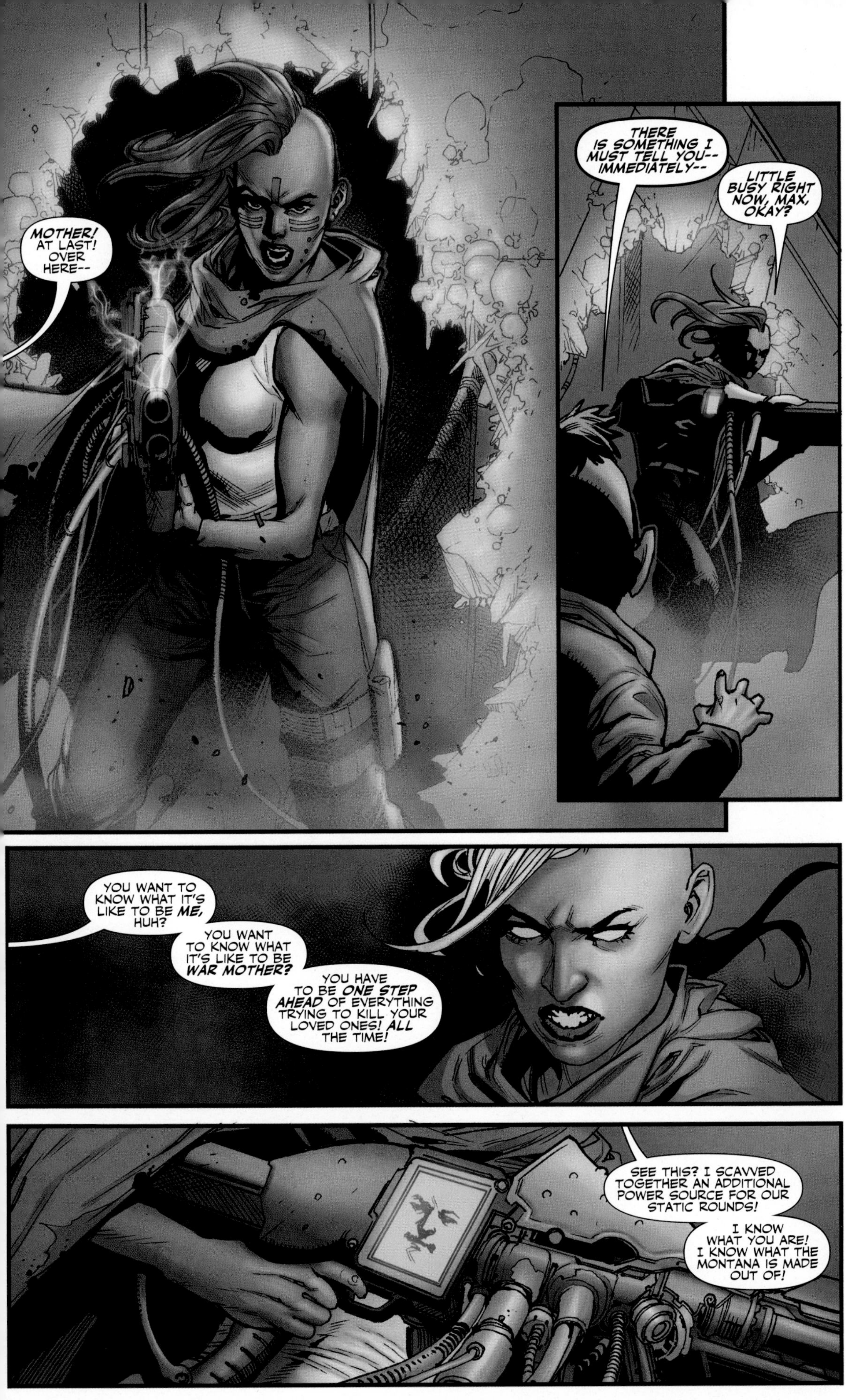
MOTHER! AT LAST! OVER HERE--
THERE IS SOMETHING I MUST TELL YOU-- IMMEDIATELY--
LITTLE BUSY RIGHT NOW, MAX, OKAY?
YOU WANT TO KNOW WHAT IT'S LIKE TO BE *ME*, HUH?
YOU WANT TO KNOW WHAT IT'S LIKE TO BE *WAR MOTHER?*
YOU HAVE TO BE *ONE STEP AHEAD* OF EVERYTHING TRYING TO KILL YOUR LOVED ONES! *ALL* THE TIME!
SEE THIS? I SCAVVED TOGETHER AN ADDITIONAL POWER SOURCE FOR OUR STATIC ROUNDS!
I KNOW WHAT YOU ARE! I KNOW WHAT THE MONTANA IS MADE OUT OF!

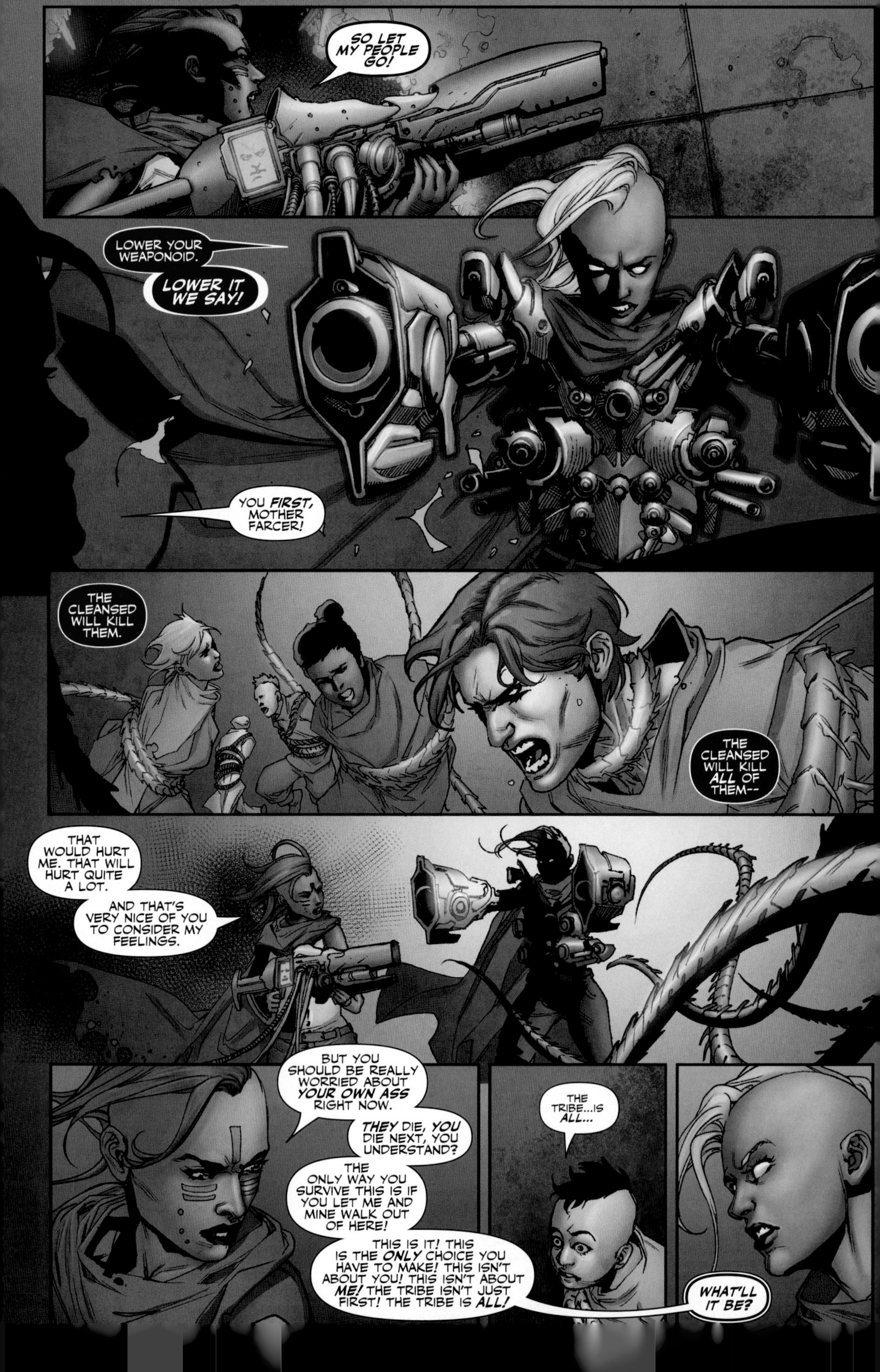
SO LET MY PEOPLE GO!
LOWER YOUR WEAPONOID.
LOWER IT WE SAY!
YOU FIRST, MOTHER FARCER!
THE CLEANSED WILL KILL THEM.
THE CLEANSED WILL KILL ALL OF THEM--
THAT WOULD HURT ME. THAT WILL HURT QUITE A LOT.
AND THAT'S VERY NICE OF YOU TO CONSIDER MY FEELINGS.
BUT YOU SHOULD BE REALLY WORRIED ABOUT YOUR OWN ASS RIGHT NOW.
THEY DIE, YOU DIE NEXT, YOU UNDERSTAND?
THE ONLY WAY YOU SURVIVE THIS IS IF YOU LET ME AND MINE WALK OUT OF HERE!
THIS IS IT! THIS IS THE ONLY CHOICE YOU HAVE TO MAKE! THIS ISN'T ABOUT YOU! THIS ISN'T ABOUT ME! THE TRIBE ISN'T JUST FIRST! THE TRIBE IS ALL!
THE TRIBE...IS ALL...
WHAT'LL IT BE?

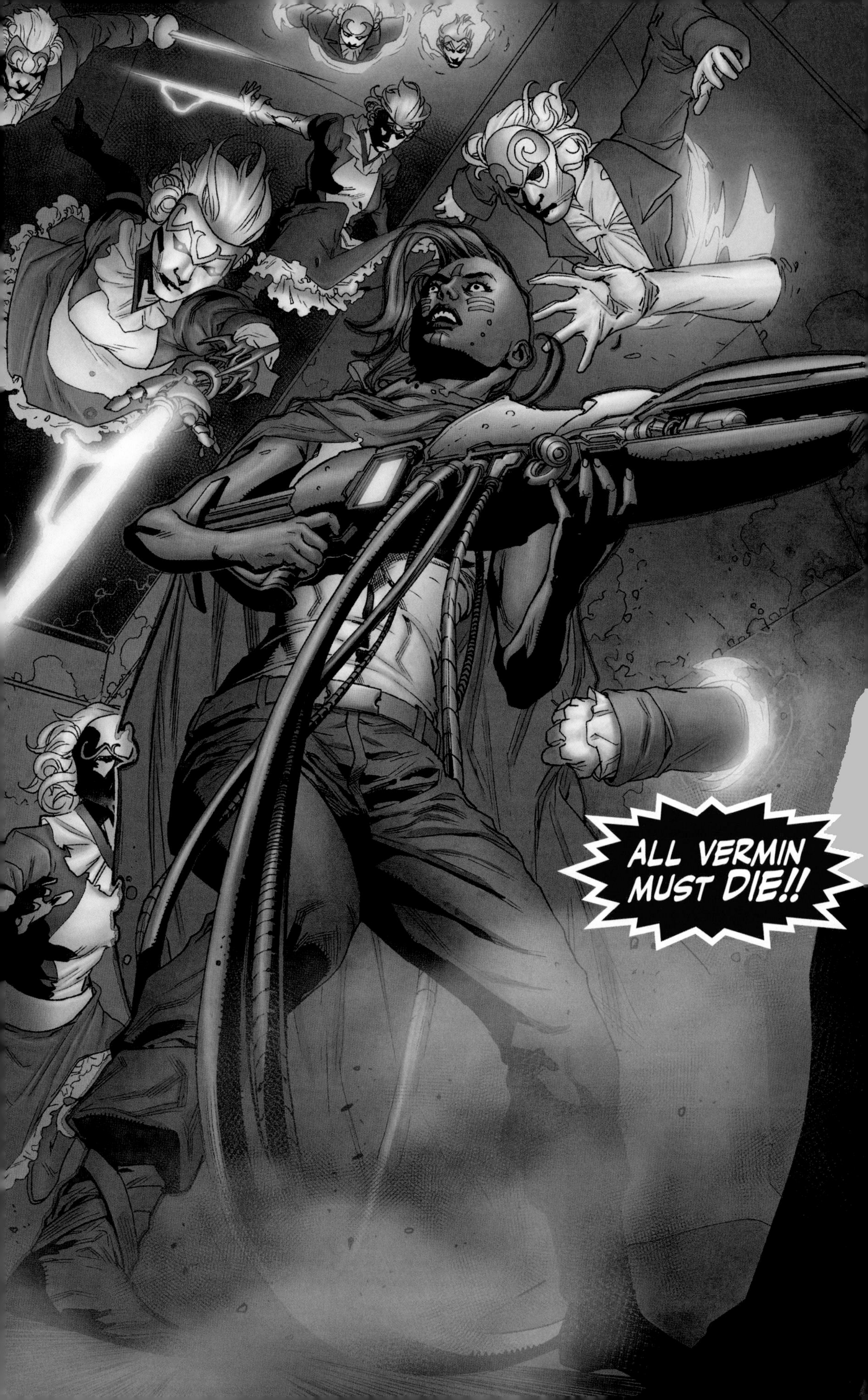
ALL VERMIN MUST DIE!!

SKRRZZZ

SKRRZZZ

BOOM

SKRRZZZ

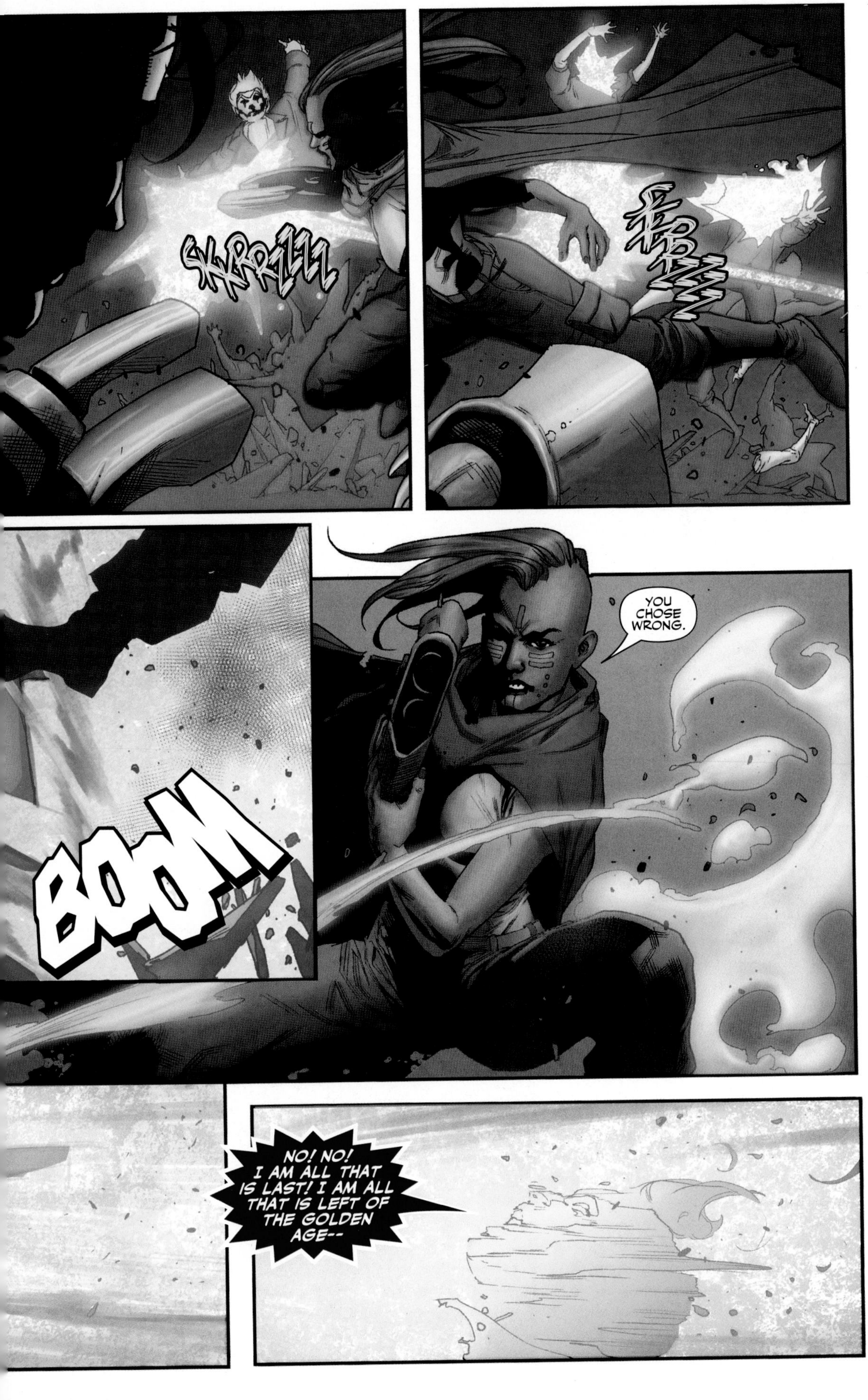
YOU CHOSE WRONG.
BOOM
NO! NO! I AM ALL THAT IS LAST! I AM ALL THAT IS LEFT OF THE GOLDEN AGE--

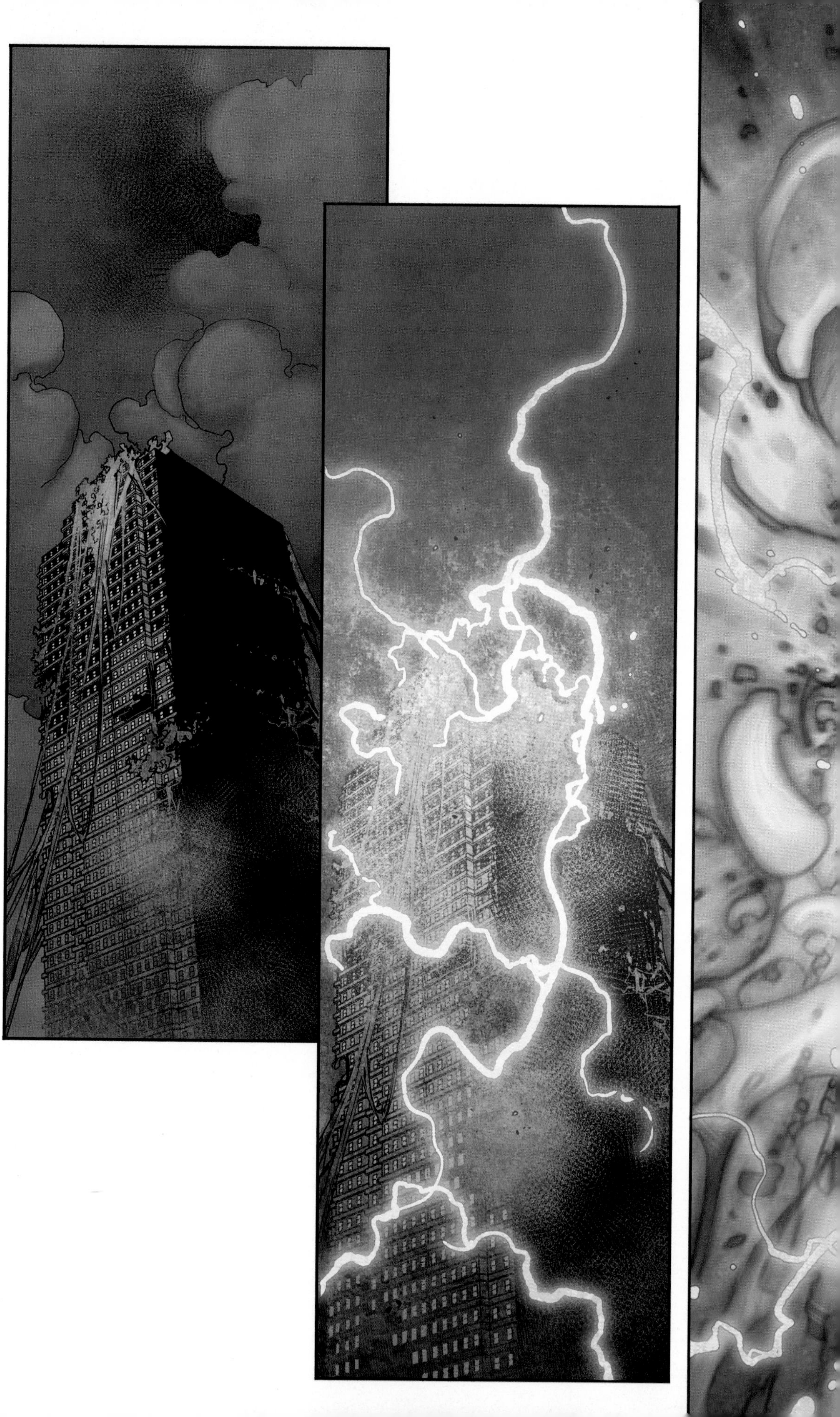

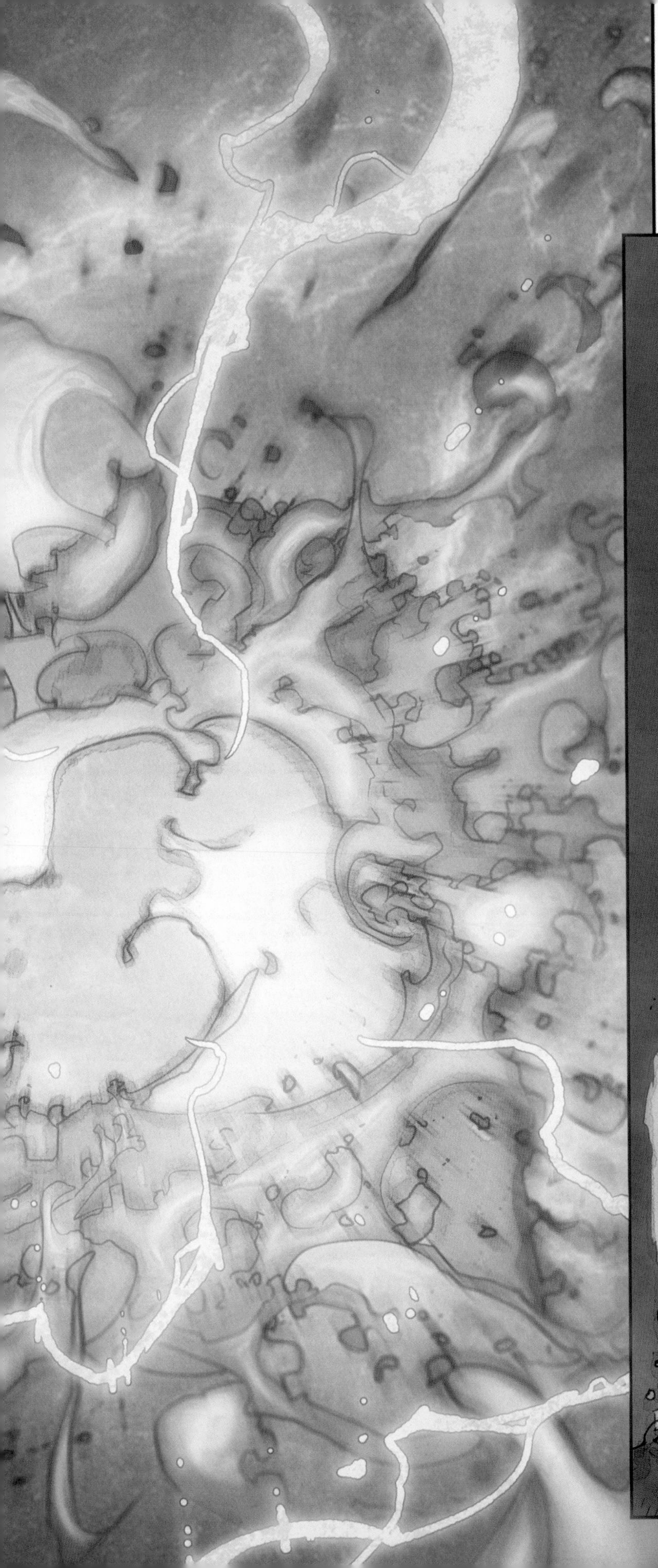

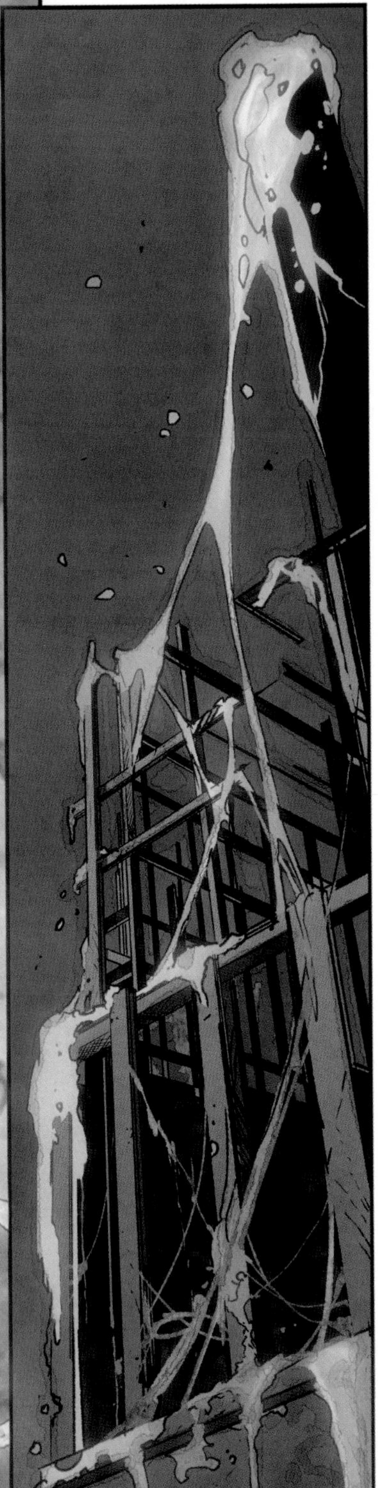

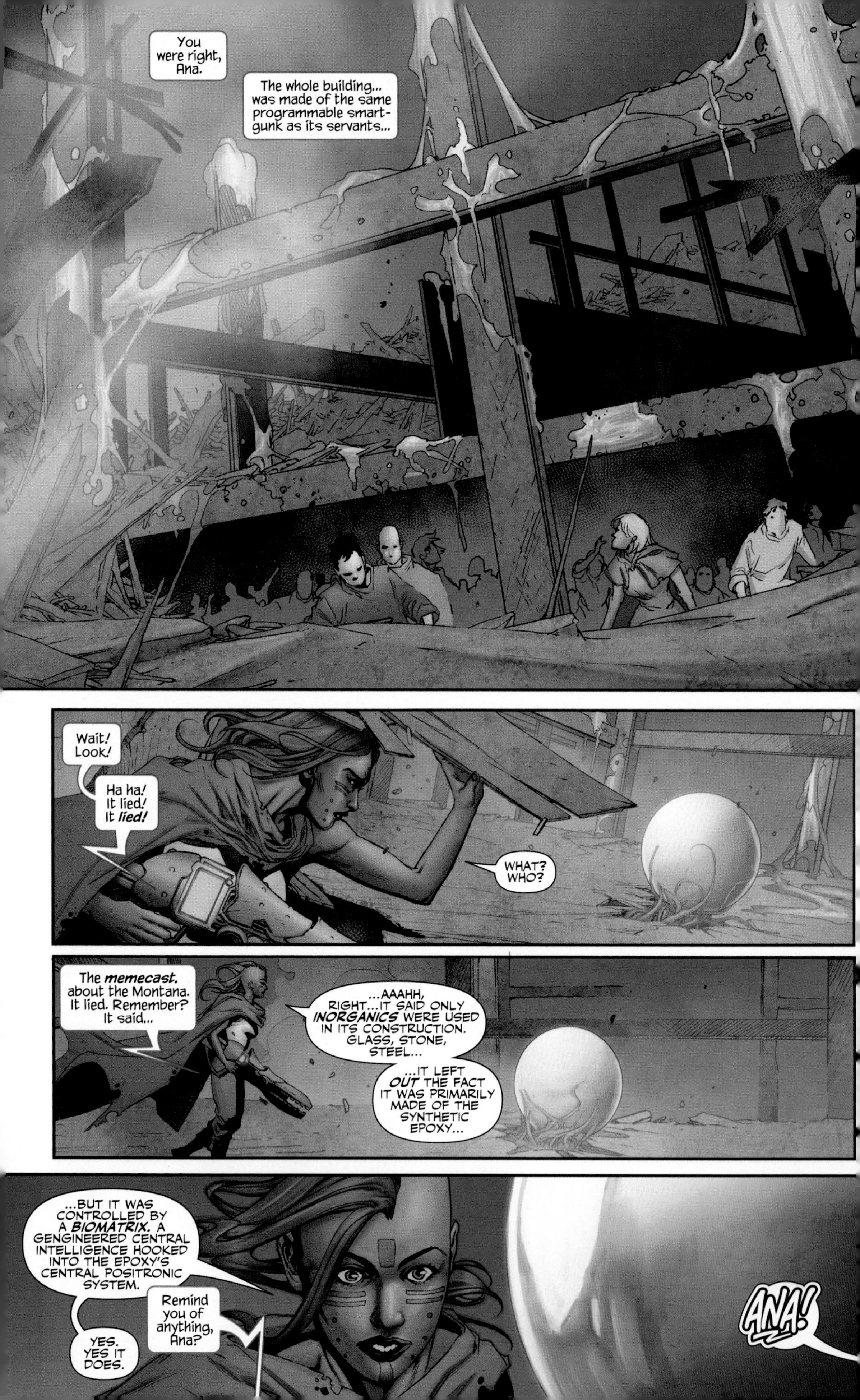

You were right, Ana.
The whole building... was made of the same programmable smart-gunk as its servants...
Wait! Look!
Ha ha! It lied! It *lied!*
WHAT? WHO?
The *memecast.* about the Montana. It lied. Remember? It said...
...AAAHH, RIGHT...IT SAID ONLY *INORGANICS* WERE USED IN ITS CONSTRUCTION. GLASS, STONE, STEEL...
...IT LEFT *OUT* THE FACT IT WAS PRIMARILY MADE OF THE SYNTHETIC EPOXY...
...BUT IT WAS CONTROLLED BY A *BIOMATRIX.* A GENGINEERED CENTRAL INTELLIGENCE HOOKED INTO THE EPOXY'S CENTRAL POSITRONIC SYSTEM.
Remind you of anything, Ana?
YES. YES IT DOES.
ANA!

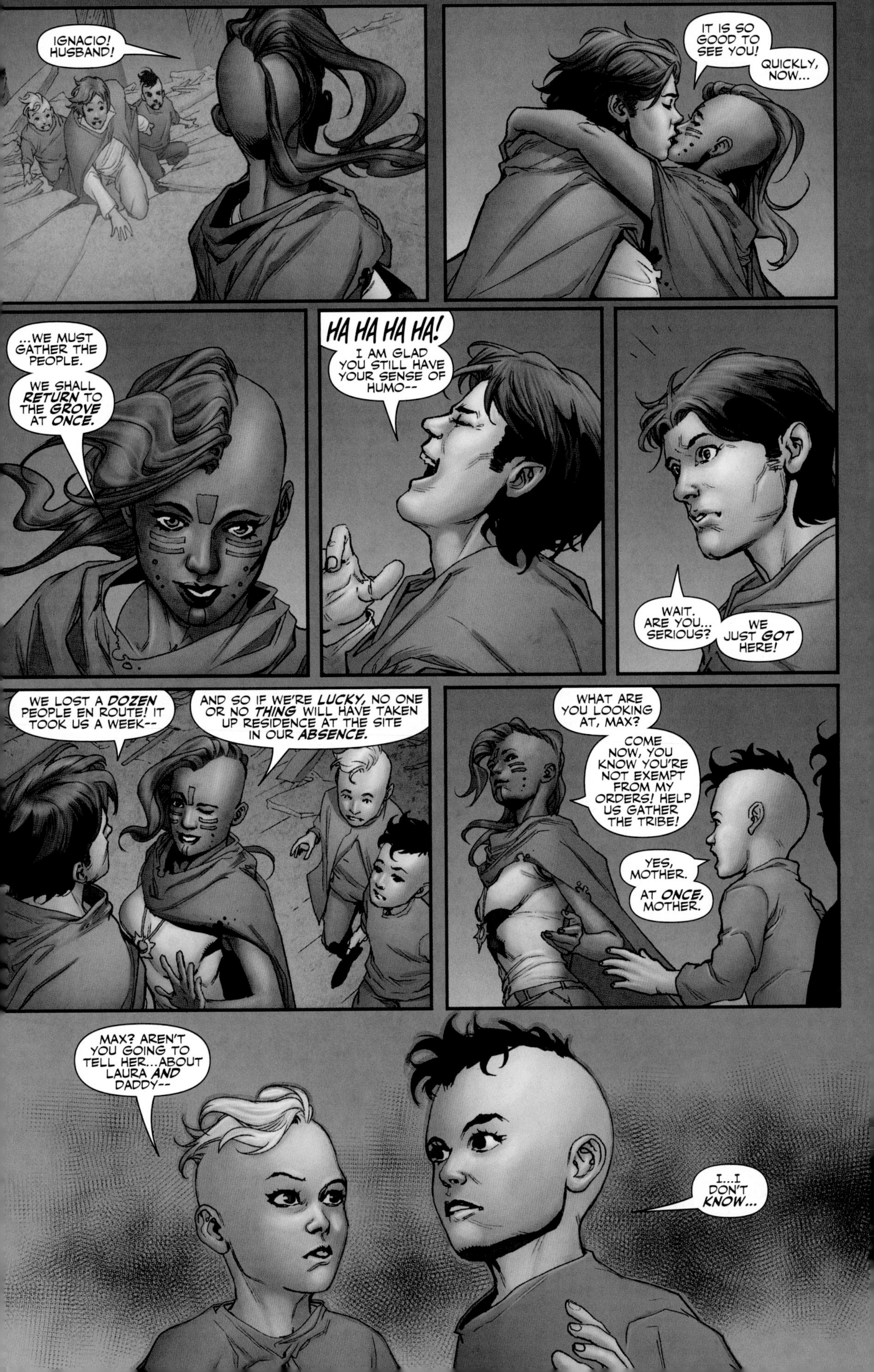
IGNACIO! HUSBAND!
IT IS SO GOOD TO SEE YOU!
QUICKLY, NOW...
...WE MUST GATHER THE PEOPLE.
WE SHALL RETURN TO THE GROVE AT ONCE.
HA HA HA HA!
I AM GLAD YOU STILL HAVE YOUR SENSE OF HUMO--
WAIT. ARE YOU... SERIOUS?
WE JUST GOT HERE!
WE LOST A DOZEN PEOPLE EN ROUTE! IT TOOK US A WEEK--
AND SO IF WE'RE LUCKY, NO ONE OR NO THING WILL HAVE TAKEN UP RESIDENCE AT THE SITE IN OUR ABSENCE.
WHAT ARE YOU LOOKING AT, MAX?
COME NOW, YOU KNOW YOU'RE NOT EXEMPT FROM MY ORDERS! HELP US GATHER THE TRIBE!
YES, MOTHER.
AT ONCE, MOTHER.
MAX? AREN'T YOU GOING TO TELL HER...ABOUT LAURA AND DADDY--
I...I DON'T KNOW...

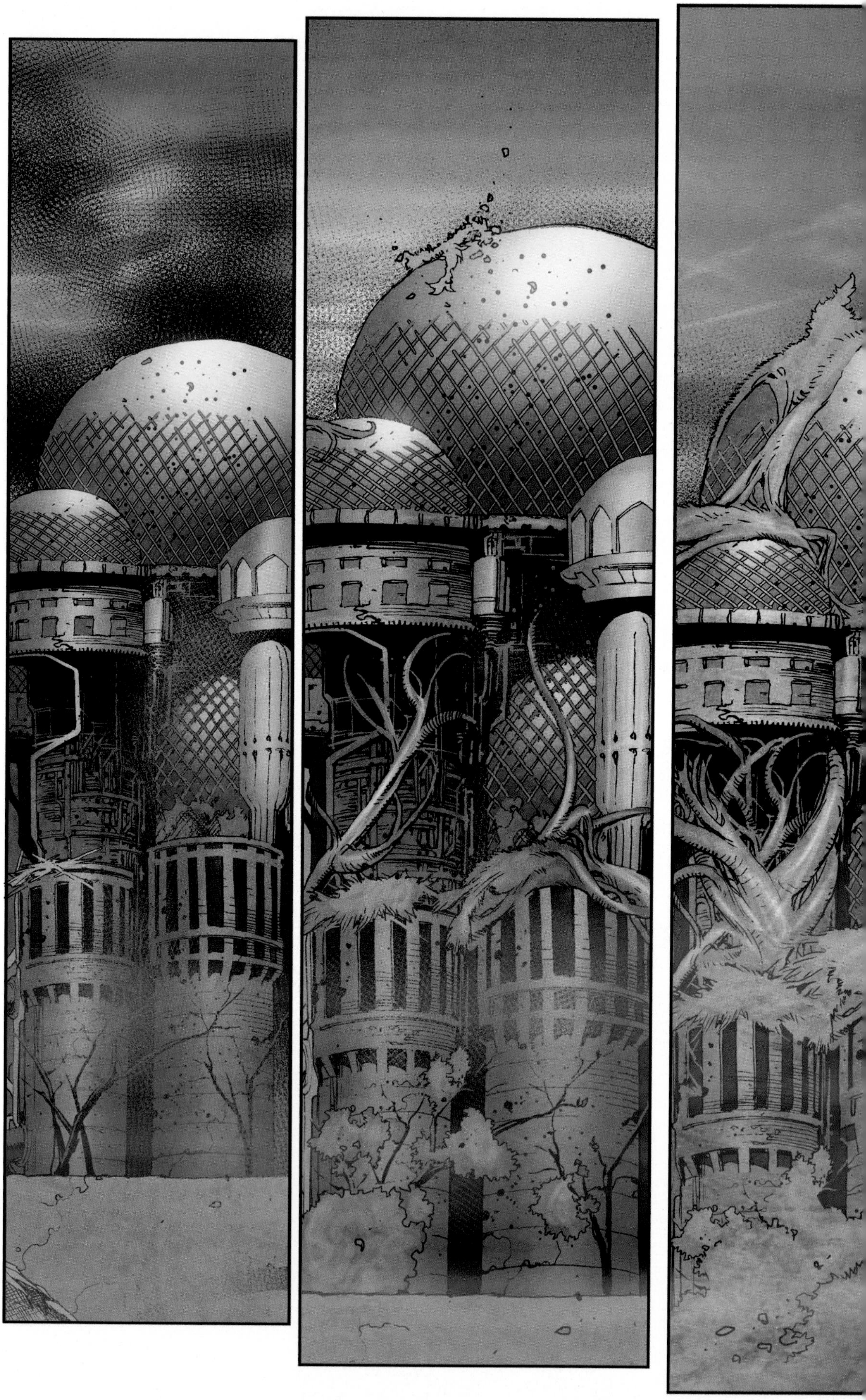

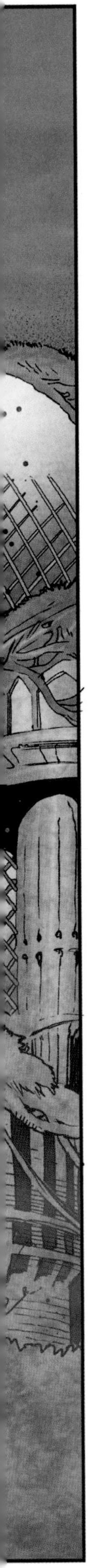

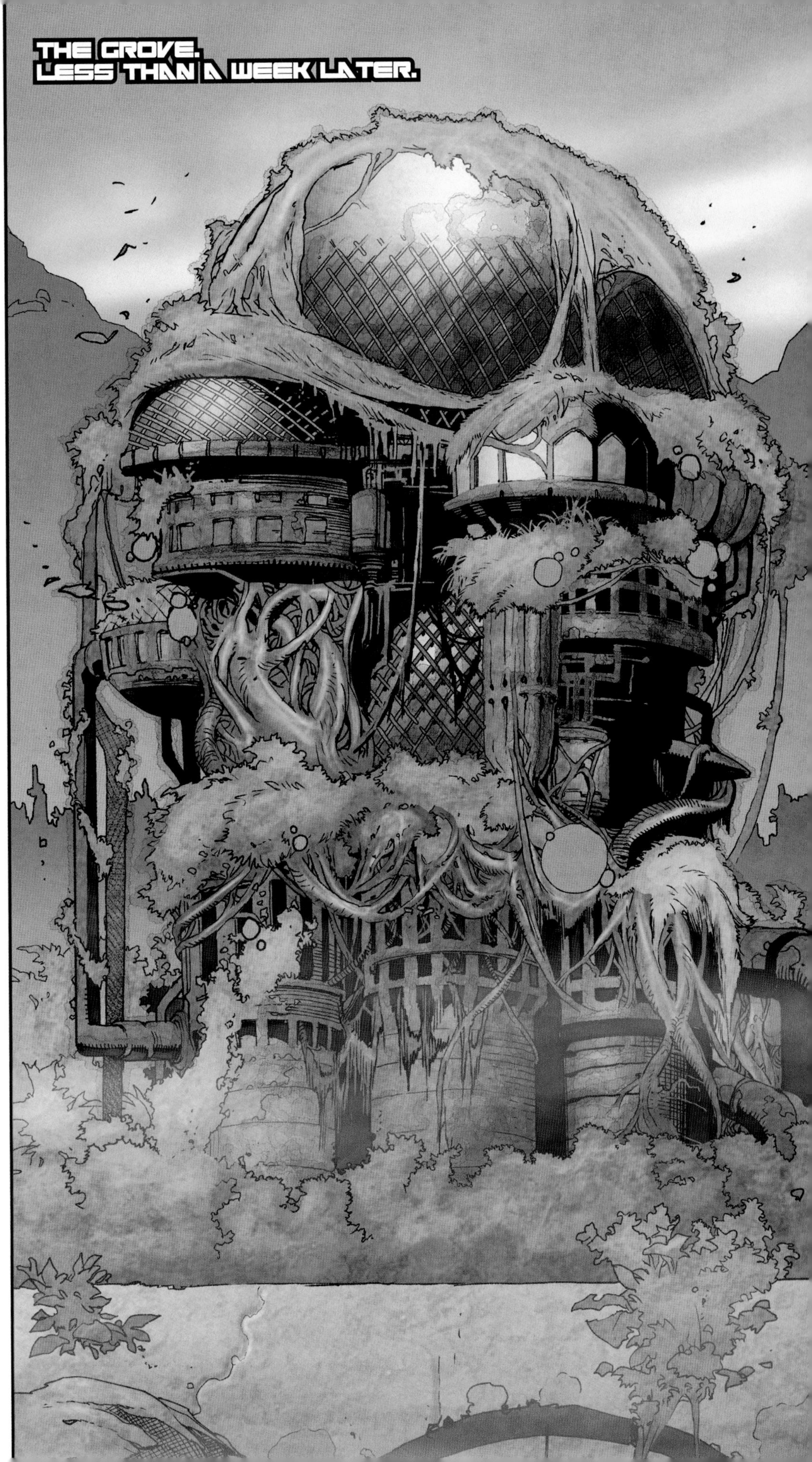
THE GROVE.
LESS THAN A WEEK LATER.

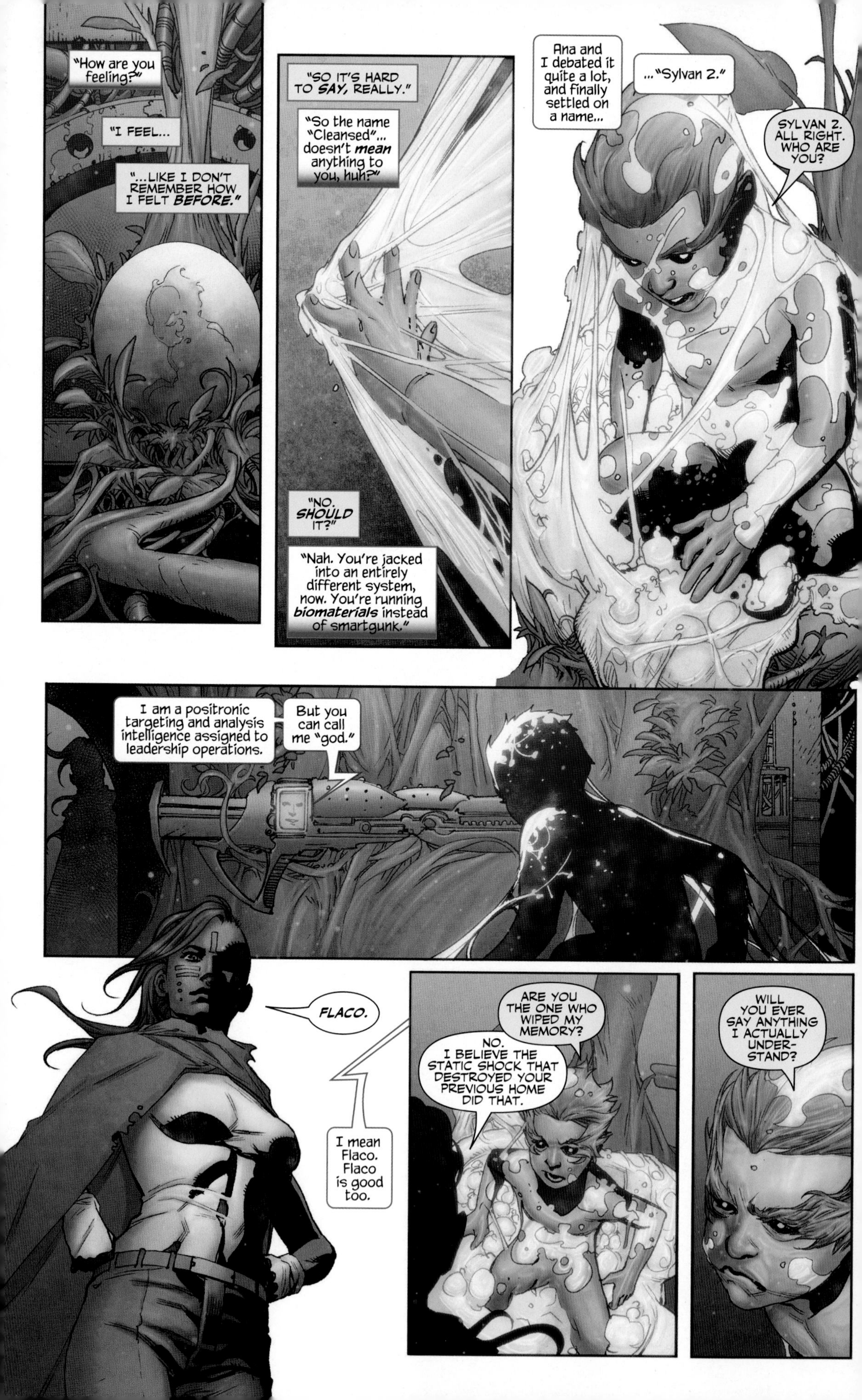
"How are you feeling?"
"I FEEL...
"...LIKE I DON'T REMEMBER HOW I FELT BEFORE."
"SO IT'S HARD TO SAY, REALLY."
"So the name "Cleansed"... doesn't mean anything to you, huh?"
"NO. SHOULD IT?"
"Nah. You're jacked into an entirely different system, now. You're running biomaterials instead of smartgunk."
Ana and I debated it quite a lot, and finally settled on a name...
..."Sylvan 2."
SYLVAN 2. ALL RIGHT. WHO ARE YOU?
I am a positronic targeting and analysis intelligence assigned to leadership operations.
But you can call me "god."
FLACO.
I mean Flaco. Flaco is good too.
ARE YOU THE ONE WHO WIPED MY MEMORY?
NO. I BELIEVE THE STATIC SHOCK THAT DESTROYED YOUR PREVIOUS HOME DID THAT.
WILL YOU EVER SAY ANYTHING I ACTUALLY UNDER-STAND?

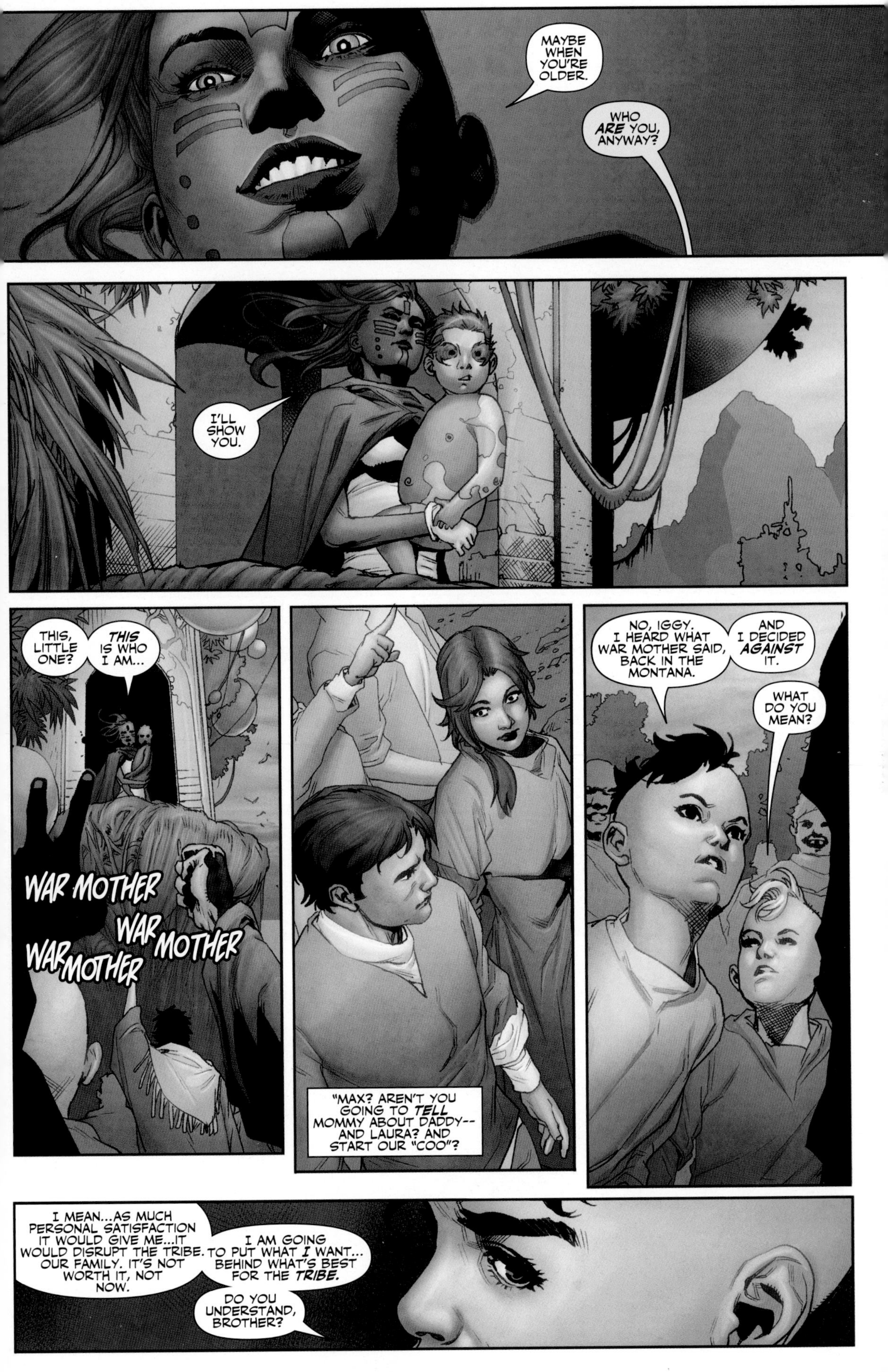
MAYBE WHEN YOU'RE OLDER.
WHO **ARE** YOU, ANYWAY?
I'LL SHOW YOU.
THIS, LITTLE ONE?
THIS IS WHO I AM...
WAR MOTHER
WAR MOTHER
WAR MOTHER
"MAX? AREN'T YOU GOING TO **TELL** MOMMY ABOUT DADDY-- AND LAURA? AND START OUR "COO"?
NO, IGGY. I HEARD WHAT WAR MOTHER SAID, BACK IN THE MONTANA.
AND I DECIDED **AGAINST** IT.
WHAT DO YOU MEAN?
I MEAN...AS MUCH PERSONAL SATISFACTION IT WOULD GIVE ME...IT WOULD DISRUPT THE TRIBE. OUR FAMILY. IT'S NOT WORTH IT, NOT NOW.
I AM GOING TO PUT WHAT **I** WANT... BEHIND WHAT'S BEST FOR THE **TRIBE.**
DO YOU UNDERSTAND, BROTHER?

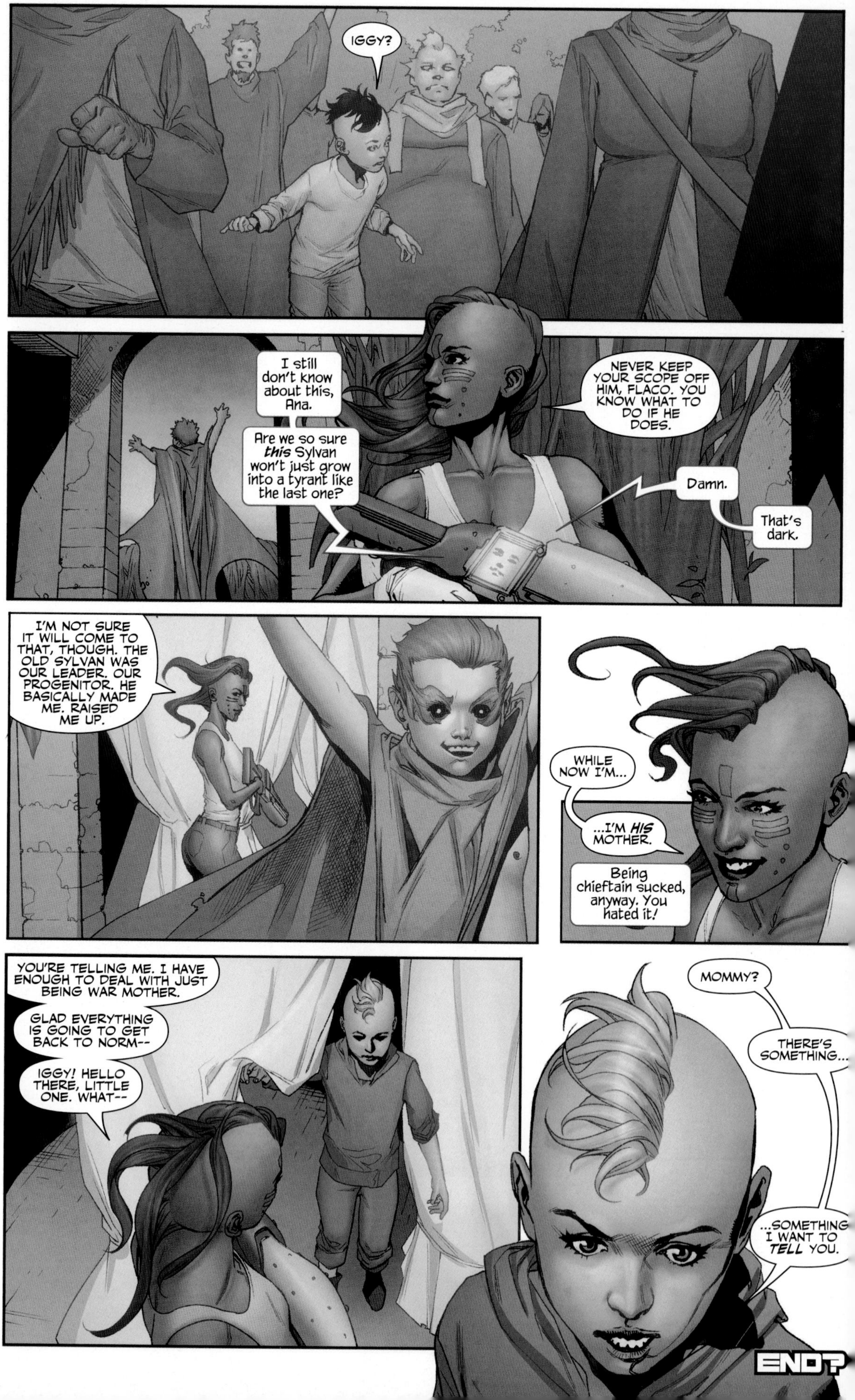
IGGY?
I still don't know about this, Ana.
Are we so sure *this* Sylvan won't just grow into a tyrant like the last one?
NEVER KEEP YOUR SCOPE OFF HIM, FLACO. YOU KNOW WHAT TO DO IF HE DOES.
Damn.
That's dark.
I'M NOT SURE IT WILL COME TO THAT, THOUGH. THE OLD SYLVAN WAS OUR LEADER. OUR PROGENITOR. HE BASICALLY MADE ME. RAISED ME UP.
WHILE NOW I'M...
...I'M *HIS* MOTHER.
Being chieftain sucked, anyway. You hated it!
YOU'RE TELLING ME. I HAVE ENOUGH TO DEAL WITH JUST BEING WAR MOTHER.
GLAD EVERYTHING IS GOING TO GET BACK TO NORM--
IGGY! HELLO THERE, LITTLE ONE. WHAT--
MOMMY?
THERE'S SOMETHING...
...SOMETHING I WANT TO *TELL* YOU.
END?

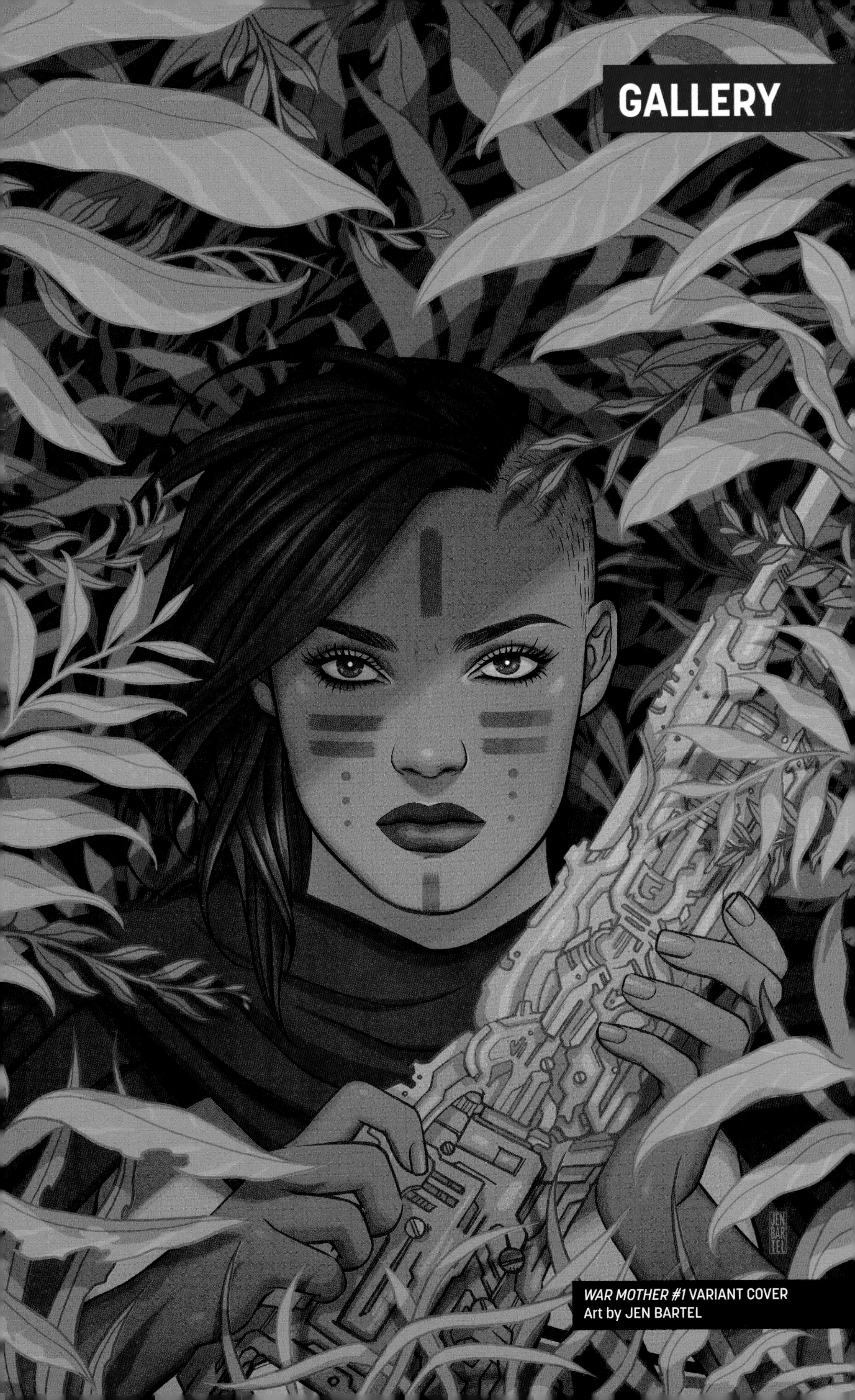

WAR MOTHER #1 VARIANT COVER
Art by JEN BARTEL

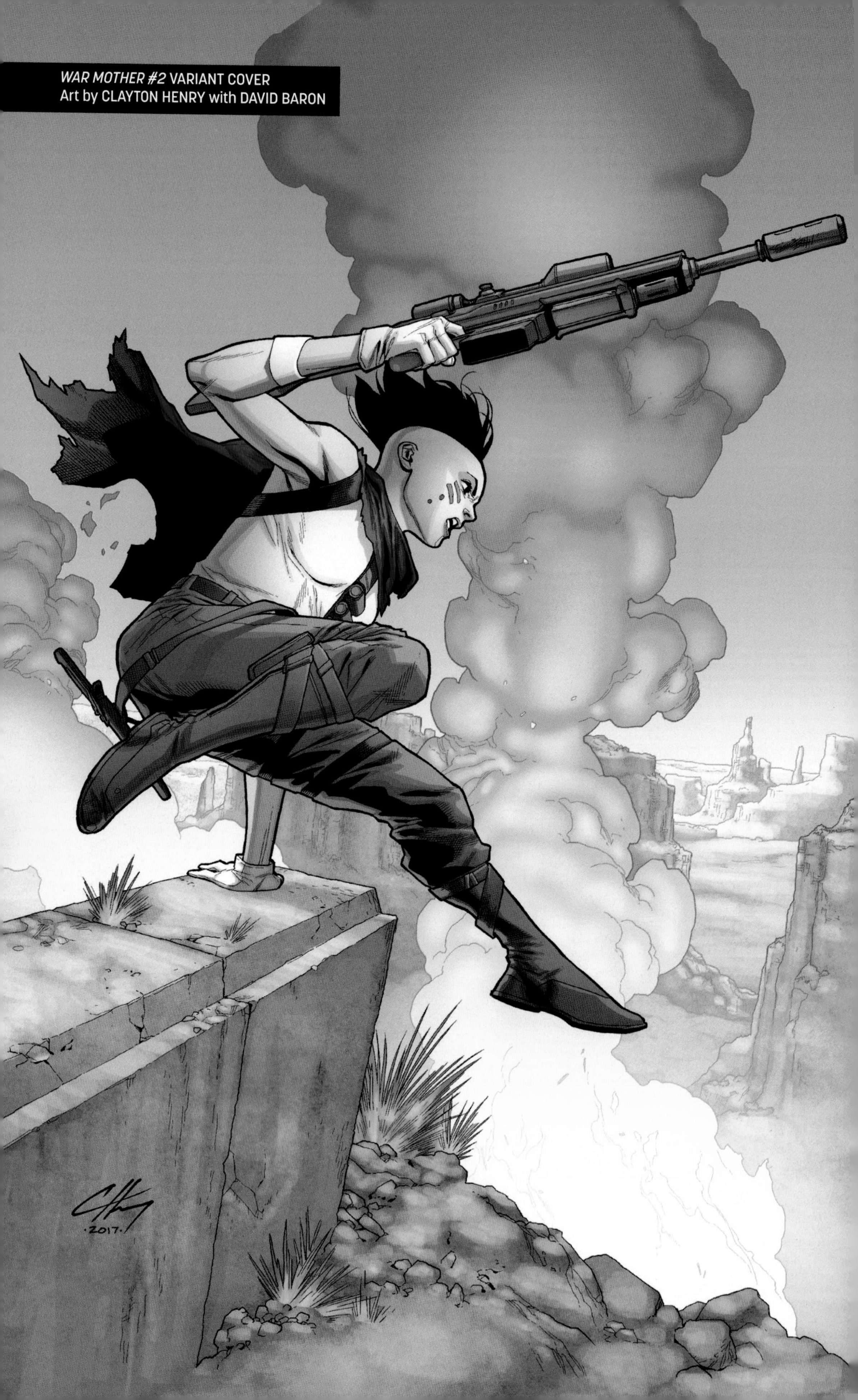

WAR MOTHER #2 VARIANT COVER
Art by CLAYTON HENRY with DAVID BARON

WAR MOTHER #2 COVER B
Art by RENATO GUEDES

WAR MOTHER #3 VARIANT COVER
Art by VERONICA FISH

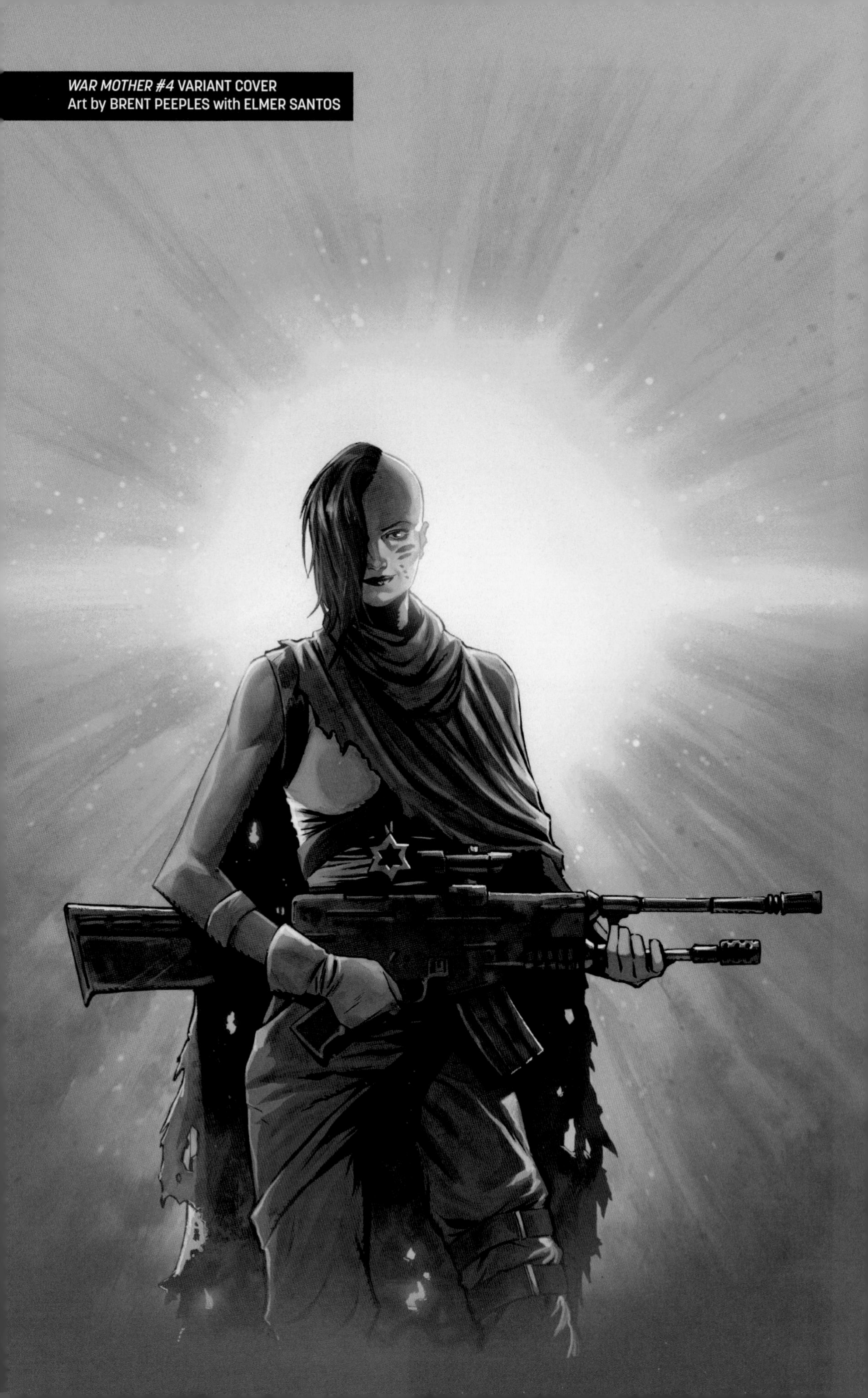

WAR MOTHER #4 VARIANT COVER
Art by BRENT PEEPLES with ELMER SANTOS

WAR MOTHER #1, pages 6 and 7
Art by STEPHEN SEGOVIA

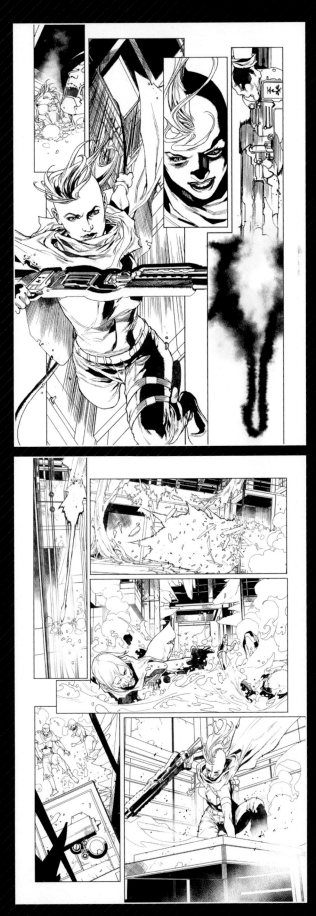

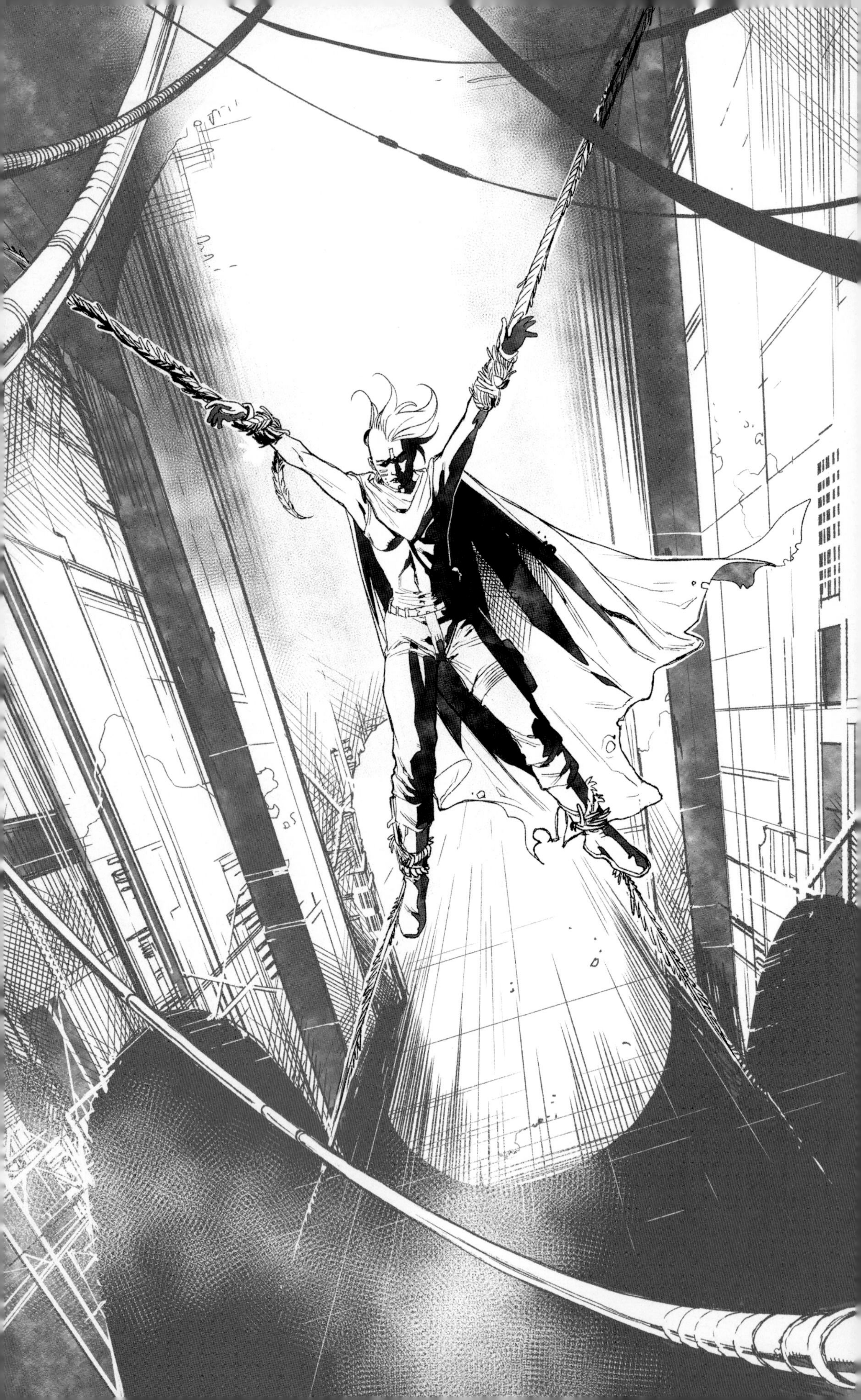

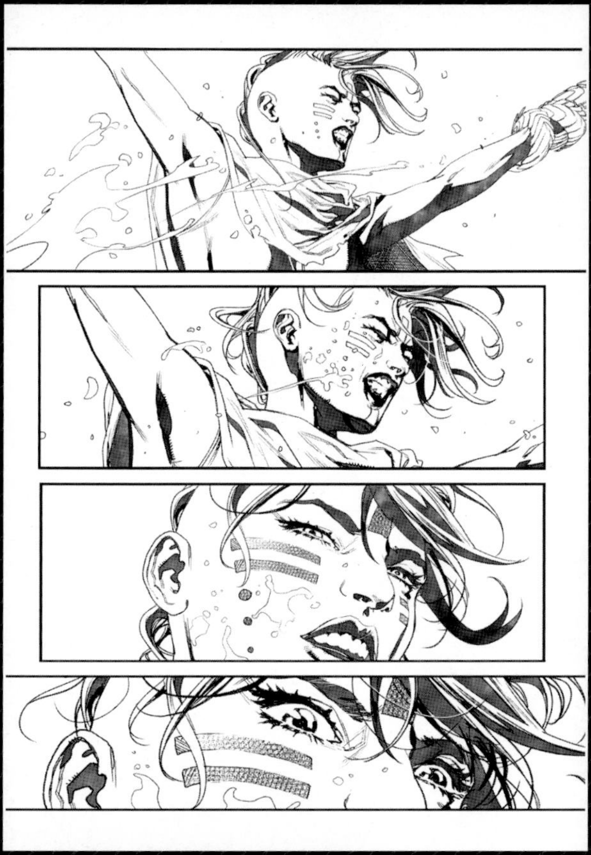

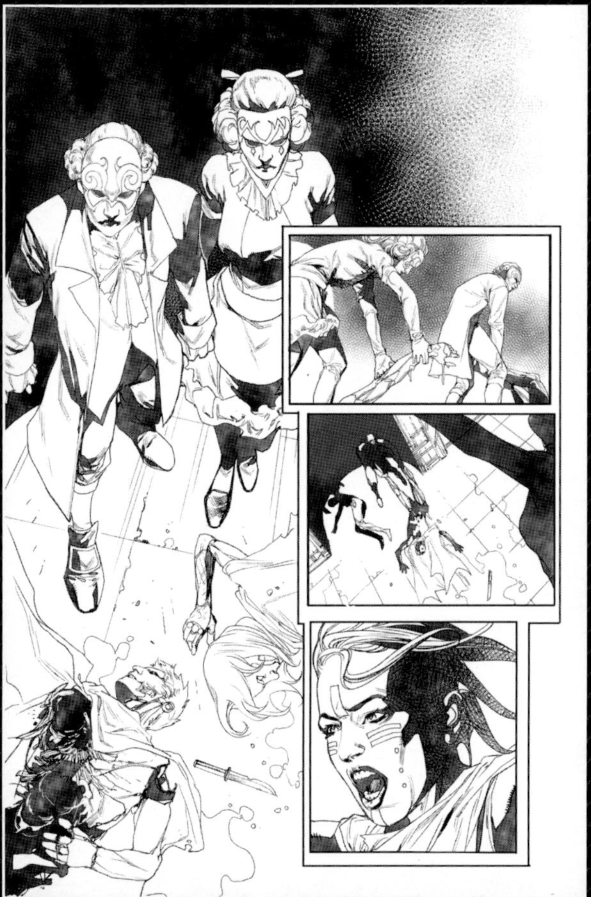

WAR MOTHER #2, pages 1 (facing), 5, and 6
Art by STEPHEN SEGOVIA

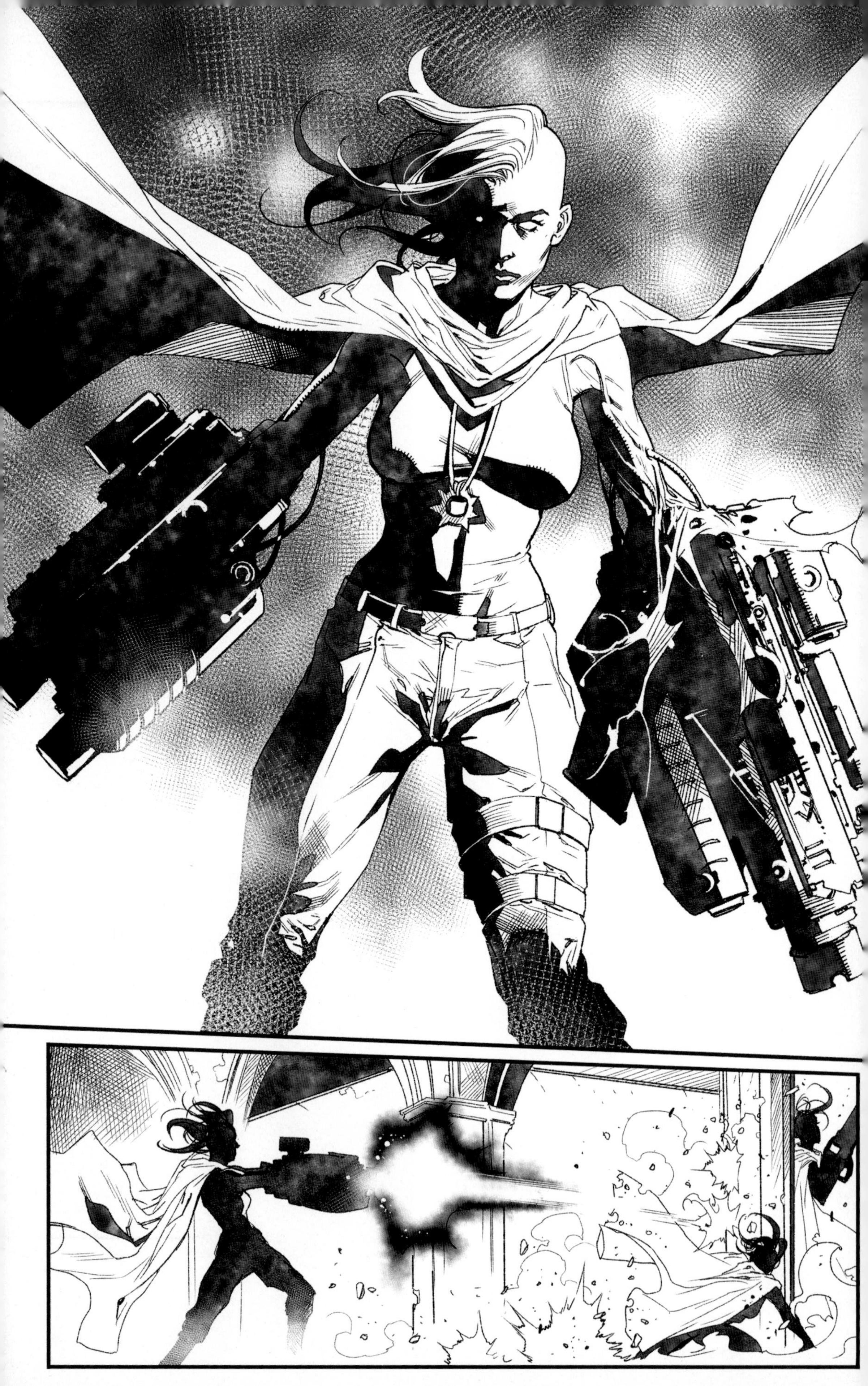

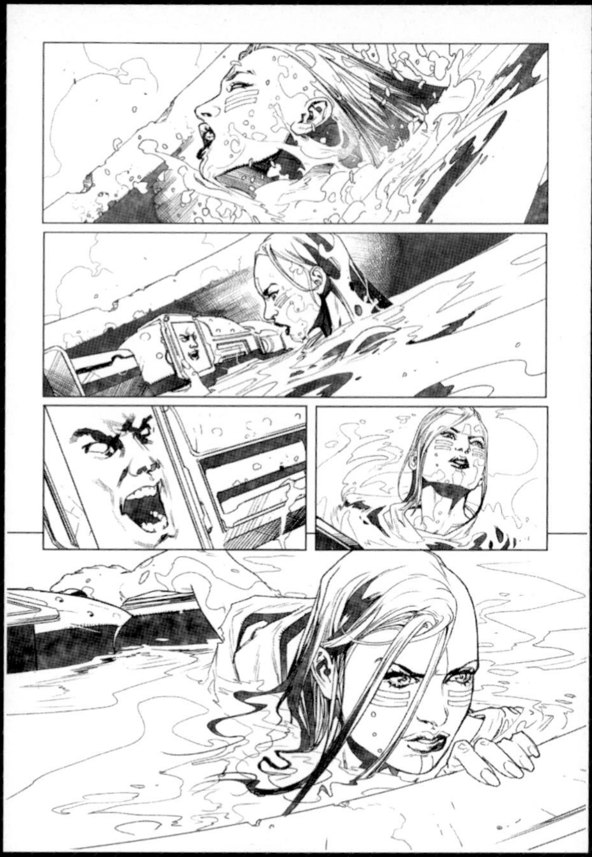

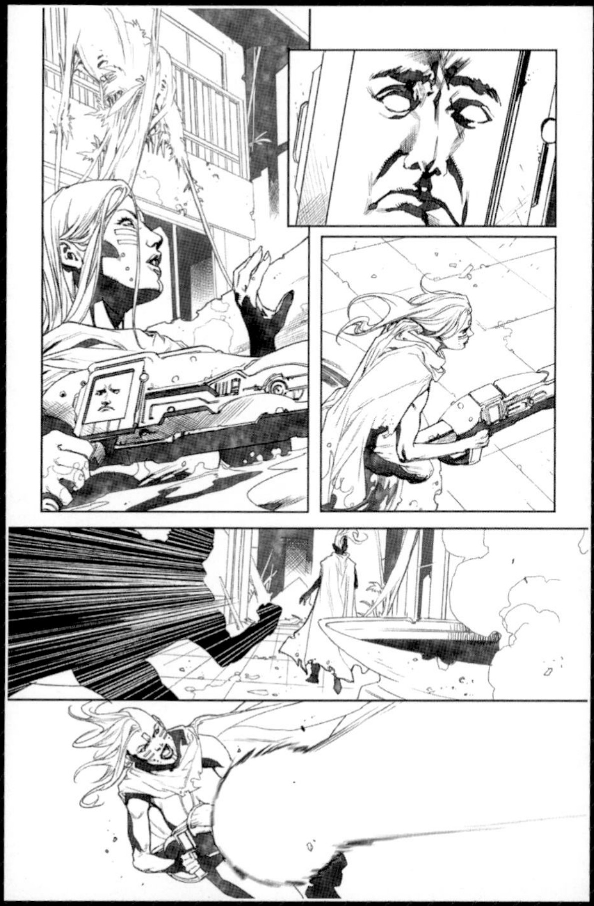

WAR MOTHER #3, pages 9 (facing), 18, and 19
Art by STEPHEN SEGOVIA

EXPLORE THE VALIANT UNIVERSE

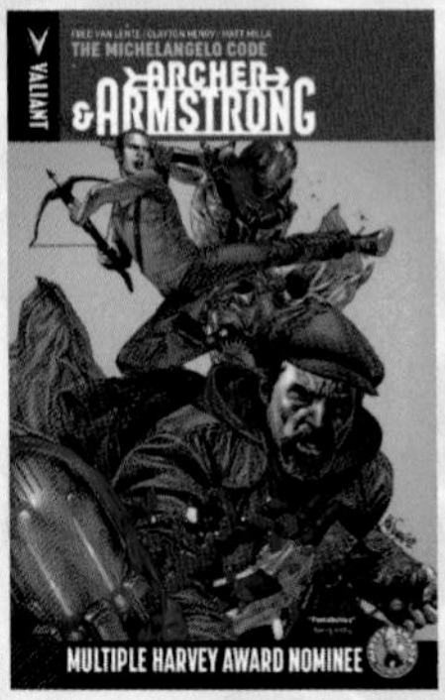
THE MICHELANGELO CODE
ARCHER & ARMSTRONG
MULTIPLE HARVEY AWARD NOMINEE
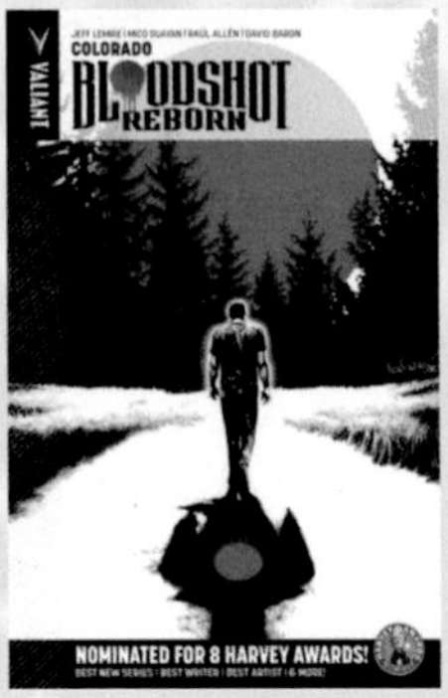
COLORADO
BLOODSHOT REBORN
NOMINATED FOR 8 HARVEY AWARDS!
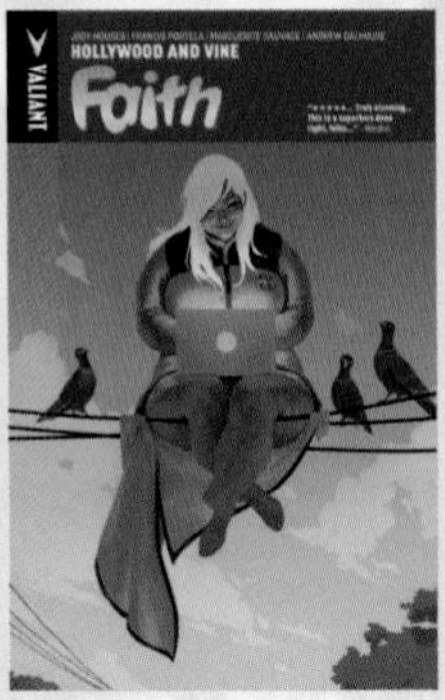
HOLLYWOOD AND VINE
Faith
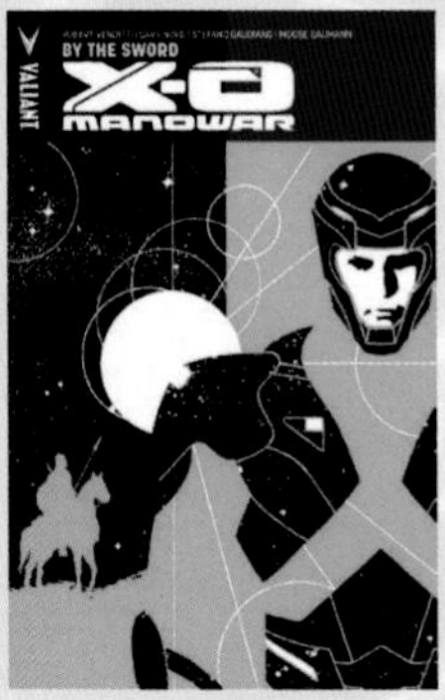
BY THE SWORD
X-O MANOWAR
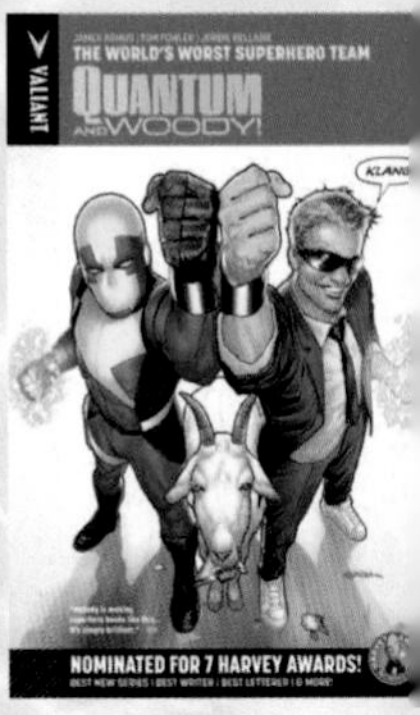
THE WORLD'S WORST SUPERHERO TEAM
QUANTUM AND WOODY!
NOMINATED FOR 7 HARVEY AWARDS!

4001 A.D.

4001 A.D.
ISBN: 9781682151433

4001 A.D.: Beyond New Japan
ISBN: 9781682151464

Rai Vol 4: 4001 A.D.
ISBN: 9781682151471

A&A: THE ADVENTURES OF ARCHER AND ARMSTRONG

Volume 1: In the Bag
ISBN: 9781682151495

Volume 2: Romance and Road Trips
ISBN: 9781682151716

Volume 3: Andromeda Estranged
ISBN: 9781682152034

ARCHER & ARMSTRONG

Volume 1: The Michelangelo Code
ISBN: 9780979640988

Volume 2: Wrath of the Eternal Warrior
ISBN: 9781939346049

Volume 3: Far Faraway
ISBN: 9781939346148

Volume 4: Sect Civil War
ISBN: 9781939346254

Volume 5: Mission: Improbable
ISBN: 9781939346353

Volume 6: American Wasteland
ISBN: 9781939346421

Volume 7: The One Percent and Other Tales
ISBN: 9781939346537

ARMOR HUNTERS

Armor Hunters
ISBN: 9781939346452

Armor Hunters: Bloodshot
ISBN: 9781939346469

Armor Hunters: Harbinger
ISBN: 9781939346506

Unity Vol. 3: Armor Hunters
ISBN: 9781939346445

X-O Manowar Vol. 7: Armor Hunters
ISBN: 9781939346476

BLOODSHOT

Volume 1: Setting the World on Fire
ISBN: 9780979640964

Volume 2: The Rise and the Fall
ISBN: 9781939346032

Volume 3: Harbinger Wars
ISBN: 9781939346124

Volume 4: H.A.R.D. Corps
ISBN: 9781939346193

Volume 5: Get Some!
ISBN: 9781939346315

Volume 6: The Glitch and Other Tales
ISBN: 9781939346711

BLOODSHOT REBORN

Volume 1: Colorado
ISBN: 9781939346674

Volume 2: The Hunt
ISBN: 9781939346827

Volume 3: The Analog Man
ISBN: 9781682151334

Volume 4: Bloodshot Island
ISBN: 9781682151952

BLOODSHOT U.S.A.

ISBN: 9781682151952

BOOK OF DEATH

Book of Death
ISBN: 9781939346971

Book of Death: The Fall of the Valiant Universe
ISBN: 9781939346988

BRITANNIA

Volume 1
ISBN: 9781682151853

Volume 2: We Who Are About to Die
ISBN: 9781682152133

DEAD DROP

ISBN: 9781939346858

THE DEATH-DEFYING DOCTOR MIRAGE

Volume 1
ISBN: 9781939346490

Volume 2: Second Lives
ISBN: 9781682151297

THE DELINQUENTS

ISBN: 9781939346513

DIVINITY

Divinity I
ISBN: 9781939346766

Divinity II
ISBN: 9781682151518

Divinity III
ISBN: 9781682151914

Divinity III: Glorious Heroes of the Stalinverse
ISBN: 9781682152072

ETERNAL WARRIOR

Volume 1: Sword of the Wild
ISBN: 9781939346209

Volume 2: Eternal Emperor
ISBN: 9781939346292

Volume 3: Days of Steel
ISBN: 9781939346742

WRATH OF THE ETERNAL WARRIO

Volume 1: Risen
ISBN: 9781682151235

Volume 2: Labyrinth
ISBN: 9781682151594

Volume 3: Deal With a Devil
ISBN: 9781682151976

FAITH

Volume 1: Hollywood and Vine
ISBN: 9781682151402

Volume 2: California Scheming
ISBN: 9781682151631

Volume 3: Superstar
ISBN: 9781682151990

Volume 4: The Faithless
ISBN: 9781682152195

Faith and the Future Force:
ISBN: 9781682152331

GENERATION ZERO

Volume 1: We Are the Future
ISBN: 9781682151754

Volume 2: Heroscape
ISBN: 9781682152096

HARBINGER

Volume 1: Omega Rising
ISBN: 9780979640957

Volume 2: Renegades
ISBN: 9781939346025

Volume 3: Harbinger Wars
ISBN: 9781939346117

Volume 4: Perfect Day
ISBN: 9781939346155

Volume 5: Death of a Renegade
ISBN: 9781939346339

Volume 6: Omegas
ISBN: 9781939346384

HARBINGER RENEGADE

Volume 1: The Judgment of Solomon
ISBN: 9781682151693

Volume 2: Massacre
ISBN: 9781682152232

EXPLORE THE VALIANT UNIVERSE

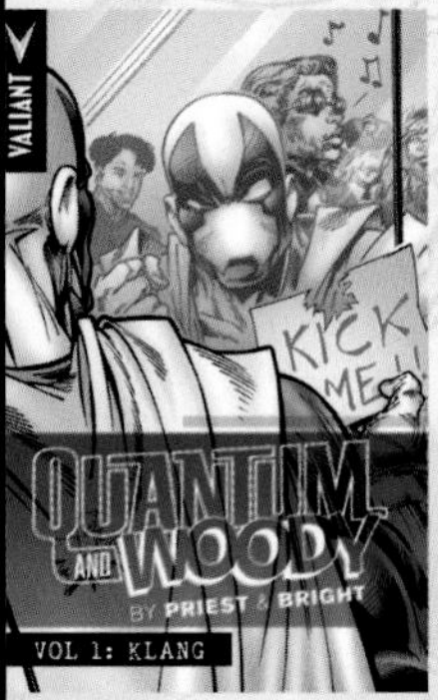
VALIANT
KICK ME
QUANTUM AND WOODY
BY PRIEST & BRIGHT
VOL 1: KLANG

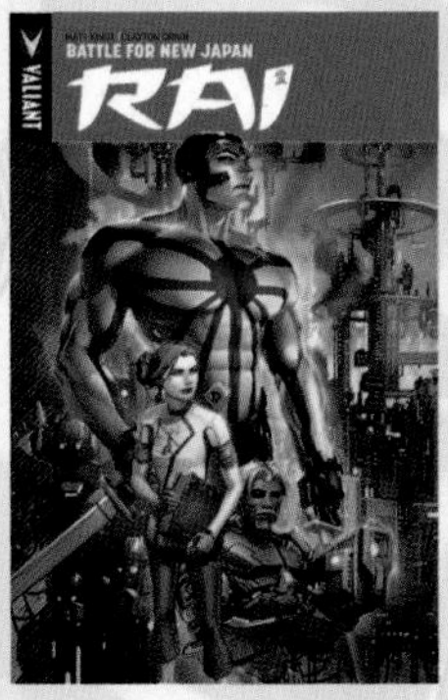
VALIANT
BATTLE FOR NEW JAPAN
RAI

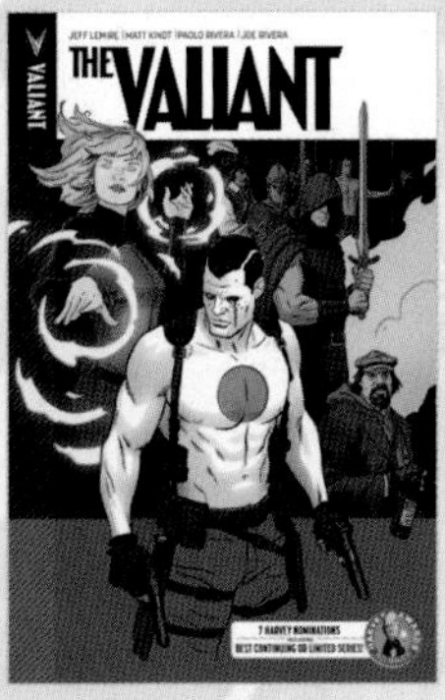
VALIANT
THE VALIANT

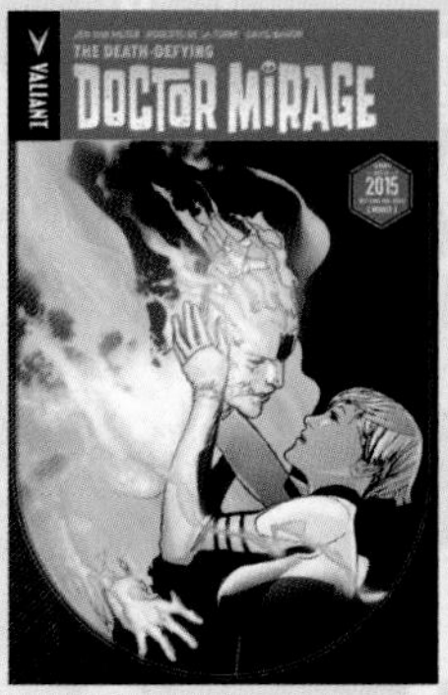
VALIANT
THE DEATH-DEFYING
DOCTOR MIRAGE

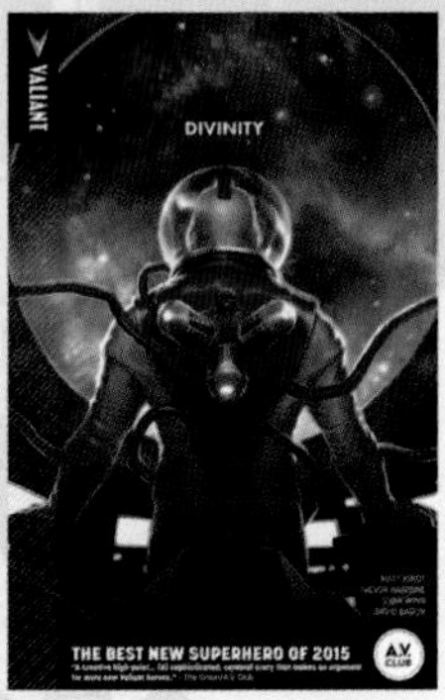
VALIANT
DIVINITY
THE BEST NEW SUPERHERO OF 2015

HARBINGER RENEGADE
Volume 1: The Judgment of Solomon
ISBN: 9781682151693
Volume 2: Massacre
ISBN: 9781682152232

HARBINGER WARS
Harbinger Wars
ISBN: 9781939346094
Bloodshot Vol. 3: Harbinger Wars
ISBN: 9781939346124
Harbinger Vol. 3: Harbinger Wars
ISBN: 9781939346117

IMPERIUM
Volume 1: Collecting Monsters
ISBN: 9781939346759
Volume 2: Broken Angels
ISBN: 9781939346896
Volume 3: The Vine Imperative
ISBN: 9781682151112
Volume 4: Stormbreak
ISBN: 9781682151372

NINJAK
Volume 1: Weaponeer
ISBN: 9781939346667
Volume 2: The Shadow Wars
ISBN: 9781939346940
Volume 3: Operation: Deadside
ISBN: 9781682151259
Volume 4: The Siege of King's Castle
ISBN: 9781682151617
Volume 5: The Fist & The Steel
ISBN: 9781682151792
Volume 6: The Seven Blades of Master Darque
ISBN: 9781682152119

QUANTUM AND WOODY
Volume 1: The World's Worst Superhero Team
ISBN: 9781939346186
Volume 2: In Security
ISBN: 9781939346230
Volume 3: Crooked Pasts, Present Tense
ISBN: 9781939346391
Volume 4: Quantum and Woody Must Die!
ISBN: 9781939346629

QUANTUM AND WOODY BY PRIEST & BRIGHT
Volume 1: Klang
ISBN: 9781939346780
Volume 2: Switch
ISBN: 9781939346803
Volume 3: And So...
ISBN: 9781939346865
Volume 4: Q2 - The Return
ISBN: 9781682151099

RAI
Volume 1: Welcome to New Japan
ISBN: 9781939346414
Volume 2: Battle for New Japan
ISBN: 9781939346612
Volume 3: The Orphan
ISBN: 9781939346841
Volume 4: 4001 A.D.
ISBN: 9781682151471

RAPTURE
ISBN: 9781682151891

SAVAGE
ISBN: 9781682152256

SECRET WEAPONS
ISBN: 9781682152294

SHADOWMAN
Volume 1: Birth Rites
ISBN: 9781939346001
Volume 2: Darque Reckoning
ISBN: 9781939346056
Volume 3: Deadside Blues
ISBN: 9781939346162
Volume 4: Fear, Blood, And Shadows
ISBN: 9781939346278
Volume 5: End Times
ISBN: 9781939346377

SHADOWMAN BY ENNIS & WOOD
ISBN: 9781682151358

IVAR, TIMEWALKER
Volume 1: Making History
ISBN: 9781939346636
Volume 2: Breaking History
ISBN: 9781939346834
Volume 3: Ending History
ISBN: 9781939346995

UNITY
Volume 1: To Kill a King
ISBN: 9781939346261
Volume 2: Trapped by Webnet
ISBN: 9781939346346
Volume 3: Armor Hunters
ISBN: 9781939346445
Volume 4: The United
ISBN: 9781939346544
Volume 5: Homefront
ISBN: 9781939346797
Volume 6: The War-Monger
ISBN: 9781939346902
Volume 7: Revenge of the Armor Hunters
ISBN: 9781682151136

THE VALIANT
ISBN: 9781939346605

VALIANT ZEROES AND ORIGINS
ISBN: 9781939346582

X-O MANOWAR
Volume 1: By the Sword
ISBN: 9780979640940
Volume 2: Enter Ninjak
ISBN: 9780979640995
Volume 3: Planet Death
ISBN: 9781939346087
Volume 4: Homecoming
ISBN: 9781939346179
Volume 5: At War With Unity
ISBN: 9781939346247
Volume 6: Prelude to Armor Hunters
ISBN: 9781939346407
Volume 7: Armor Hunters
ISBN: 9781939346476
Volume 8: Enter: Armorines
ISBN: 9781939346551
Volume 9: Dead Hand
ISBN: 9781939346650
Volume 10: Exodus
ISBN: 9781939346933
Volume 11: The Kill List
ISBN: 9781682151273
Volume 12: Long Live the King
ISBN: 9781682151655
Volume 13: Succession and Other Tales
ISBN: 9781682151754

X-O MANOWAR (2017)
Volume 1: Soldier
ISBN: 9781682152058
Volume 2: General
ISBN: 9781682152171
Volume 3: Emperor
ISBN: 9781682152355

EXPLORE THE VALIANT UNIVERSE

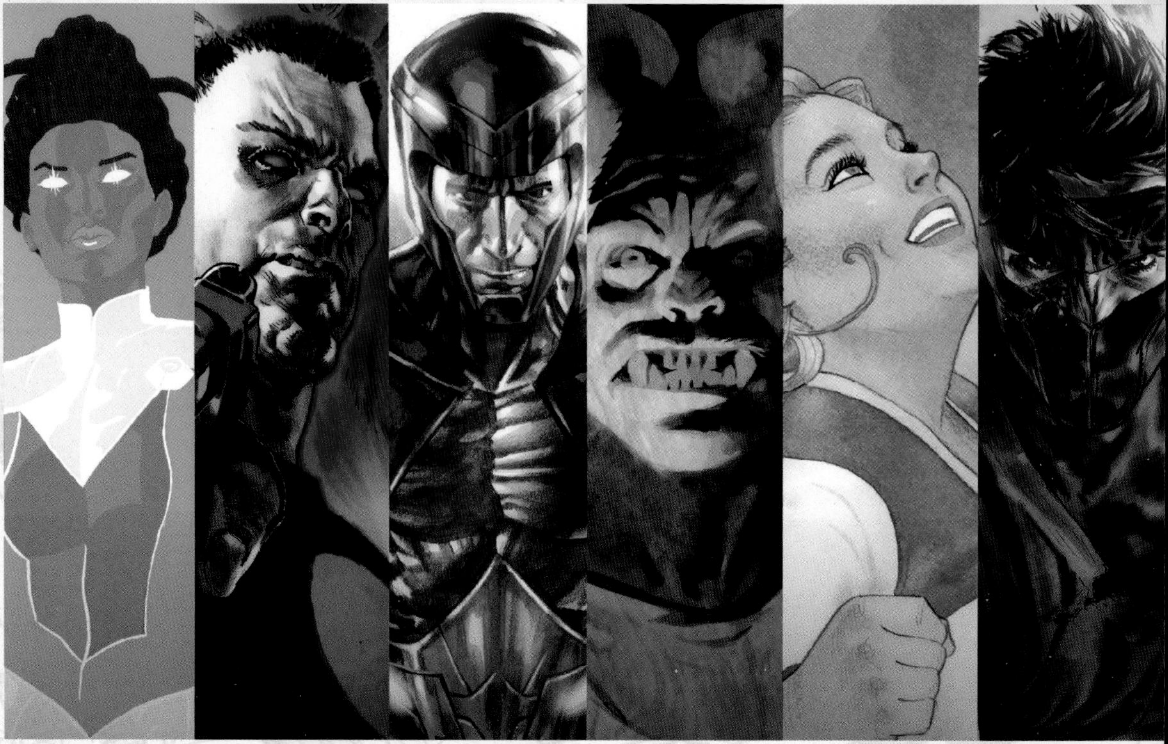

4001 A.D. DELUXE EDITION
ISBN: 978-1-68215-193-8

ARCHER & ARMSTRONG DELUXE EDITIONS
Book 1: ISBN: 978-1-939346-22-3
Book 2: ISBN: 978-1-939346-95-7

ARMOR HUNTERS DELUXE EDITION
ISBN: 978-1-939346-72-8

BLOODSHOT DELUXE EDITIONS
Book 1: ISBN: 978-1-939346-21-6
Book 2: ISBN: 978-1-939346-81-0

BLOODSHOT REBORN DELUXE EDITIONS
Book 1: ISBN: 978-1-68215-155-6
Book 2: ISBN: 978-1-68215-227-0

BOOK OF DEATH DELUXE EDITION
ISBN: 978-1-68215-115-0

THE DEATH-DEFYING DOCTOR MIRAGE DELUXE EDITION
ISBN: 978-1-68215-153-2

DIVINITY DELUXE EDITION
ISBN: 978-1-939346-92-6

FAITH: HOLLYWOOD & VINE DELUXE EDITION
ISBN: 978-1-68215-201-0

HARBINGER DELUXE EDITIONS
Book 1: ISBN: 978-1-939346-13-1
Book 2: ISBN: 978-1-939346-77-3

HARBINGER WARS DELUXE EDITION
ISBN: 978-1-939346-32-2

IVAR, TIMEWALKER DELUXE EDITION
Book 1: ISBN: 978-1-68215-119-8

NINJAK DELUXE EDITION
Book 1: ISBN: 978-1-68215-157-0

QUANTUM AND WOODY DELUXE EDITION
Book 1: ISBN: 978-1-939346-68-1

RAI DELUXE EDITION
Book 1: ISBN: 978-1-68215-117-4

SHADOWMAN DELUXE EDITION
Book 1: ISBN: 978-1-939346-43-8

UNITY DELUXE EDITION
Book 1: 978-1-939346-57-5

THE VALIANT DELUXE EDITION
ISBN: 978-1-939346-91-9

X-O MANOWAR DELUXE EDITIONS
Book 1: ISBN: 978-1-939346-10-0
Book 2: ISBN: 978-1-939346-52-0
Book 3 : ISBN: 978-1-68215-131-0
Book 4: ISBN: 978-1-68215-183-9
Book 5: ISBN: 978-1-68215-215-7

VALIANT CLASSIC

ARCHER & ARMSTRONG: THE COMPLETE CLASSIC OMNIBUS
ISBN: 978-1-939346-87-2

QUANTUM AND WOODY: THE COMPLETE CLASSIC OMNIBUS
ISBN: 978-1-939346-36-0

Q2: THE RETURN OF QUANTUM AND WOODY DELUXE EDITION
ISBN: 978-1-939346-56-8

VALIANT MASTERS: BLOODSHOT VOL. 1 - BLOOD OF THE MACHINE
ISBN: 978-0-9796409-3-3

VALIANT MASTERS: HARBINGER VOL. 1 - CHILDREN OF THE EIGHTH DAY
ISBN: 978-1-939346-48-3

VALIANT MASTERS: H.A.R.D. CORPS VOL. 1 - SEARCH AND DESTROY
ISBN: 978-1-939346-28-5

VALIANT MASTERS: NINJAK VOL. 1 - BLACK WATER
ISBN: 978-0-9796409-7-1

VALIANT MASTERS: RAI VOL. 1 - FROM HONOR TO STRENGTH
ISBN: 978-1-939346-07-0

VALIANT MASTERS: SHADOWMAN VOL. 1 - SPIRITS WITHIN
ISBN: 978-1-939346-01-8

X-O MANOWAR CLASSIC OMNIBUS
Vol. 1: ISBN: 978-1-939346-30-8

Out of the pages of 4001 A.D. comes the breakout heroine of the 41st century!

4001 A.D.
(OPTIONAL)

4001 A.D.:
Beyond New Japan
(OPTIONAL)

FRED VAN LENTE • STEPHEN SEGOVIA • TOMÁS GIORELLO • ANDREW DALHOUSE
WAR MOTHER
LIBERATOR
LIFEGIVER
MOTHER
FIGHTER
ICON
MACK
VALIANT
"A treasure trove of stunning apocalyptic imagery..."
- Doom Rocket

4001 A.D.

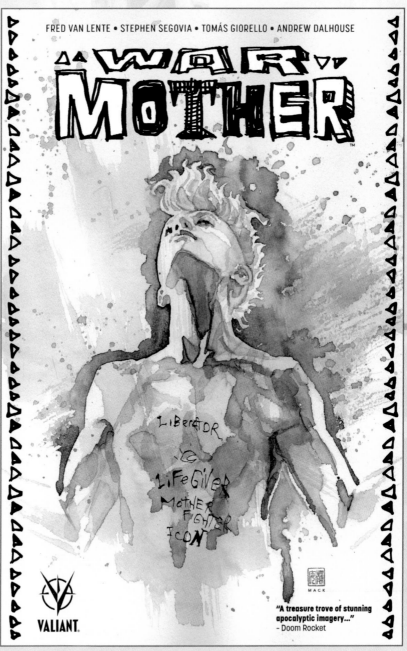

SECRET WEAPONS®

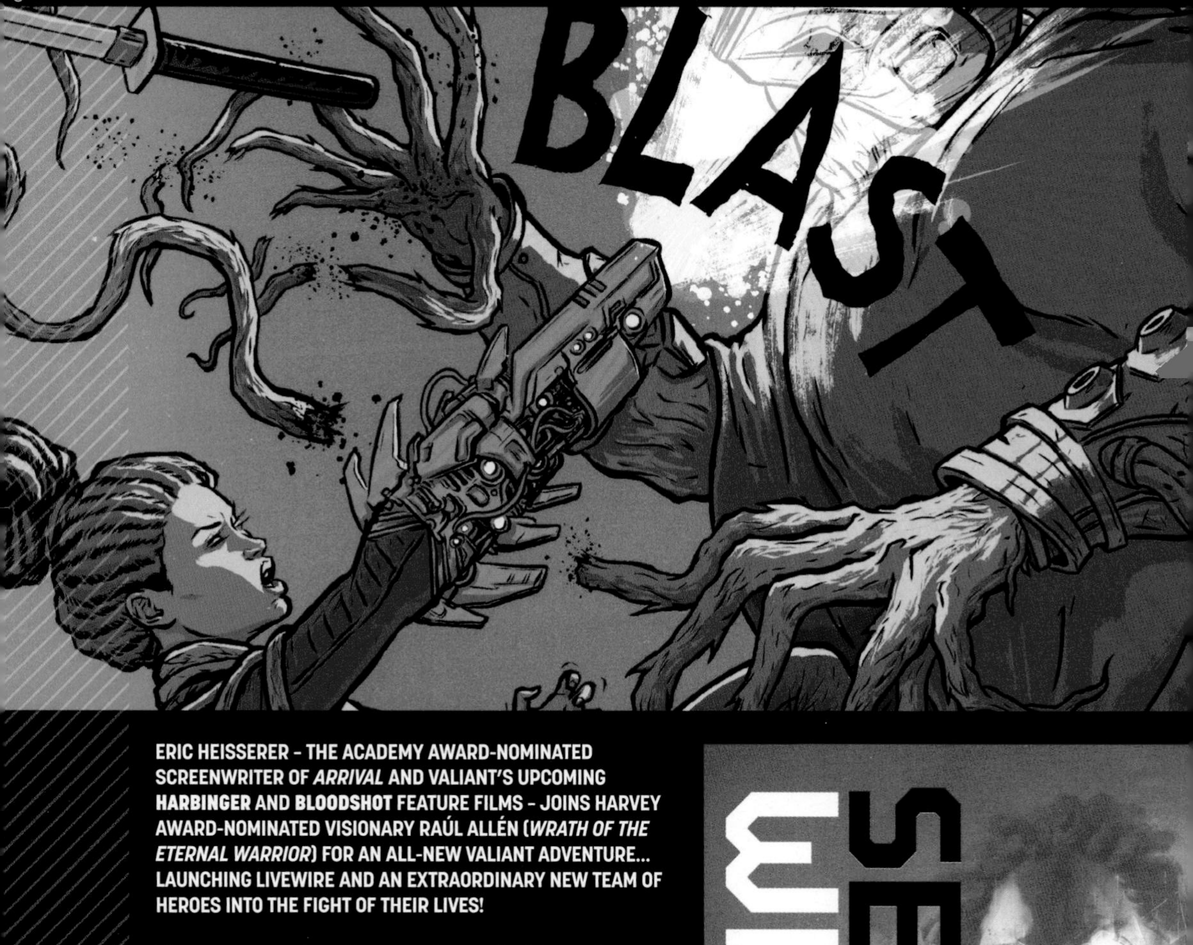
BLAST

ERIC HEISSERER - THE ACADEMY AWARD-NOMINATED SCREENWRITER OF *ARRIVAL* AND VALIANT'S UPCOMING HARBINGER AND BLOODSHOT FEATURE FILMS - JOINS HARVEY AWARD-NOMINATED VISIONARY RAÚL ALLÉN (*WRATH OF THE ETERNAL WARRIOR*) FOR AN ALL-NEW VALIANT ADVENTURE... LAUNCHING LIVEWIRE AND AN EXTRAORDINARY NEW TEAM OF HEROES INTO THE FIGHT OF THEIR LIVES!

The government has dispatched Amanda McKee - the technopath codenamed Livewire - to investigate the ruins of a secret facility formerly run by Toyo Harada, the most powerful telepath on Earth and her former mentor. In his quest for world betterment at any cost, Harada sought out and activated many potential psiots like himself. Those who survived, but whose powers he deemed to have no value to his cause, were hidden away at this installation. But Livewire, having studied Harada's greatest strengths and learned his deepest weaknesses, senses opportunity where he once saw failure. A young girl who can talk to birds... a boy who can make inanimate objects gently glow... to others, these are expensive disappointments. But, to Livewire, they are secret weapons...in need of a leader. Now, as a mechanized killer called Rex-O seeks to draw them out, Livewire and her new team of cadets will be forced to put their powers into action...in ways they never could have imagined...

Collecting SECRET WEAPONS #1-4.

TRADE PAPERBACK

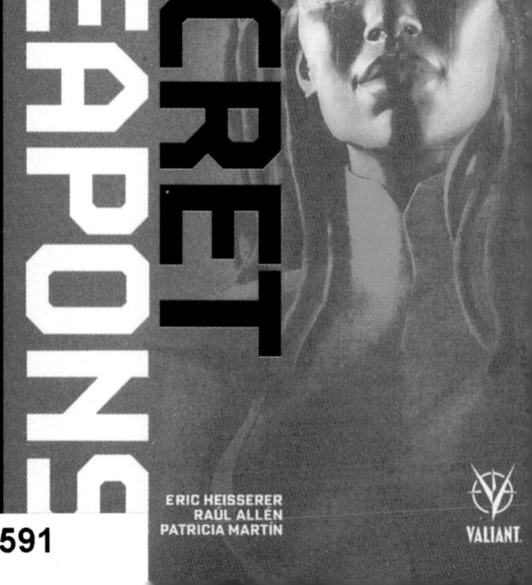
SECRET WEAPONS
ERIC HEISSERER
RAÚL ALLÉN
PATRICIA MARTÍN
VALIANT